The Art of Better Retail Banking

THE ART OF BETTER RETAIL BANKING

Supportable Predictions on the Future of Retail Banking

Hugh Croxford
Frank Abramson
Alex Jablonowski

JOHN WILEY & SONS, LTD

Other Wiley Editorial Offices

Library of Congress Cataloging-in-Publication Data

Croxford, Hugh.
    The art of better retail banking : supportable predictions on the future of retail banking /
Hugh Croxford, Frank Abramson, Alex Jablonowski.
        p.   cm.
    Includes index.
    ISBN 0-470-01320-6
    1. Banks and banking–Great Britain.   2. Consumer credit–Great Britain.
I. Abramson, Frank.   II. Jablonowski, Alex.   III. Title.
HG2988.C68   2005
332.1′2′0941—dc22   2004027085

British Library Cataloguing in Publication Data
A catalogue record for this book is available from the British Library

ISBN 0-470-01320-6

Typeset in 10/12 Times by TechBooks, New Delhi, India
Printed and bound in Great Britain by TJ International Ltd, Padstow, Cornwall, UK
This book is printed on acid-free paper responsibly manufactured from sustainable forestry
in which at least two trees are planted for each one used for paper production.

Contents

Preface

It looks like the big retail banks are going to inherit the earth, but they will not get it all.

Banking is a single industry incorporating a dozen businesses, such as corporate banking, investment banking, small business banking, wealth management, capital markets, and so on. Another one of these is retail banking. Retail banking is characterised by large numbers of customers, accounts and transactions, a variety of products and services, a high level of dependency on technology and terrific levels of cooperation between banks, retailers, businesses and consumers.

Our objective with this book is to discuss retail banking with a view to identifying changes that will materially improve the value proposition for retail banking customers, and benefit the bank and its owners – all three at the same time. Ambitious, or what?

This is timely. Banks have more capacity than they can use; consumers will need a bank account to receive government benefits; and banks continue consolidating into a small number of large banks. This consolidation may be a good thing, or it may be a bad thing. Certainly, smaller banks will have to develop successful strategies to compete, and only competition will benefit customers. One hope could be that even if we do end up with a handful of banks, they will at least compete with each other, and not enjoy comfortable, benign competition between themselves. But that might be to dream. We must have real competition.

It is difficult to see that competition only coming from within the entrenched UK banking industry will have a significant market impact. A good idea from one competitor within the UK can be picked up and emulated or copied quickly. But banks from outside the UK, or companies from other industries, such as the supermarkets and retailers, competing with UK banks will present more fireworks. New entrants have no mobility barriers or existing banking customers to consider, which gives them more flexibility. They can introduce new ideas to the market, and, if consumers embrace those ideas, then the incumbents may have to struggle to compete. Equally, UK banks could also go and do what they do best in other countries.

Perhaps the UK retail banking industry consolidation will continue to the point where nearly all retail banking will end up in five banks or less. This is a distinctly possible outcome. After all, the largest five banks already account for 80 % of banking assets by value, and the largest eight account for 95 %. But for some of them that asset total includes significant global activities. In UK retail banking there is less concentration. For example, five banks account for 60 % of mortgages and 65 % of new mortgages, but that is consolidating too. In small business banking the same applies, with the top five holding some 70 % of that market.

But realise this, it is the smaller banks or new banks that introduced most of the innovations that have benefited retail banking customers. It was the smaller or new banks that forced entry into the planned big bank monopoly of the clearing system, that provided free consumer banking, dropped annual fees for credit cards, paid interest on current accounts, offered white label/affinity credit cards and mortgages, introduced offset accounts, fielded high-rate savings accounts, supported non-prime lending, focused on very specific markets, assumed community responsibilities and encouraged entrepreneurs. Phone banking, now widespread, came from smaller banks, as did PC home banking. It was the building societies that were able to offer the best rates for savings and mortgages. It was Internet banking from new and small banks that spurred the big banks into that. It seems that the small are driven by opportunity, the large by competitive threat and cost reduction opportunities. This makes sense.

Why would large, happy banks want to initiate any of those things, since the only outcome for them would be to introduce costs, thereby reducing profits? This is not to say that the large banks haven't introduced large and valued changes, such as direct debits, debit cards and ATMs, and more recently the chip and PIN cards. But these initiatives were driven primarily by the profitability improvements that would accrue to themselves. For them, by making handsome profits, they have been able to generate capital with which to grow their asset bases, gobble up others and – well, yes – consolidate. Absolutely nothing wrong with that. The family tree of a large bank will show one hundred or more mergers and acquisitions over a hundred years.

Despite this long trend of consolidation, retail and small business banking might not necessarily continue in this way in the UK. Not least because of growing customer power, the capabilities of various technologies and the government competition rules. The banking industry may be at an inflexion point. New business models might prove so attractive that the inevitability of further concentration may be slowed down, even halted. There are signs that this could happen. If better banking can be delivered, through some mixture of products, rates, fees, terms and conditions and service, and if investors can achieve good and predictable returns on their bank investments, then the trends in retail banking could change markedly over the next five or ten years, which is a short period of time in banking. The large banks may really need to begin putting their customers first and place their pricing on a fairer basis. Small and new banks might introduce products that are priced considerably better. What will the large banks do, what will the new and small banks do, what will the mid-sized ones do, how will consumers and small businesses respond? Who knows?

This book seeks to explain the situation and the opportunities. It uses facts, experience and logic to argue the positions. Only a basic familiarity with banking is assumed.

The most important aspects of retail banking are addressed in some depth. We've tried to keep the book short and readable, and gone into some detail to explain the science, the engineering and the pivotal change force, which we believe to be the art of banking. The art is largely missing today. Necessarily there are some 'soft' concepts that we cannot 'prove', but we have incorporated these and done our best to discuss them, because some will prove to be powerful influences, and a few will be very powerful.

Let's face it; this book has to be as much about customer behaviour as anything else, and their behaviour will be the single most powerful force. Much of the rest is about organisational behaviour, and this will determine the effectiveness of both the banks' responses to consumer needs and their initiatives to meet opportunities.

Just how confidently can these customer and organisational behaviours be predicted? Who is going to decide how the retail banking industry evolves?

WE WILL DECIDE THE FUTURE OF RETAIL BANKING. YOU, ME, HIM, HER AND THEM, AND EVERYONE LIKE US

Unlike politics where we get wheeled out to vote for one of two and a half candidates as Prime Minister every four years, 'we, the people' have an immense amount of power to change banking for the better. We can vote as often and whenever we feel like it, simply by opening or closing accounts. If it makes sense to do so, we should use our votes.

In the UK, we consumers are today borrowing about £1 000 000 000 000 from banks. That's a trillion pounds, or one thousand billion pounds, or one million million pounds. It sounds like, it looks like, and it is, a lot. That's an average of about £20 000 per head, or about £40 000 per household, which is admittedly a pretty useless statistic because almost none of us are average. This appears more frightening than it is. About 80 % of this debt is in mortgages. So, on average, that leaves us borrowing £4 000 each on credit cards, store cards, loans and overdrafts. More likely, those of us in our first half of life average £8 000 debt, and those in the second half, a lot less. Inland Revenue figures, based on income from savings and investments, show that 50 % of taxpayers account for only 5 % of the wealth, excluding property (it was 11 % of the wealth just eight years ago). Most of us have money in banks as well, for instance, in our current and savings accounts. This adds up to something like the same amount – the bank has to get the deposits to make the loans. If indeed we are a nation of borrowers, then we must be a nation of savers too.

The largest source of retail banking revenue is made from the spread between the interest rates paid on deposits and the interest rate paid on loans. That's about 1 % in the mortgage business, and can be 10 % in the credit card business. Let's say that the spread averaged out at 2 %. So, in very round numbers, the retail banks make £20 billion revenue from that £1 trillion each year. They also have fees and charges that make them about a quarter as much again. So their total retail banking income is £25 billion. They have costs for staff and stuff, which takes away about 40 %, leaving £15 billion. Other deductions, like bad loans, push this down a little further. And finally, the government charges 30 % Corporation Tax, which leaves retail banks with about £10 billion of profit after tax. If the spread was 3 %, then a bank could aspire to make a 30 % ROE, which would be good for them. Useless average or not, that £10 billion equates to about £400 of bank profit per household per year, which is a little over £1 per day. It's actually less than 50 p per citizen per day. Not so terrifying considering what banks do for us. That's the way it is, and we see little wrong with this aspect, as we explain.

There are two sides to consider – the customers and the investors. The bank is bang in the middle. Bang, that is, as in the firing line.

To support the £1 trillion loans in the UK, the regulators require investors in the bank to stump up about £40 billion of their money as equity, and this is at risk. If all goes extremely well, and £10 billion profit is made on the £40 billion equity, it's a very good investment, giving a post-tax return on equity (ROE) of 25 % (10/40). If it goes well enough, and they make a £5 billion profit, then they get a 12.5 % ROE (5/40). If they make nothing, then they get a zero return. If they lose £1 billion, then they lose a billion of their equity. So the investors pressure the banks to 'do good'. Wouldn't you?

But the customers keep demanding more. More service, more beneficial rates, more 'kindness', indeed, more of anything they can get. What they really want is better banking. Why shouldn't they?

So, in the blue corner, we have customers pushing for better banking, and in the red corner, we have investors pushing for high and sustainable returns on their investment in the bank. The referees are the banking regulators and the equities market, both with formidable powers at their disposal.

Left to its own devices, a bank will place its priorities with the investors – the investors do own the bank after all. The bank will work to improve its performance. It might address the customer propositions, thus to gain market share and grow revenues. However, the most likely first actions will focus on increasing the profit and improving the bank's efficiency. This will inevitably lead to a decline in the staff/customer ratio – staff being the dominant cost for a bank. The bank views most staff interactions with customers as inefficiencies or necessary overheads.

Still, for all that, the customers want better banking. This may or may not mean efficiency to the banks, but it definitely does mean effectiveness to the customers. The regulators want, and the government needs, a sound and honest banking industry. But

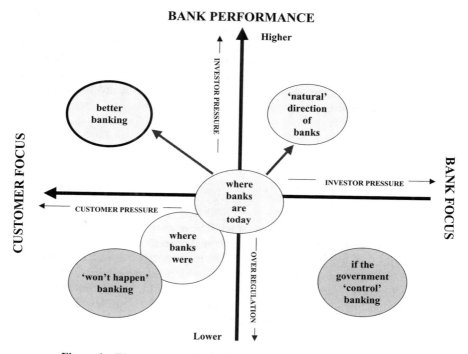

Figure 1 The pressures upon banks and the possible future directions

they seem to have difficulty in selecting their tool of choice between a small screw-driver and a sledgehammer to monitor and regulate the industry. So they will tend to drive the bank to lower performance. If performance is lowered, there is no way that customers will benefit. And the picture for all this is shown in Figure 1.

We think that retail banking is 'up for grabs'. It looks like it is ready for some good competition from within the banking industry or from elsewhere.

It is our view that better retail banking is possible, that consumers will embrace it, and that it will benefit the investors.

Better banking will not originate from the largest banks, but once again from small, mid-sized or new banks. The large banks will follow if they see a threat or an opportunity.

It will be relatively easy for small, mid-sized and new banks to deliver, but difficult for them to achieve the large numbers of customers required.

It will be relatively difficult for established banks to deliver because of their complexities, but easy for them to achieve scale and attract customers.

Small and new banks have an additional challenge – the capital investment requirement to achieve the necessary scale is large. Only serious players could, and should, even try.

It is likely that the first banks to successfully define, develop and offer better banking will enjoy a migration of customers from their competitors towards themselves if, and only if, consumers respond by recognising that it is better, and so much better that it warrants them opening an account. Such migration will seriously damage the laggards.

We can all enjoy better banking. The customer in using it and having their needs met; the staff in getting more satisfaction from their jobs; and the investor from better investment performance.

TARGET READERSHIP

This book has been written with several audiences in mind – an interesting challenge in itself:

- *Bank staff* – a small percentage of retail bank staff are looking to gain insight into the strategic, financial, marketing and operating activities of the organisations they work for. Whilst their jobs may concentrate on a few aspects of the business, many might appreciate a view of the wider picture, and how it all fits together. When you tell people that you work for a bank they politely say 'that must be interesting', when in fact they are thinking 'how boring'. This book will nail that problem. Not only is retail banking not boring, but it is worthwhile doing, and helps make the dreams of many people come true. Too few people have jobs with these positive characteristics. But beware; retail banking is not an easy subject.
- *Senior managers of financial institutions* – bankers in leadership roles will appreciate an informative, provocative and constructive overview of the retail banking sector. They may even feel such a book is overdue. The existing diet of banking books, articles and media opinions does not seem very stimulating. Often, books are only a repeat of what has been done before, but now done better. Sometimes in banking it may seem that nothing is new, and it has all been said before. This book does have new things to say, and will be uncomfortable in parts for most.
- *Those interested in the banking industry* – this covers a whole range of suppliers, partners, marketers, journalists, vendors and what have you. In particular, we acknowledge the role of information technology (IT) and discuss it at length. Banks, and particularly the retail banking parts, are one of the largest users of IT hardware, software and a variety of outsourced services. It helps to better understand your customers' business.
- *Investors* – Analysis of banks is anchored on past performance and finance. We believe that banks' abilities to provide better banking to their served markets and to take more control over their own destinies will determine success in the future more than it has in the past. No bank will be able to drift and be successful. We can even see the compound competence of management becoming

as important as compound interest itself. Analysis and extrapolation will usefully continue, but management strategies and their successful execution will be increasingly influential, and these require investor judgement on top of the analysis.

• *Customers* – if anybody stands to benefit from better banking, it is the customers. Anyone interested in the dynamics of retail and small business banking, for personal or business reasons, will find this an enlightening and rewarding read. Banks have their problems too.

• *Students* – students studying business, especially those who are considering banking as a career, could do worse than realise that banking isn't boring, it isn't simple, and it is evolving at high speed. If you are offered a job in investment banking with Goldman Sachs or others, we suggest you take it. But for the other 99.9 % of us, ground level is a good place to be. Although this book is not aimed at academia, lecturers may see it as a reading list candidate because it does recognise the continuous state of change and the uncertainties that abound in the business. And what's wrong with a bit of controversy? This book may do little to help pass exams, but it will lead to a better understanding and feel for the whole subject. With all respect to academia, there is no difference between theory and practice, except in practice.

• *Regulators, politicians and government officials* – it seems to us that a better understanding of the retail banking business would do no harm in helping the development of creative, practical and sensible solutions for the public and the government. It could help avoid the unintended consequences of poorly thought out initiatives imposed on the public and banks, and lead to helpful, realistic products that won't need to be changed after only a short period.

What is known about retail banking has been written about many times. What is not known is more fun. The danger is that because it is not known, it could be wrong. But then again, it could be more or less right.

BOOK STRUCTURE

There are two parts to this book. The first part – Chapters one to five – seeks to establish an awareness and understanding of what retail banking is about. Those really familiar with retail banking should still browse through these chapters; they are not meant to be a boring primer, even though the first two or three chapters get dangerously close. The intent is to establish a common understanding, so that in the second part, we can raise and widen the overall level and scope of the debate. Nobody gets left behind. Whoever you are, there is stuff in the first part that you didn't know!

Following the introductory chapter, the second chapter looks at the basic model, and is largely concerned with the results of the science involved with banking. It is a simple and limited view, but no less accurate for that, and covers the fundamental raison d'être of retail banking.

The third chapter, on account types and delivery channels, is centred on the engineering that transforms the science into the products and services that the customers see. It gives an appreciation of the range of activities in a retail bank.

The fourth chapter discusses the challenges, using bank figures from the banks' annual reports, to size and scope the realities and opportunities.

The fifth chapter revolves around information technology (IT). In our opinion, the area of IT and its predecessor, data processing, have made enormous contributions to retail banking, but have now become the largest obstacles to better banking. The thorough integration of IT into the retail banking business is poised to be the catalyst that will enable better banking to emerge.

In the second part – Chapters six to ten – we leave banking certainties behind. We spin our wheels, and take some risks and liberties. Like each of us authors, no reader will agree with it all.

Chapter six concentrates on the real world of business. It relies heavily on observation of non-bank businesses, on a few home truths and cold facts. There is no reason for retail banking to behave differently to other businesses. We relate the retail banking planet to the real world that we live in. We think it all through a little, starting with the customers themselves.

Chapter seven introduces propositions on how best to proceed, given these challenges. Undoubtedly, there are other approaches out there.

In Chapter eight we look at how we should prepare for the future. Clearly, established banks cannot change overnight. There has to be an elaborate preparation period, which has already started in most banks, irrespective of their various directions. New banks don't have it easy either. We look at the most difficult of changes, those required in the mindsets of people wedded to the status quo – bankers, customers and investors, no less! The introduction of better banking will be a step change challenge, leading to significant performance improvement over some years. Such a change has deep implications for all members of the bank, customers and many others. Using some form of R&D leads to a business plan, a business model and a transition strategy.

In Chapter nine we make predictions for the direction of retail banking. We are well aware that there are multiple approaches that will make sense generally, and that some will make more sense than others for a particular bank. Our objective was to get to this point, and we can only apologise that the line to it was not as straight as we initially wanted it to be. This is biggish wave stuff, and each bank has every reason to handle these predictions with the utmost caution. Our predictions come in only two flavours – simple predictions and braver predictions from over the horizon. These predictions are based on facts and realities, not flights of fancy.

All the illustrative and arithmetic examples use simple interest and constant currency values for clarity.

Our conclusions end the book. Your critiques begin to arrive.

An outline schematic of the book structure is shown in Figure 2.

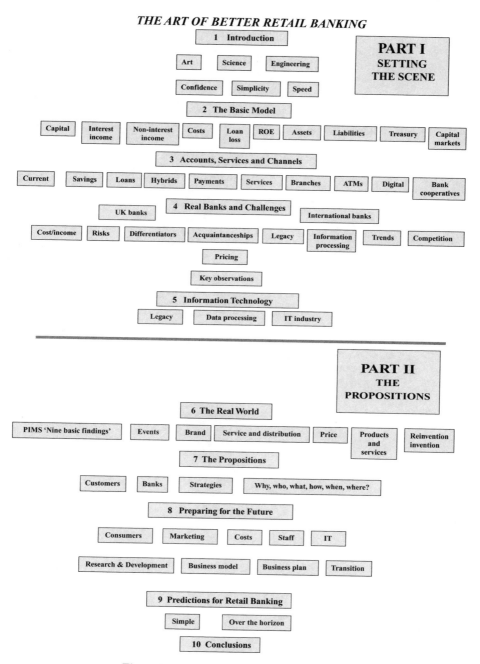

Figure 2   Schematic of the book's structure

Background and Acknowledgements

It all started out harmlessly enough, and well over a year ago. We were asked to write a White Paper on retail banking for a large IT company. This was 'simply' to identify and frame the issues facing retail banks. We agreed to do that, thinking it would only take a few days. Having worked for, and with, banks, and with many experiences in the banking business and change projects, we thought that this would be easy enough to put together.

It is only when you try and write it down on a few sheets of paper that you realise how complicated the subject of retail banking has become, and how vibrant the business is now. We found ourselves questioning everything, including assumptions that have been held by the industry and ourselves for years, assumptions that we've never seriously questioned. The more we tried to fit it all into a precise, neat and accurate document, the more it expanded to reflect the complexity of the subject. It is possible to twitter on about products, services, branches, relationships, costs, technologies and so on, but the result on just a few sheets of paper is necessarily superficial, and looks glib. At least, it looks glib to anybody who understands the business. The problem is not the depth or the complexity, although both exist. It's the width, the breadth and the number of issues that have to be considered simultaneously, along with their interactions, ricochets and consequences.

After about ten pages it was goodbye to any White Paper. However, it had become so thought provoking that we sketched out what we wanted to say. We then realised that we were talking about a book if we were to give the subject the justice it deserves.

The challenge became to write a book on banking that would be interesting, relevant, useful and current. We found few books covering the whole subject of retail banking, fewer still that came at it with a practical focus – most specialise in an aspect of the subject only. It is interesting that a favourite book, published nearly 20 years ago, has retained its punch. The book is *Retail Banking: The New Revolution in Structure and*

Strategy by J.B. Howcroft and J. Lavis. They had it right back then, and that book certainly influenced this one.

As good as the other books are in their subjects, the real challenge is to get one's arms around the interactions and interdependencies of marketing, treasury, risk, operations, IT, branches, staff, and on and on, and all at the same time. No part of a retail bank is an island. This challenge cannot be met without a strong appreciation of the business.

Another objective was to anchor the discussion to real and practical business, not to rely on unproven theories, unfounded opinions or optimistic assertions. Retail banking is a rational business operating in the real world. The PIMS material, being industry independent, fitted this need perfectly. Inevitably, we were going to have to arrive at a strategy for banks, and we questioned just what it was that made banks different from other businesses. It appears to us that this widely held belief of bankers that 'banking is different' is rarely questioned, but does not hold water. PIMS provides the pivot between Part I and Part II, and they can better expand on their material themselves. They can be found at www.PIMS-EUROPE.com.

As amateur writers, and with inevitable gaps in knowledge and experience we asked former colleagues, current senior players in financial services and others to critique various drafts, and with the benefit of their constructive criticism and help this book 'happened'. We are indebted to them all. Our families, naturally, agreed with everything we were doing! They have given us much encouragement and support. Thank you, and with our love – Liz, Mark, Andrew, Matthew and Kirsten (from Hugh); Jackie, Michelle and Warren (from Frank); Alex and Sarah, Richard and Louise, Nicholas, Katherine and Nicola (from Alex). Margaret Jablonowska was thrilled that her son, Alex, was doing an honest day's work in writing a book about banking. She was a fine applied economist, and it is sad that she will not see the finished book. And then there was the team from John Wiley & Sons, lead by Rachael Wilkie. They made everything happen, and we are most grateful for their efforts, advice and guidance, particularly to Chris Swain who shepherded us through the process.

We truly did not know what the conclusions of the book would be when we started, and the journey was not at all as planned. We hope the readers will get as much interest and fun from reading this book as we had writing it.

We have taken care with the accuracy of the facts and figures, but we do not accept liability for errors.

Hugh Croxford
Frank Abramson
Alex Jablonowski
London
Autumn 2004

About the Authors

It takes a variety of experience, skills, knowledge and respect for the subject to address as large a subject as retail banking. No single person can be an expert. The book is heavily based on experience and realism.

Frank majors in marketing, Alex in running banks, and Hugh in systems. This book is about teamwork.

HUGH CROXFORD

Hugh has had a career in banking and banking systems, primarily in the UK and USA. His first jobs were with Barclays Bank as a good old bank clerk, then as a computer operator, and then computer programmer. He joined Burroughs Corporation (now Unisys), where he worked on many sales and implementation assignments over eleven years, finally in their HQ in Detroit.

That was followed by a further ten years working with Citibank and HSBC in New York, where he was responsible for Customer Systems, and was a founding Executive Director of NYCE, the ATM/POS shared banking network.

Following a long interest in banking systems development, he joined ALLTEL Information Services in the US for several years, and was then relocated to the UK to develop European Sales. After ten years with ALLTEL he moved to Sanchez, both companies are now part of the Fidelity Group. Hugh continues to work in banking systems.

DR FRANK B. ABRAMSON

Frank's career started in pharmaceuticals, where Night Nurse was his early claim to fame, and then through FMCG and retailing into personal/retail financial services at LTSB, Citicorp and RBSG.

Frank has a rigorous and challenging approach to business strategy and measurement, new/merged business ventures, facilitating change, and developing and implementing customer-led strategies. He co-founded The Relationship Consulting Group in 1992 and clients include UK and international companies, including banks.

Frank is the non-executive Chairman of *Intramezzo*, identifying senior executives and directors to recognise and implement solutions at critical times, and a director of Verdandi, working in change management.

ALEX JABLONOWSKI

Alex had an enjoyable 30-year career with Barclays Bank during which he served in the UK, Germany, France, Korea and Egypt in various roles involving planning, retail banking, offshore banking, corporate and institutional banking. He has been responsible for IT and operations including payments and cash management, global custody, mortgage and trade services.

In Barclays Alex has been MD Banque du Caire Barclays International SAE in Egypt, Group Strategic Planning Director, MD Barclays Global Services, which is a grouping of IT and operational service businesses, and MD Corporate International responsible for corporate and institutional banking outside the UK.

Latterly he was CEO of United Bank of Kuwait PLC a London based merchant and private bank.

He now spends his time advising and speaking on banking issues and has various non-executive directorships in both the private and public sector. He enjoys technology, management coaching, and venture capital work. A linguist by education, Alex speaks French, German and Russian and some Polish, Arabic and Korean.

Part I
SETTING THE SCENE

1
Introduction

1.1 OBJECTIVE

To try to help banks provide better banking to their retail and small business markets whilst sustaining or improving their profitability is no small ambition. The banks' customers want their own lives made easier and 'fairer'. And for a bank, the number one goal is to profitably increase its number of customers and the depth of its relationships with them (more accounts, more funds, more services). Providing better banking for customers will help achieve both, whether through initiatives from established large, mid-sized or small banks, building societies, or from new banks.

Our point is not that banks have a problem, and here is a solution. It is that banks have major opportunities to provide 'better banking' to the benefit of both their customers and investors – and here is a proposition, together with some approaches to consider. Not, we must add, that banks do not know this already.

The confluence of market, societal and technological possibilities makes the present times markedly different for banks than the past. Banking has got progressively 'better' over the years, but slowly. It is a question of whether this pace of improvement could happen faster, how that could happen, and what the consequences would be. Retail banking has noticeably changed from a mature market with benign competition into a growth market with aggressive competition. The more one understands about the retail banking business, the more exciting it becomes.

Change could happen a great deal faster than we are used to. Change in retail banking has been slower than, say, in corporate banking. The retail banking market is huge, with relatively few environmental factors. In a slow moving business, as retail banking has been, decisions tend to be cumulative and irreversible, so although decisions have been fewer and more widely spaced out, they are more fundamental and critical.

The choice is not between evolutionary changes and new, revolutionary approaches. Both are involved. We attempt to support both a faster evolution of the industry and safe progress with the more revolutionary ideas within the industry.

In order to cover the ground, the book breezes along trying to avoid detours – and failing on occasions. But this is a complicated business, and it is right that the complexities are acknowledged and explained to some level so that readers with a wide variance of knowledge and experience of the subject can appreciate the forces at work. We give explanations and opt for generalised, supportable numbers instead of closely calculated ones. This approach does not compromise the facts or the messages. It starts from where we are now, only occasionally looking back, usually to see the unintended consequences – *why did we do that?*

If important opportunities do exist for banking improvement, they can only become evident from reviewing, analysing and challenging the basics, and adjusting and changing some of them. Banks try to do this as a habit, usually driven by budgetary disciplines such as imposing a 5 % budget reduction across the board. This process is a driving enabler behind centralising, distributing, outsourcing, off shoring, automating, merging, acquiring, divesting, reorganising and the many smaller activities. With such actions, the anticipated results can usually be calculated and are generally achieved; the more so as banks emulate their competitors' successful changes, thus further derisking the process. In the main, these changes are safe and strongly biased towards the internal performance of the bank. There are many examples of organisational and departmental improvements over the years where manual work has been automated, and merged and duplicated operations rationalised, thus reducing costs.

Such changes as mergers, acquisitions and automation decisions are usually clear and unambiguous opportunities. There are certainly strong, strategic overtones, but it is tactics to us. The basics with the most promise for an established bank are the more pervasive issues. Actions to address pervasive issues can improve the entire bank in a substantial way by fundamentally strengthening its abilities to compete in the market, as judged by the public at large, and by significantly improving its cost structures.

Opposition to such changes is abundant and comes from all parts of a bank. Such change suggestions have been 'no-go' areas because they are agreed to be 'can't do' initiatives. It is no surprise when the various parts of the bank close ranks to ward off major disruptions. But it is now precisely these pervasive basics that need to be considered and addressed. Sorry about that.

The evidence that some, at least a few, of the pervasive basics must change to effect a step improvement comes from almost every other industry, but rarely comes from the industry leaders. Step improvements have come from fundamental change within many industries, and the key drivers have been new, customer-focused businesses. Somehow the majority of retail banking has deterred or deflected such change.

To banking customers, other than for certain account types and those often kick-started by government/taxation influences, the products and services that banks offer today are much the same as they were five, ten or even twenty years ago.

From the inside of a bank looking out, it might well seem like the last decade has been dramatic. Indeed, many hundreds of branches and many thousands of jobs have gone, as examples. But it does not seem so dramatic to customers looking in from the outside. The benefits of these significant efforts have not been shared with the customers in important, obvious and tangible ways. To the contrary, there are fewer branches, a growing confusion with product choice and bottomless interactive voice response units. The benefits of these changes have largely been private – for the bank itself and its investors/owners. There is nothing necessarily wrong with that, but as the customers see it, there have been few important benefits.

The customers will ultimately decide what is better, or worse. Whether they choose to do anything about it is a wholly different matter. Slow improvements have not made for many memorable customer benefits. Banks seem reluctant to improve the customer value propositions except in the face of competitive threats or regulatory requirements. New mortgage types, credit card rates, the payment of interest on current accounts, facilitating the transfer of accounts between banks and not charging for ATM transactions are all examples where the large banks have grudgingly 'given' customers an improvement in the last five years or so – spurred by competition or, at the industry level, by the regulators.

1.2   SCIENCE AND ENGINEERING

Of the many facets to retail banking, surprisingly few directly concern serving customers, or indeed the customers themselves. The majority of the facets, however complex, are all operationally, mathematically, procedurally, legally, regulatorily or otherwise precisely defined. They are handled successfully through controls, procedures, processes and experience, and occupy the majority of all the staff time. We view these facets as the *science* and *engineering* of banking (Figure 1.1). Customers see a bank and are happily unaware of the majority of the science and engineering behind it. As far as it goes, that is as it should be.

Figure 1.1   The science and engineering of banking

But customers want to see the *art* of banking, to see the finished picture, with themselves in it. If they are unaware of what is behind the bank, they are not much wiser as to what is in the front of the bank either, be that a branch, the telephone, Internet or mail. What most customers usually discern is brusqueness, an absence of real help – a choice of 'take it or leave it'. Banks usually project their art poorly, but the art is what the customer wants to see more of.

Few can associate retail banking with art. How could you today? But real retailers most definitely practise art. A retail store is some combination of a stage set, an experience, a pleasure and a purpose. Otherwise it is going out of business. There are those consumers, no names, who can have a good day shopping without buying anything! Is this art from the retailers, or what?

A small number of the ill-defined facets of art exist in bank management, and present unusual, unexpected and random difficulties. How can we help a customer? Is there something that they would like to discuss? Are we approachable? On a larger scale, bank management is deciding on what the bank should do, and why, how and when they should do it. These decisions are not easily handled, and the consequences of mishandling them can be huge. Banking history, over the last ten years in particular, shows that to tread new paths, to be creative, to have new ideas and to be original is always difficult and can be dangerous. But without using these freedoms, how else will we prosper in the overall market? By contrast, retailers at large, shops to you and us, are quite the opposite, with new formats pushing the old to one side.

1.3   SCIENCE, ART AND ENGINEERING

So, banking is no longer just science and engineering (Figure 1.2). Not if a bank is in retailing.

Figure 1.2   Banking is not just about science and engineering

The science challenge in banking is largely wrapped up, and the regulators themselves rely in part on the science. There are innumerable books on the subject and its many topics. Bank product management is primarily based on the science of returns, risks, economics, demographics, and so on.

In the interests of expediency, engineering then fits it into the status quo of the engineering infrastructure. The engineering aspect of banking is well understood too, usually coming under the word *operations*. Bank operations include technologies of many kinds. These technologies are raw materials for banks, as important as iron, steel, steam and bricks were to the Victorians. In fact, many great 'works' have been the result of an engineering operational capability or technology push. We can think of bridges, roads, railways, buildings, ships, aircraft, water mains and countless other engineering achievements, all based on various technologies. In banking, the branch network, ATM and EFT/POS networks, payments and clearing systems are great works and are visible to customers. The back office processing, invisible to customers, is a staggering achievement, as measured by the many millions of transactions being processed daily, error free. But we can also think of many engineering monstrosities. Engineering does tend to push itself towards its greater usage. It relies heavily on the science, but it does not always produce the desired outcome.

In banking, the engineering influence ranges widely, from customer interactions with the bank and the daily operations, through to mergers and acquisitions, and indeed divestments. On the one hand, customers unknowingly depend on the engineering and take it for granted. On the other hand, the forms to be completed, the correspondence received, what is allowed and what is not allowed, and most other frustrations experienced have their roots in the engineering. The engineering is in a continuous state of slow change (Figure 1.3).

Figure 1.3   The aspects of banking and the ease with which each changes

The art of banking is where this book is aimed. Fundamentally, art is a maverick that should pull in the science and engineering to support it. Entrepreneurs have art, banks do not do art. The framework for action in banks hinders or precludes effective entrepreneurial responses to opportunities.

Bank management has total freedom to practise the art of banking as it sees fit, assuming that the engineers (sales, service, operations and IT staff) and the scientists (mathematicians, economists, lawyers, actuaries, statisticians, demographers, taxation specialists) in turn, can support the 'work'. Banks can influence their art more easily than their engineering, and they have to live within the science and quasi-science anyway.

The central point is that to provide better banking, which in turn will inevitably mean to excel at banking, will require a step change from where most banks are today. Extraordinary customer growth and product sales in retail banking will not come through adding rococo work on to what is there already.

Most bank staff are paid to directly or indirectly fulfil engineering roles. Yes, they are. Simply helping a customer fill out a form is primarily in order to 'feed' the engineering requirements; back office staff resolve problems that the 'system' cannot handle; others pore over reports from the system. A high proportion of the staff are, in effect, system operatives. We use the word *system* throughout the book to mean the total banking system – the way things get done around here.

Much of this staff, perhaps a half of the total, are back office and support staff, invisible to customers and feeding data into the system and responding to its outputs. These activities do not add value or increase productivity. That is, it is not something that customers are prepared to pay for. One definition of productivity is the amount by which the value of the raw materials used is increased. These functions do not increase the value. The branch staff that helped the customer fill out the form may have added some value, but the back office and support staff did not.

Few staff are paid to fulfil art roles, although it must be said that half of the entire staff do bring elements of art into their jobs. The helpful and knowledgeable branch employee can be an important piece of the little art that the customer actually does see.

Engineering improvements are difficult and expensive to implement, and are becoming fewer and farther between. They will continue, but there are diminishing returns, if not limits, to squeezing, optimising, standardising, reorganising, and so on.

Increasingly, banks will want to look into the opportunities of improvement through addressing the art of banking and fundamentally changing the way that they do business.

Introducing an improvement in performance, specifically visible to the bank customers, will require a greater emphasis on the art of banking, simply because customers cannot decide what is better if they cannot see or experience it. Whatever this mysterious thing called 'service' is, it is a poor substitute.

We need to understand what our bank *should* be doing, not only what it must do and what it can do.

1.4 A BRIEF LOOK BACK, AND THE CULTURE OF RETAIL BANKING

The history of banking is a fascinating subject, but not for this book. Still, let's understand a little of why retail banks behave the way they do, and the challenge of the change facing them. It will only take a few paragraphs.

Banks, as we now know them, come from two main gene pools. The first was what we would today call commercial banks. Often, these started with agriculture, lending to their farmer clients, hence the banking characterisation of an overdraft as being 'from seed time to harvest'. They started to take deposits and issue local bank notes. With industrialisation, they widened their business into the towns and took deposits from, and loaned money to, commerce and industry. They enabled businesses to pay each other, that is, to clear cheques, often through a branch or bank in London, hence the expression *clearing bank*. Over time, they amalgamated and became national institutions.

The second gene pool, the mutual movements of savings banks, building societies and credit unions had different roots. They developed in the towns as 'friendly societies', self-help credit unions helping their members to buy houses and essential items. To borrow, you had to save first. Money was in short supply and the ability to borrow was a privilege that had to be earned. In recent years many major building societies have demutualised and broken away from their roots to become banks. The Nationwide is by far the largest of the 63 mutual building societies now in the UK. Credit unions have never featured as large in the UK as they do in the US, Canada, Ireland and Australia.

The long period up into the eighties was the golden age of the traditional bank manager, an important figure in society, but actually only accessible to people with money, not to the great unbanked who comprised most of society. The bank manager of old is largely a myth, because they acted like private bankers to their most lucrative clients. The non-myth is that the local bank managers were able to make decisions within defined limits. Today, we do not miss the bank manager; we miss the local autonomy and local decisions based on local knowledge and local contacts. The bank manager often made a little phone call and problems were fixed.

That's enough history for some cultural points to be made. Clearing banks typically served people who had money: landowners, people in business and commerce, professionals. Ordinary people went to the building societies for their basic deposit and loan services; theirs was essentially a cash society. These basic divisions started breaking down during the 1960s when the consumer economy took off. All boats rose with the tide of increasing affluence, we all started needing bank accounts to transact – now watch Central Europe, and its banks, grow.

Until relatively recently, a strong mixture of commercialism and public duty ran through both banks and building societies. Staff entered from school and worked their way up from cashier, potentially and in fact, right to the top. The career was from cradle to grave, staff rarely changed banks – that was viewed as treason. Integrity, probity, risk aversion and conservatism were the core values. The core skills were managing process and risk to avoid losses. Career progress was slow and steady with little fast tracking. Despite the formality, there was a strong underlying egalitarian streak. With strong union representation, banks had the feel of a workers' co-operative. Bonuses were unknown. Salaries were modest, but status, pensions and subsidised staff mortgages (the ability to acquire a good house at a beneficial rate) were superior. There was little or no individual performance management. To echo Woody Allen, 80 % of success was turning up. There were few marketing or retailing skills. Training was mainly about the banks' processes – monkey see, monkey do.

Up until the eighties, the government fixed the levels of loan interest rates and the amounts that could be loaned, and the banks themselves set the deposit rates. There was little competition between banks, and none from elsewhere. Mutual banks and building societies were under no pressure to maximise profits – their priority was serving their members/customers. Banks were regarded as utilities by the equity markets – producing dull and steady profits, with share prices to match.

This all changed in the 1970s and 1980s when the government effectively deregulated financial services, which then proceeded to let rip. When the horse bolted, the government had to subsequently reregulate somewhat during the 1990s, for prudential and consumer protection reasons. Financial services boomed. However, it was on the back of a culture and operational infrastructure built for a different time to do different things. It is no surprise that with its strong, historic legacy, banking is still culturally somewhat schizophrenic. How can we nice, honest, trustworthy, conscientious, gentle people handle a tough, competitive market?

Within a period of some 25 years we moved from simple loans and deposits to a wide range of lending and savings products, became dependent on oodles of technology, and entered into real competition from other banks and other companies. All this meant rapid change within a powerful ethos. Staff now move jobs more frequently; they no longer anticipate a lifetime career with one employer. More people are coming into banking from other industries and disciplines – retailing, marketing, IT. Performance management and bonuses are the norm, and pressures on staff to sell and generate revenue have increased, even at the expense of the customer. The world has changed and banking continues to move slowly away from its historic roots. The danger is that it moves too far away from its core values. Of course, products, branches and staff need to be modernised and attuned to customers' changing needs. But equally, customers did trust and respect banks as they were. These qualities need to be retained, maybe regained a little. They are a prerequisite to relationships, and the basis of any advisory selling effort.

1.5   THE VIEW FROM THE BRIDGE

So what does it feel like to be a bank or building society Chief Executive Officer (CEO)? Even compared with just ten years ago, banking has become a more complex and challenging business. It makes increasing demands of its leaders. They now need to be deeply competent in leadership and management and need a profound understanding of the key drivers of their business. Before we weep tears for the CEO we must also recognise that banking can be enormous fun, and this fun is now well paid. Pensions are good. The mortgage may be nothing to write home about, but the stock options are.

Banks and their CEOs do not enjoy a good press. It comes with the patch – branch closures, mis-selling, excessive bank charges, fat cat salaries – the list is long. Apart from the occasional knighthood, the bankers are rarely commended for their contribution to society, even though, as any economist will confirm, a stable and efficient banking system is essential for national economic growth and wellbeing (there aren't too many things that economists all agree on). The UK has one of the most effective and efficient banking systems in the world.

The key to surviving in the CEO job is being able to balance a wide range of complex, demanding, interacting and often conflicting pressures. If the bank is publicly quoted, market expectations need to be satisfied. These include meeting forecasts, rolling out new products and creating new business lines, avoiding unforeseen cost spikes and credit losses and having a good story on cost control. To satisfy market expectations requires the setting of business growth strategies and targets; seeking out and evaluating new capital investment opportunities; gaining new customers and retaining existing ones; improving the customer experience; repositioning, upgrading and reconfiguring the branch network; managing and upgrading an increasingly complex IT and operational infrastructure; and so on. Staff-related matters, such as the development of team play, raising staff competencies and equipping those competencies so they can be effective, are at least as important as any of the other tasks.

A reputation problem such as mis-selling, unanticipated losses or some series of problems can have a major impact on the share price. If the problems are not addressed quickly and effectively, the CEO's job will be at risk. If the regulators impose fines, they are but pinpricks to a bank in financial terms, but in terms of public trust they are potentially dangerous, and largely immeasurable in their consequences.

Who would have foreseen that Midland Bank, the largest bank in the world in the 1950s would be taken over by a former colonial bank, or that NatWest would succumb to a hostile takeover by a regional Scottish bank, or how close to the brink Abbey National was taken by its trading book problems? Banking remains a risky business – the price of failure is high for investors and the bank leadership. Plenty of CEOs have been pushed. Few choose to jump.

Pressures from the regulator, the FSA (Financial Services Authority), can be a major worry. Like the market, they do not appreciate surprises. If they occur too frequently, or if there is a major failure, they will review the quality of the bank's management. An increasing emphasis is being placed on compliance with new conduct of business regulations and codes, designed to ensure that banks have the best interests of their customers at heart and that they are being treated responsibly and fairly. The implementation of banking law is becoming increasingly demanding. Key members of the management team have their own statutory responsibilities, but the buck stops with the CEO. Gone are the days of a quiet fireside chat with the Bank of England. The FSA, extensive remedial work, possibly a large and public fine, and the attendant uncomfortable and intrusive investigations have now replaced that. In the extreme, there is the prospect of draconian personal sanctions against key senior managers, including the CEO. If the institutional shareholders don't get you first, the FSA will.

1.6 WE HAVE TO START FROM WHERE WE ARE

The obvious explanation as to why banks have been able to avoid making changes is that the demand for banking is large, inevitable and growing. Retail banking is not a zero sum game. This is because consumers and businesses increasingly need banks. They have few options but to go to banks. Also, for the investors in a bank, the returns on the equity employed by a bank in terms of dividends and equity appreciation in general have been, and are, sufficiently high that there is no prima facie case to want or need to change. Such change as we have seen in other businesses has been driven by customers deserting a company or its products, or by the company needing to improve its returns to attract investment, or repel predators, or the emergence of new varieties of competitor. The stimulus has been competition for customers, and to a lesser extent competition for capital. Market competition in the banking sector, and the response to such competition, has been gentler because neither the customers nor the shareholders feel disenchanted with the status quo. Generally, there is an excess of capital in banking so it is not a scarce resource to be competed for. Also, the customers, the ultimate target of competition, doubt that another bank will be that much different from their existing bank. They might be right. Growth, as always, was driven by need, but the selection of a bank was largely determined by access to a branch and these were sited in a catchment area. The number of branches that a bank had really did matter. The selection of a bank today is less influenced by branch numbers and access than it was.

In a nutshell, few clearly better banks and banking products or services have appeared. The nearest any group has come was the building societies. In fact, at their peak in the eighties they attracted over 50 % of all personal liquid assets and financed over 75 % of mortgages by volume and value. They were the retail savings and mortgage banks for mortals. Those remaining are an economic, regulatory and institutional phenomenon that may fulfil the needs and expectations of the personal sector better than the banks. They enjoy cheaper cost structures and certain fiscal advantages, and have a unique control over their simpler balance sheets enabling them to lead price competition. Unfortunately for society, in our opinion, many have demutualised and converted into banks, at the wish of their own customers. A cash windfall is a powerful force. In banking timeframes, Cheltenham & Gloucester, Halifax, Abbey National, Bradford & Bingley and Northern Rock transferred almost a half of building society mortgages and savings into the banking sector at a stroke.

1.7   ARE BANKS 'UNPOPULAR'?

A challenge for banks is to address the failure, or lack of effective attempts, to establish better communications between the banks and their customers. The public at large has a jaundiced view of banking as a business. Their prejudices against the banking industry are fortified annually when banking profits are announced and newspapers trumpet 'profits of £233 per second' for some bank or another. The fact that 'the bank made £60 000 profit per employee', with each employee being paid £20 000, would be eyebrow raising except that the bank had to attract about £6 million in deposits per employee to do so. Over half a million people in the UK work directly or indirectly in retail banking, and the investors in banks make some 15 % return on their investment, by putting their capital at risk. A fair proportion of bank customers have made a higher return on their house value in recent years with no long-term risk to their capital, and the enjoyment of a place to live.

Customers do not easily recognise, or openly acknowledge, how important banks are in their lives. Banks truly do make things possible for their customers. Home ownership, financial security, credit, and the ability to make and receive payments are basic requirements of life for most consumers. Small businesses regularly rely on bank assistance to fund their operations, handle payments and even their billing. By virtue of the banking industry, and the sensible usage of it by customers, a raft of other things follow, such as home improvements, cars, holidays, education, health and peace of mind.

Given that, how has it arrived that the mass of the public feels nothing towards their bank or the banking industry, and yet when surveyed they will willingly state that they are happy with their bank and are unlikely to change? Customers seem resigned to the status quo. Only 4 % of consumers in the UK change their current account in any year – it's 2 % in France and 14 % in the USA. Most of this is a direct result of population movements and the geographic coverage of the banks – not customer dissatisfaction. This book can play a small part in explaining some of the issues in banking, and addressing some of the misunderstandings surrounding banks. Misunderstandings, it must be said, that are held as much by bank staff as by their customers.

The correct answer(s) to the single question 'what would make me change my bank?' will lead to major changes in the market. The right answer to a second question 'why would I ask my bank to help me meet this new need I have?' would shake the market.

Actually, UK banks are not unpopular, but don't tell them that. Many surveys say that bank customers are mostly 'satisfied' or 'very satisfied' with their banks. That's not press worthy copy however. The 'unpopularity' may in truth be something that stems from isolated incidents, inconvenience, inflexibilities and the large, envied profits. The popular media print ten column inches of unflattering banking stories to every inch of positive recognition. The reality is not that skewed, and the public knows it.

1.8 THE PATH TO POPULAR POPULARITY

It is not apparent to customers that banks put much effort into providing solutions that address life situations, as opposed to simply providing products that resolve down to a commercial, contractual arrangement. That's because banks don't. There are no solutions, just the components (products) that can be used by customers to build their own solutions for themselves. There is no fitness-for-purpose guarantee, that's for sure. The mortgage comes closest, having been specifically designed for buying a house or apartment – but the property market has changed greatly, and mortgages not much.

Customers get little value from bank staff because the staff are focused on these components, not on the problem for which the customer is seeking a solution. Of course, customers usually do not tell the staff what problem they want to address, and they may doubt whether the staff would 'understand' and be able to give meaningful advice, or suspect that they would just try to sell them a product.

An analogy might be the difference between a garage that fixes and looks after your car, with a store that sells car parts. Another might be travel agencies who will increasingly have to advise on, and sell, travel and holiday solutions, not just package tours, air tickets and hotel reservations. Do you, or anybody you know, use a travel agent to buy airline tickets? Such purchases, and importantly the planning of itineraries and schedules, are being made using the Internet because we can see entire flight schedules, and evaluate our options of times, costs and convenience. We now want our needs met – we want solutions more tailored to our needs.

Additionally, bank processes generate many activities spawning internal work, which impacts speed and accuracy. Few books on banking spend time on addressing customer needs, fewer still on the importance of bank staff and their potential for contribution. Few look at technology outside of its engineering context. These three aspects are of paramount importance because banks revolve around people, processes and technology. Combined, these dictate the effectiveness of the bank in its chosen markets and the costs of running the bank.

No bank can do better than meet its customers' real needs at the lowest cost, while earning its shareholders good and sustainable returns on their investment. In all commercial life this is the business 'sweet spot'.

Our premise, developed in the second part of the book, is that banks will be more popular if they set out their capabilities in terms of solutions that help customers meet life events and opportunities, rather than just supplying the components for them to build the solutions for themselves. You can argue that this may be a cosmetic change, and we wouldn't completely disagree. But it is the change needed, so banks should do it.

1.9   AND GET THIS TOO . . .

The public is far more financially aware and competent in banking matters than they were. In 2003, some 30 % of all home mortgage business was in refinancing to fixed rate mortgages, pending the foreseen rise in interest rates. That's not a display of ignorance or lethargy. The public 'knew' that rates would rise, and they did five times, and the public did something about it. Similarly, some 30 % of private car owners chose over the years to insure with Direct Line or Churchill (both now in the RBS Group). Another estimate is that 250 000 small business accounts changed banks in 2003.

Don't rely on lethargy. We look to the velocity of account changing to increase. What are the consumers' tolerances to poor rates and service? And we're not talking about just a tenth of a percent on the rates charged and paid here, that's not going to influence many people. It has to be more than that to attract attention.

People's jobs today have taught many to understand finance, spreadsheets, measurement, performance, incentives, negotiating, understanding and profitability goals. Newspapers have personal finance supplements. Perhaps many people do have a long way to go, but they will get there. In the meantime, if they themselves can't understand something, they have friends/parents/colleagues who can help them. Peculiar this, people don't want to go to a bank for assistance, and the bank doesn't want them to either.

When it comes to consumer financial matters, are the customers beginning to know more than the bank staff they speak to? Can a 50-year-old customer relate to a 25-year-old staff member in terms of experience and understanding? Can the bank employee discuss the customer needs only in terms of their bank's products? Might the customer feel embarrassed at his or her own ignorance of the subject, and will the staff member take the time to explain?

Where is the value to be added by the bank staff member? Knowing which forms to fill in? It's a little early to bring this in yet, but this is the crux of the situation. The bank and its investors want to see better productivity because this has a tremendous influence on the bank's operational performance. Customers equally like to experience productivity, but they see it as courteous, knowledgeable and efficient service. These are two sides of the same coin. However, the second case has to happen for the first to be achieved. The staff ability to add value for the customer is synonymous with the bank's productivity. Unfortunately, it will cost a bundle to attain the productivity.

1.10 CHANGE IS IN THE AIR – CONFIDENCE, SIMPLICITY, SPEED

There is change in the air for retail banking. We all see the competition heating up across media, mail and physical changes in the branches. We see supermarkets and new names appearing selling financial products. We see the pace quickening – but where is it going?

The lessons from successful changes are that a bank must have confidence in its strategies, simplicity in its actions and speed in its change implementation. It is not insulting to suggest that many strategies have come from observing competitor behaviour, or indeed from the feeling that 'doing something' is better than doing nothing. Change in itself is not necessarily progress. The chosen strategies may not be 'provable' in the scientific or engineering senses, and there may be no precedents to follow. Enough West End stage shows open and hurriedly close to demonstrate the difficulties associated with art. Predicting what customers will pay to see, hear or experience is by no means a science, and whilst the engineering of lights, staging and special effects has power, it cannot greatly impact the audience if the art is not there in the customers' eyes. Confidence for the bank can only truly come from a certainty that customers will buy. To the extent that it is not easy to accurately divine customer reaction, the word courage may be more appropriate than confidence.

Simplicity is valued by both the customers and by the bank. The easier it is for the customers to understand, the more comfortable they will be. The simpler the bank proposition is, the easier it is for the bank to develop, market and support.

Speed is not an attribute usually associated with retail banking. But speed is known to be a vital contributor to successful, new initiatives. Speed maximises market advantage and wrong-foots competitors. Speed curtails drift away from the original objectives. Speed minimises the costs of introducing changes, because there are fewer changes over a short period.

New initiatives will need to be exercised confidently, quickly and inexpensively, and the risks involved managed out to the maximum extent possible.

2
The Basic Model

Retail banking is based on a simple, straightforward model. Some people and enterprises have a surplus of funds, and some have a deficit of funds. In fact, most of us have both – a surplus of short-term funds in current and savings accounts, and a deficit in long-term funds filled principally by mortgages. Banks borrow from those in surplus and lend to those in deficit. The bank makes an interest rate spread between the two. In addition, the bank provides ancillary services for which they can charge fees as customers use them, although some of these services are bundled in with customer accounts.

Customers with surplus funds will not individually risk lending money to their neighbours, friends or family – or to their plumber, landlord or vicar. So, the bank pays its customers from zero to five-point-something percent on their current, savings and term deposit accounts (deposits/liabilities), and it charges from five to twenty percent to people who want to borrow the same money (loans/assets). This pure 'spread' of interest rates in retail customer funds is about 5 %, that is, you get 2 % on savings and pay 7 % on loans, or some such similar figures. Overall in a bank, with all things considered, this margin is nearer 2 %–3 % because there are substantial interbank and corporate deposits and loan balances at skinny margins, cash, and other factors. For a bank primarily in the mortgage business it is around just 1 %. In the UK, the minimum loan amount is usually £1000. A good rate available for savings is around 5 %, and for a loan is something around 6.5 %, which gives a spread of only 1.5 %. Still, we'll take the real margin of the active funds in retail banking to be about 3 %. Most accounts have modest balances and customers don't shop around except where larger amounts are involved.

This bank intermediation role removes all risk from both borrower and lender. Few people are prepared to lend £1000 to a friend at 7 %, let alone somebody they don't know. Of those that do, few will get £1070 back after the year is up, certainly not from the money they loaned to their children. With a bank as intermediary, the lender/depositor/saver is definitely getting, say, 4 % on their savings and their capital is safe, and the borrower is definitely paying, say, 7 % on their loan, the terms of which they can completely rely upon. Everybody is happy. The bank makes revenue from the *net interest income*, this being the spread, the difference between the interest it earns from borrowers and the interest it pays to depositors.

This is not a bad deal for any of the parties. The proof being that we all do it. More than half of a retail bank's revenue, perhaps three-quarters, comes from this intermediation role in the form of net interest income.

In addition, the bank offers a number of services usually anchored to the customer's funds in some way. These include payment services, insurance, money transmission, advisory services, securities brokerage services, investment and taxation services, trust and will services, card and factoring services, and more.

The bank either requires the customer to pay a fee, or the fee is bundled into the overall cost of the account relationship. For instance, a bank provides cheque and standing order processing, which are costly. It will either charge the customer, say, £4 per month, or waive the fee if the average balance is kept above, say, £500. All the service fees added together represent the *non-interest income* for the bank, which is their other major source of income. This non-interest income totals some 15 %–35 % of the size of the net interest income in a retail bank.

That's the model then. The bank earns a spread between its borrowers and depositors, and it charges fees for services it offers. If enough customers deposit and lend, and make use of the services, then happiness for the bank will surely follow – and all based on providing customers with the products and services that they need, when they need them.

Most of the public and bank staff see retail banking as just this, and they resent these margins and fees. Altruism is not the word that springs to their minds. One supposes that if the spread was much reduced, and the fees halved, then the entire world would embrace the banking industry as its favourite experience, since it helps make their many dreams of advancement come true. Unfortunately, even this would not be true. Life isn't fair.

2.1 PROFIT AND RETURN ON EQUITY

We need to appreciate that it is not quite so easy or clear cut for the banks themselves. All companies are in business to make a profit. That is, they need to make more than it costs them to be in business. A company that is twice as big as a competitor will expect to make twice as much profit, or thereabouts. For a company 100 times bigger the same logic applies. The big banks are truly huge. So they make truly huge profits, quite in proportion to their size, and with some advantages from scale economies, which is size again. By the same token, a company making double the profit of a competitor is likely to be twice as big, or thereabouts.

Many people get upset at the size of bank profits, but they know this to be true. Those with little work experience, such as many politicians, can get apoplectic over the size of bank profits. However, plus or minus a little, retail banks make about 1 % on their assets after tax. The bank assets are mainly the consumers' mortgage and loan accounts. If others don't like banks making one percent on their loans, they must get together and work on alternatives. Building societies and credit unions are two alternative models.

Companies need capital to get started and to keep operating. In the case of banks, investors provide the capital in return for which they receive equity in the company, which means that they 'own' a part of the company. Capital, investment and equity are tightly related. The company's profits and the investors' return on the equity they own (ROE) are closely correlated. The ROE (return on equity) is a performance measure that is standard across all commercial businesses, including banks. It can be used to compare company performances from bank to bank, from company to company, from bank to company. So we use the ROE, rather than the profit itself, to discuss investor returns. ROE is, by definition, a normalised performance measure between commercial companies of any size, in any business.

The investment/capital needed by banks is not for buildings, factories, inventories and plant as manufacturing companies might need, but rather for the capital required by the regulators for a bank to operate. This capital, moreover, is required mainly to protect the bank's customer deposits.

Customers want better banking. Bank shareholders/investors/owners (essentially all the same) want a better ROE – and 10 % is not enough, 15 % is the norm and 20 % is good. They do risk their investment, and their returns are not guaranteed.

2.2 CAPITAL REQUIREMENTS

The banking regulatory authorities set the capital requirement of banks. This is set internationally, not on a country-by-country basis – the rules are largely identical for every bank in the world.

Customer deposit and savings accounts are a bank's major liabilities, in that they have to repay them to the customers in accordance with their account agreements. Customer loans are the bank's main assets, in that they have an agreement with customers that the customer will pay the loan back as contracted.

A bank is not allowed to just borrow from one group of customers (deposits/liabilities) and lend to another (loans/assets). If it did, and some of the borrowers didn't repay their loans, then the bank wouldn't be able to repay its depositors' money in turn. The bank is obliged to keep some of its own funds, raised primarily from shareholders and debt-holders, as bank capital. A banking licence is a prerequisite to allow an institution to accept customer deposits. Pretty much any company can lend money to consumers, because the risk is entirely with the lender. But to borrow money from a consumer, where the risk is on the consumer, requires that the holder of the deposits hold a banking licence to ensure that these funds are used prudently and that the customers' deposits are safe. Be glad.

In order for a bank to make loans, using its customers' deposit accounts to fund the loan, the regulators require the bank to hold some minimum amount of capital. The precise amount of this capital varies depending on the types and amounts of the loans, and can range from about 2 % to 8 % of the total value of the loans (assets). This capital is to support and absorb risks, including the non-repayment of loans, and to comply with regulatory capital adequacy requirements that exist to protect bank customers, and ultimately the banking system itself. If loans are not repaid, then the bank has to pay out, first from operational profits and then by drawing upon this capital if necessary – that is, if the bank makes a loss. Thus the customers' deposits are not put anywhere near the front line of risk. To further give confidence in a bank, to its customers, its investors, other banks and the regulators alike, the bank management may be required, or choose, to boost its capital further, to 10 % or more of the value of the loans, this extra capital being 'prudential' capital. Be gladder.

The amount of the capital requirement needed for a bank is a complex subject. It varies from bank to bank, primarily due to the riskiness of the bank's loans and the regulator's view of the bank and its business. The amount is set as percentages of the various types of loan that the bank makes.

A secured loan, such as a mortgage, is judged to be less risky than a personal unsecured loan because, in the extreme, the bank can sell the property and recover the loan amount. An unsecured loan, such as an outstanding balance on a credit card, is judged to be more risky. A loan to another bank is deemed to be of little risk. The regulators prescribe the formulae by which the capital requirement is to be calculated.

About one half of the capital must come by way of investor equity, which is investor cash, and this is where we are focusing. For our purposes in this book, primarily in the examples that follow, we are going to say that the equity capital requirement for a secured loan like a mortgage is 2 % of the value of the loan; that the capital requirement for an unsecured loan like a personal loan or a credit card is 4 % of the loan amount; and for a loan to another bank it is 1 %. These are fair numbers to use, and close to the facts.

This equity capital has a name in banking – it accounts for most of the *Tier I capital*. Overall, in a large, multibusiness bank, this Tier I capital is 4.55 % for the UK. The only reason you need to know this here is because there are some tables later on that refer to Tier I capital and the returns on it. The return on equity, ROE, is essentially the return on this Tier I capital.

Just for the sake of completeness, there is Tier II capital as well, and this accounts for the other half of the capital. This is in the form of bank bonds that can be issued up to an amount equivalent to the Tier I capital. These bonds are 'subordinated', which means that in the event of liquidation the bondholders' claims are met only after depositors have been paid, but they do rank ahead of shareholders.

The Tier I shareholder equity is totally at risk, and if the bank makes large losses, this capital will be drawn on to protect the bank's depositors. The bank does not guarantee the shareholders' rate of return on their investment, but rather the return they receive depends on the performance of the bank. The returns that the investor receives are in the form of dividends and the appreciation in the value of the shares. The investor buys shares in the bank, but the cost of the shares, which is their market value, varies depending on how well or poorly the bank is performing. The investors realise that a run of 'bad luck', or more likely bad management, could lead to the value of their investment being reduced. On the other hand, a run of 'good luck', or superior management, would see them making a larger return on their investment as its market value increases. Also, banks pay dividends to their shareholders each year based on the bank performance. Either way, the investor wants a return on their investment that is in line with the risks that they are taking, as compared to alternative risk/return investment choices that they could make in other banks or other industries. The investor ownership is mainly in the form of buying equity shares. The market value of this equity fluctuates widely based on the market perception of the anticipated impacts of fiscal, economic, market and customer forces at play, and importantly, the quality of the bank's management, as demonstrated by its success over a number of years.

By the way, most of the equity capital comes from institutional investors, often acting on behalf of ordinary people. Institutional investors, pension funds in particular, hold a large proportion of bank equity. Savings in unit trusts, and most equity securities funds, will have a proportion of their value invested in financial services equity. In large measure, bank investors are directly or indirectly the same people who are bank customers. In fact, most of us, the public, are involved up to our eyeballs in banking – as depositors, borrowers and proxy investors.

2.3 INTEREST SPREAD AND INTEREST MARGIN

If the bank pays a depositor 4 % on a £1000 deposit, and a borrower pays the bank 7 % on a personal loan of £1000, the spread is 3 %. The bank will therefore make £30 of net interest income in a year.

The equity capital required to support this loan, based on the previous section where we highlighted that an unsecured loan must be backed by 4 % of equity capital, is £40 (Tier I capital). That is, the £40 equity that it has tied up in the loan as the capital requirement makes a return of £30 (3 % of £1000), which is a 75 % basic return before costs and other deductions are made. This example is not wide of the mark. The basic return can be higher. Consider a credit card charging 16 % for a spread of 12 %. The same arithmetic gives a basic return of 300 % (the bank earns £120 on its £40 equity).

If it were not for the staff, branches, networks, computers and a lot else, the operating costs would be close to zero. It is only a ledger entry after all. The law of large numbers suggests that when one of the bank's many customers wants to deposit £1000, another customer wants to borrow it. Yes, there are some costs, but a 75 % basic return. *How difficult can this business be?*

This explains why there are 30 000 banks in the world. It cannot be that difficult to be an average performing bank, and few fail. By contrast, think restaurants and retailers. Retail banking can be a glorious business.

Much of banking is about numbers, and the two most important ones are the two we have now addressed, the capital ratio – which is the amount of capital needed to support the loans (assets) – and the spread that is made between deposits and loans. The core profit made by the bank is the difference between what it earned and paid in interest, which is its net interest income, minus its operating costs. This profit is the profit the bank made through the intelligent use of the investors' capital – specifically who to lend to at what rate. The more profit made with the capital, the greater will be the investor return. The interest spread is related particularly to the risk of the loan. The greater the risk of the loan not being repaid, the higher the loan rate, and therefore the spread, and the larger the amount of capital required.

Figure 2.1 illustrates the risk/reward nature of the retail banking business. On this basis, the profits are larger the higher the risk, so should we make more unsecured (high-risk) loans than secured (low-risk) loans? That is for management to decide.

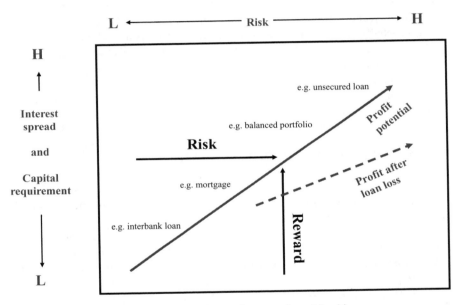

Figure 2.1   The risk/reward nature of retail banking

The higher the risk, the higher the reward or revenue, provided that the loans are repaid, which is the main risk aspect. Also, as the risk increases, so the capital requirement increases. If we use double the capital to make a loan, then we need to make double the profit to make the same return on the capital used.

We have talked of an average 3 % spread. Consider a credit card or some other unsecured personal loan. These might have an average spread of 5 %. A mortgage will be much lower (it's safer) at 1 %.

Now, should a bank lend £100 000 for a single mortgage (secured loan), or have 100 customers each borrowing £1000 in personal loans (unsecured loans)? Again, as we highlighted in the previous section, a mortgage requires about 2 % of its value to be held as equity, in this case £2000; and an unsecured loan requires 4 % to be held as equity, in this case £4000. The net interest income from the mortgage at 1 % is £1000, which gives a basic return on the equity of 50 % (1000/2000), with pretty much no risk. The comparable figure for the unsecured loans at a spread of 5 % is a basic return on the equity of 125 % (5000/4000). So you see, banks like to make unsecured loans, assuming they get their lending credit models right and the customers repay. If just one of the hundred loans wasn't repaid, then they would only make 100 % (4000/4000). If three of the loans weren't repaid it would be 50 % (2000/4000), the same return as for the mortgage. An unsecured lending business might well expect a loss in the range of 2 %, which, in this case, equates to a 75 % basic return (3000/4000).

We will be picking up on this a little later. Suffice to say at this point that the objective is to generate both good and sustainable returns on the capital used, and the greater the risk, the less sustainable the returns.

A spreadsheet follows to show these two numbers of interest spread and equity (Tier I) varying over limited ranges of value (Figure 2.2). It highlights five types of

TIER I CAPITAL RATIOS % (EQUITY)

of ASSETS SPREAD %	1%	2%	3%	4%	5%	6%	7%	
10.00	1000.00%	500.00%	333.33%	250.00%	200.00%	166.67%	142.86%	
9.00	900.00%	450.00%	300.00%	225.00%	180.00%	150.00%	128.57%	
8.00	800.00%	400.00%	266.67%	200.00%	160.00%	133.33%	114.29%	
7.50	750.00%	375.00%	250.00%	187.50%	150.00%	125.00%	107.14%	credit cards
7.00	700.00%	350.00%	233.33%	175.00%	140.00%	116.67%	100.00%	
6.50	650.00%	325.00%	216.67%	162.50%	130.00%	108.33%	92.86%	
6.00	600.00%	300.00%	200.00%	150.00%	120.00%	100.00%	85.71%	
5.50	550.00%	275.00%	183.33%	137.50%	110.00%	91.67%	78.57%	
5.00	500.00%	250.00%	166.67%	125.00%	100.00%	83.33%	71.43%	unsecured loans
4.75	475.00%	237.50%	158.33%	118.75%	95.00%	79.17%	67.86%	
4.50	450.00%	225.00%	150.00%	112.50%	90.00%	75.00%	64.29%	
4.25	425.00%	212.50%	141.67%	106.25%	85.00%	70.83%	60.71%	
4.00	400.00%	200.00%	133.33%	100.00%	80.00%	66.67%	57.14%	
3.75	375.00%	187.50%	125.00%	93.75%	75.00%	62.50%	53.57%	
3.50	350.00%	175.00%	116.67%	87.50%	70.00%	58.33%	50.00%	
3.25	325.00%	162.50%	108.33%	81.25%	65.00%	54.17%	46.43%	
3.00	300.00%	150.00%	100.00%	75.00%	60.00%	50.00%	42.86%	higher quality unsecured loans
2.75	275.00%	137.50%	91.67%	68.75%	55.00%	45.83%	39.29%	
2.50	250.00%	125.00%	83.33%	62.50%	50.00%	41.67%	35.71%	
2.25	225.00%	112.50%	75.00%	56.25%	45.00%	37.50%	32.14%	
2.00	200.00%	100.00%	66.67%	50.00%	40.00%	33.33%	28.57%	
1.75	175.00%	87.50%	58.33%	43.75%	35.00%	29.17%	25.00%	'blended' spread of all lending
1.50	150.00%	75.00%	50.00%	37.50%	30.00%	25.00%	21.43%	
1.25	125.00%	62.50%	41.67%	31.25%	25.00%	20.83%	17.86%	
1.00	100.00%	50.00%	33.33%	25.00%	20.00%	16.67%	14.29%	
0.75	75.00%	37.50%	25.00%	18.75%	15.00%	12.50%	10.71%	mortgages
0.50	50.00%	25.00%	16.67%	12.50%	10.00%	8.33%	7.14%	
0.25	25.00%	12.50%	8.33%	6.25%	5.00%	4.17%	3.57%	
0.00	0.00%	0.00%	0.00%	0.00%	0.00%	0.00%	0.00%	interbank

Figure 2.2 Basic net interest income return – varying spreads and Tier I capital ratios (Please note that these calculations are simplified in the interests of clarity, and the returns are marginally understated here, so as not to scare the horses)

lending – credit cards, unsecured loans, higher quality unsecured loans, mortgages (secured loans) and interbank loans.

These two numbers, the equity capital ratio and the net interest spread, give the basic return on the Tier I capital/equity. The lower the Tier I capital/equity ratio, and the higher the spread, the greater the return. The regulatory requirements won't allow you to have an equity ratio much under about 4 %, and other banks competing for your customers prevent you making an overall spread much above 3 %. With 4 % equity and a 3 % spread, as in the example above, the basic return highlighted is 75 %. This example is typical of unsecured loans (such as personal loans to known customers) that charge higher rates than do secured loans (mortgages).

The return of 75 % is the spread of 3 % divided by the equity ratio 4 % as a percentage. Note that similar returns can be made with higher equity levels and larger spreads, or with lower equity levels and lower spreads. For instance, one bubble on the chart is referred to as higher quality unsecured loans. This may be a customer seen as a rock solid credit risk. Again, a riskier loan in the judgement of the bank requires the borrower to pay a higher rate, and for the bank to provide more capital to back it.

In practice, if a bank can manage the risk well, then the requirement of the extra capital is more than offset by the increased revenue of the higher spread. Banks look to lend funds on a risk basis, provided that they are comfortable with the risks taken, and their abilities to monitor and measure that risk. That's the reasoning behind credit checks and credit scoring.

Yep, these basic returns are too good to be true. These returns are wickedly high. So read on.

2.4 NON-INTEREST INCOME (FEES AND COMMISSIONS)

But first, these basic returns go even higher!

That return of 75 % (£30 revenue on £40 equity) that we used in our example seems like it should be enough, but that is not all. The bank also charges fees. So let us assume that the bank gets a further £20 in fees from the borrower in the above example for 'arranging' the loan, and charging 2 % to do it, now giving it £50 revenue. That would boost the return to 125 % in the first year of the loan from the previous 75 %. The customer might also buy insurance so that the loan would be repaid if the customer had an event happen that would make repayment difficult, as identified in the policy. Such fees and commissions form the non-interest income for the bank. The bank does not need to hold significant capital/equity for its fee- or commission-based services. Of course, this additional profit without the need for equity means that on the equity that they do use for their lending activities, the bank enjoys higher returns. A currency bureau de change can have terrifically high returns on the little equity it uses, even with a limited market size. There are enough of them in the airports as evidence.

Only lending requires significant equity, and that is in order to protect the depositing customers who provide the funds for the loans.

Banks also charge fees for many of their other services to cover costs such as handling transactions against current accounts, for converting currencies or for wiring funds abroad. Additionally, banks may directly or indirectly provide many other products, such as insurance and equity brokerage, for which they also charge fees or earn commissions. The banks are now beginning to sell electricity and telephone services to their customers, acting as sales agents for others and earning a sales commission.

All these fees and commissions together form the second large source of revenue, the non-interest income. So, in our example, the bank is making a 125 % return on the investor capital (£50 revenue on £40 capital). *What a business.*

Yep, these basic returns are now outrageous. So read on some more.

Well, yes it is a good business, but not that good.

2.5 COSTS AND THE COST/INCOME RATIO

The costs a bank incurs to run its operation are large, comparable in size to the net interest income itself. For comparison purposes, costs can be expressed as the cost/income ratio percentage. These costs cover staff, premises, equipment, computers, telecommunications and much else. A bank with a cost/income ratio of 55 % will spend £55 for every £100 of the income it makes from its net interest income (spread) and non-interest income (fees). The majority of costs are related directly or indirectly to bank staffing costs. For our example, we will use a cost/income ratio of 55 %. The income from the loan was £50, £30 (from the spread) and £20 (the loan origination fee), so that means that it cost the bank £27.50 (55 % of £50) to administer the £1000 loan in our example. A loan application had to be processed and authorised. The £1,000 was transferred to the customer's account. At the very least, two statements were sent through the mail to the customer in the year to advise that the loan had been made, and that it had matured. In between, no doubt other costs were incurred. The customer phoned up a couple of times with a question. And so on. It's easy to incur £27.50 of cost. Suppose that a bank employee costs £22 000 per annum to cover salary, office costs, medical, pension and so on. So, over a year with about 220 working days, the employee costs £100 per day. Therefore, the £27.50 will pay for about two hours' worth of employee time over the life of the loan. That's ignoring processing costs, branch costs, the costs of preparing and mailing customer statements, and so on.

The cost/income ratio covers all accounts and gives some average measure for a specific business. It is clear that a loan for £10 000 would not incur costs ten times that of a £1000 loan. But that's averages for you. In the specific case of a small £100 loan, the bank allows an automatic overdraft to the customer's current account, which avoids all the hassle and cost for customer and bank. The customer could alternatively use their credit card, which is also a highly automated method. Personal bank loans normally start at £1000.

2.6   LOAN LOSSES

Some customers, for a variety of reasons, may not repay their loan. This is usually around the 1 % to 2 % mark by loan value. There is also a fraud risk, which amounted to £450 million on UK credit cards in 2003 as an example, which is included in this. These loan losses have to be covered/paid for. As a percentage, the loan loss may be small as compared to some of the other percentages flying around, such as the cost/income ratio. In fact, it has huge leverage on performance, as we will see.

2.7   TAXATION

And then there is corporation tax on the bank's profit at a rate of 30 %, about which little can be done.

2.8   OUR LOAN OF £1000

Returning to our loan of £1000, the bank is making a 3 % spread and it has 4 % of the loan amount as equity tied up in the loan. There is a 2 % fee for giving the loan. The bank has a 55 % cost/income ratio. We have a loan loss rate of 1 % of the value of the loan, and a corporate tax rate of 30 %.

1.   The £1000 loan at 3 % spread returns £30 on the £40 equity, which is a 75 % yield.
2.   We add the non-interest income amount (loan origination fee) of £20 to the net interest income. That gives us a 125 % (£50) yield.
3.   Since we have costs, a cost/income ratio of 55 %, then we reduce the £50 (125 %) yield by multiplying the £50 by (100 − 55 %), leaving £22.50. That's the return left after we've removed the costs (56.25 %).
4.   Now we deduct the loan loss provision from the new total. The loan loss provision in this example is 1 % of the loan value, which is £10. So (£22.50 − £10) = £12.50 (31.25 %).
5.   Finally, the government wants tax of 30 % of the remaining yield. Multiplying £12.50 by (100 − 30 %) gives us £8.75 (21.9 %), which is the return on our £40 equity.

1.	Net interest income	£30.00	
2.	Non-interest income	20.00	loan fee at 2 % of loan
	Total income	50.00	
3.	Operating expense	27.50	55 % of total revenue
	Profit before provision	22.50	
4.	Loan loss provision	10.00	at, say, 1 % of loan value
	Profit before tax	12.50	
5.	Tax	3.75	30 % taxation
	Profit	**£8.75**	

Since we worked that out on a £1000 loan, the return on the £40 equity is 21.9 % (8.75/40.00). This final return, after all deductions, is the return on equity ROE %.

That took some of the fun out of it, knocking the return from 125 % to 21.9 %.

In well-regulated, more stable economies, this 21.9 % return from a bank, as we have here, is terrific. Most bank returns cluster around the mid-teens. Anyway, a sustainable 20 % return in most large industries and businesses is not common.

With these large percentages of 55 %, 30 %, 21.9 % floating around, and even the spread of 3 %, you could be forgiven for glossing over the smallest percentage of them all – the loan loss provision of 1 % in the example. But you will see that it alone nearly halved the profit. In fact, it took nearly three times as much as the government with its 30 % slab. Had the loan loss been 2.25 % it would have wiped out the profit. Clearly, a bank has to be careful as to whom it lends money. The loan loss impact is so large because it is a percentage of the loan, whereas all the other deductions are a percentage of the revenue.

By the way, had we halved the spread and the fee, as alluded to earlier as what customers would like, we would be giving the borrower the unsecured loan at 5.5 % instead of 7 %, and reducing the fee to £10, then the profit would be £0.90, which is a 2.25 % return. This would not attract investors. If we were to reduce the depositor rate to compensate we would lose our depositors to competitors. Either way, the inevitable result would be that the bank would cease to exist.

In this case we assumed that one in a hundred customers would not repay their loan, which was the loan loss provision of 1 %. Had two customers in a hundred not repaid their loans, then we would be in the ditch. Had our customer paid the interest and fees, but only given us £990 back instead of the £1000, we would also have suffered. It's all a bit tight, don't you think?

Figure 2.3 shows a variety of loans for differing amounts, rates and costs, based on precisely the same arithmetic as before with varying factors. These all use simple interest as in our example.

First year of loan examples

Examples	1	2	3	4	5	6	7	8	9	10	11
Loan amount	£1,000	1,000	100	2,000	5,000	10,000	5,000	10,000	20,000	100,000	100,000
Interest spread	3.00%	3.00%	3.00%	3.00%	3.00%	3.00%	2.75%	2.75%	2.75%	1.25%	1.00%
Tier I capital/equity requirement as % of loan	4%	4%	4%	4%	4%	4%	4%	4%	4%	2%	2%
Fee for loan as % of loan (annualised)	2.00%	2.00%	0.00%	1.00%	1.00%	1.00%	1.50%	1.50%	1.50%	0.00%	0.00%
Cost/income ratio	55%	75%	25%	55%	50%	45%	55%	55%	55%	40%	40%
Loan loss rate as % of loan (annualised)	1.00%	1.00%	1.00%	1.00%	1.00%	1.00%	1.00%	0.75%	0.50%	0.10%	0.10%
Corporate tax rate	30%	30%	30%	30%	30%	30%	30%	30%	30%	30%	30%
Net interest income	£30.00	30.00	3.00	60.00	150.00	300.00	137.50	275.00	550.00	1,250.00	1,000.00
Non-interest income	£20.00	20.00	0.00	20.00	50.00	100.00	75.00	150.00	300.00	0.00	0.00
Total income	£50.00	50.00	3.00	80.00	200.00	400.00	212.50	425.00	850.00	1,250.00	1,000.00
Operating expense	27.50	37.50	0.75	44.00	100.00	180.00	116.88	233.75	467.50	500.00	400.00
Profit before provision	£22.50	12.50	2.25	36.00	100.00	220.00	95.63	191.25	382.50	750.00	600.00
Loan loss provision	£10.00	10.00	1.00	20.00	50.00	100.00	50.00	75.00	100.00	100.00	100.00
Profit before tax	£12.50	2.50	1.25	16.00	50.00	120.00	45.63	116.25	282.50	650.00	500.00
Tax	£3.75	0.75	0.38	4.80	15.00	36.00	13.69	34.88	84.75	195.00	150.00
Profit	£8.75	1.75	0.88	11.20	35.00	84.00	31.94	81.38	197.75	455.00	350.00
Return %	21.88%	4.38%	21.88%	14.00%	17.50%	21.00%	15.97%	20.34%	24.72%	22.75%	17.50%

Our example

A higher cost. Although we are using the cost/income ratio, it is the case that the true cost in a £1000 loan probably makes the loan unprofitable anyway.

An overdraft on a current account. Low actual cost keeps it profitable, even with no fee.

As the loan amount gets larger, the costs fall, and so profit rises.

As the loan amount gets larger, the loan loss is reduced by better credit control, and so profit improves.

Mortgages. Lower equity requirement and low loan loss.

Figure 2.3   Loans for differing amounts, rates and costs

This chart takes a simple view of a single year loan and is only to illustrate the relationship of the interest spread, risk and hence capital requirement, fees, costs and loan losses that dictate the ultimate ROE. Few loans are for exactly one year. They are revolving, or to some other schedule. There are many variations in loans in their duration, risk, rates, degree of security and size.

2.9   PERFORMANCE MEASUREMENTS

For our purposes, we have used the bank's Tier I capital, the shareholder equity and the bank's profit to calculate the return on equity (ROE) as our measure of performance, that being the most widely used and telling single measurement, requiring the least explanation. We need to look at the ROE over a number of years, say three to five, to get a good fix on a bank's performance.

There are a number of less useful and more useful measures. A common one is the return on assets (ROA). This conveys little in the way of insight on the bank. In fact, if banks are listed in order of their ROEs, which is an approximation to a listing from best to worst, it is not the same order as their ROAs. But even the ROE, which is, after all, but a single number, doesn't give the finest picture. For this, analysts use more sophisticated measures, which require more data. Banks themselves have more sophisticated measures that can rely on their intimate knowledge of their business, and on proprietary financial information not available to outsiders.

These more sophisticated measurements glory under different names, for example:

RAROC – risk adjusted return on capital
VARONE – value added return on net equity
ROEC – return on economic capital

A major additional factor in these measurements is the inclusion of risk. A bank, at its best, is a risk engine. The higher returns come from successfully selecting and managing the risks of the business. This is an increasingly important aspect of bank performance, not conveyed in the simple ROE figure.

But the ROE is good enough for us. By way of illustration, we can see how much the ROE can vary. An ROE in excess of 20 % is certainly within striking range. It can be done, and it is being done. Consider this article. We have underlined some of the points:

Sunday, June 16, 2002 Source: The Sunday Business Post – http://archives. tcm.ie/businesspost/2002/06/16/story322129.asp

Banks generate 50 % equity returns in Ireland

Sunday, June 16, 2002

By Michael Murray

Ireland's two largest banking groups, AIB and Bank of Ireland, are generating returns on equity of nearly 50 per cent in the Irish retail banking market. According to figures in the banks' latest accounts, AIB's Irish retail banking operations generated a return on equity of 50 per cent last year, while Bank of Ireland generated 47 per cent when the life and retail operations are combined for consistency purposes. The sustained high rates of return are being achieved despite interest margins narrowing and converging with those in other European countries. The returns partly reflect the banks' increased focus on fee-based, non-capital consuming activities, the scale economies that their strong positions in the Irish market give them, and their ability to drive higher volumes through their infrastructure due to the strong growth in the domestic economy. In the sterling area both banks' return on equity is lower – and much more divergent. This difference in the relative performance of the two banks in Britain reflects their different business mixes in the sterling area. BoI generated a return on equity of 20 per cent in its sterling financial services business last year compared to AIB's 41 per cent. BoI's lower returns in Britain/NI reflect its involvement in the competitive British residential mortgage market and the need to allocate extra regulatory capital to its financial advisory business, according to a BoI source. AIB, by contrast, has little involvement in British mortgages and its stronger First Trust franchise in the North also contributes to the superior sterling area returns. BoI's highest return on equity – at over 100 per cent – comes from wealth management consisting mainly of fund management which is a fee-based business that consumes little bank capital.

This is not an isolated story in banking. Ireland was booming at the time, it is true. Many points are made here, but the real story is that at some stage these banks experienced 'strategic serendipity'. That is to say, everything came together just nicely. That performance was not sustained once the serendipity moved on, although peer performance at both banks remains excellent.

The challenge is to replace strategic serendipity with strategic sustainability. Banks can fly. You take all the luck you get, but a good bank has to make much of its own 'luck' or serendipity. If it does get all or most of it 'right', then the ROE will improve over what it would otherwise have been. Most banks have had, are having, and/or will have such experiences.

As we have said, the return on equity (ROE) and return on assets (ROA) are high-level, catch-all measurements of performance. Banks have far more sophisticated measures that give finer, more appropriate measures of performance for individual businesses, organisational units and departments. However, stick to ROEs – the advanced measures require mega-mathematics and a sad home life to be truly enjoyed.

2.10 THE DIFFERENT BUSINESSES WITHIN BANKING

Although our subject is retail banking, it is useful, and will become important later, to have a little idea of the other banking businesses and what it is that makes them different to retail banking. There are large differences between banking lines of business, one to the other. Figure 2.4 illustrates the variance of four different banking businesses, one of which is retail banking, the others being corporate banking, private banking and trading/investment banking. If we look at some key differences in size, capital requirements, spreads, fees, costs, risk and performance, the chart shows how much they vary between each and every business.

Each of these seven variables is important, but perhaps the most interesting one of all is the fee income. To a bank, fee income is doubly delicious. It is revenue, and can account for more than half of the total revenue, the other half being the net interest income from the spread. So that's good in its own right. But in addition, fee income has no regulatory capital requirements to speak of, so that it greatly enhances the return on overall equity of the bank. This is why private banking and trading/investment banking earn the highest ROEs. Fees in retail banking, which we know as bank charges, are lower, at about 20–25 % of the revenue. However, retail

■ Retail/SB
● Corporate banking
✳ Private banking
○ Trading/investment banking

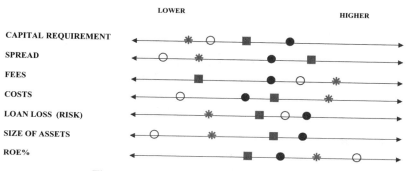

Figure 2.4 Variations in banking businesses

spreads are higher, as is the asset size of the business. Basically, staff costs aside, a dollar of fee income is preferable to a dollar of net interest income.

This diagram also illustrates that the bank-wide figures need to be known in depth and split up into the different businesses to be useful in any detailed analysis of a bank.

2.11 ASSETS, LIABILITIES, TREASURY, CAPITAL MARKETS

From the earliest days of banking, commercial banks were dominated by the opportunity to lend money to corporations. Why not? As well as providing good business they also invite their bankers to big parties and golf days. Branches were a cheap way of collecting retail deposits so that asset formation, which is making a large loan from many smaller deposits, could be achieved at good margins. Building societies handled most of the mortgages. A great deal has changed since then. In retail banks, a higher proportion of loans are now in mortgages, and personal lending has always provided attractive margins. Fewer loans based on retail deposits are now made to businesses. Where the lending operations are limited and there is an excess of deposits, as in a bank with a smaller mortgage business, or in a bank focused on attracting deposits, there will be an excess of deposits. These are 'loaned' to the parent bank, and the bank's treasury department will direct these funds through a separate corporate lending division into larger corporations, or other banks and governments who need to borrow.

In retail banking, assets are primarily loans to individuals and small businesses in the form of mortgages, personal loans, small business loans, car loans, home improvement loans, credit card balances and so on.

Another major change has been the provision of extensive payment services to depositing customers. This has added to the cost of deposits. Secondly, competition has forced varying rates of interest to be paid on these deposit accounts, thus decreasing the spread. Thirdly, the volume of corporate lending far exceeds the surplus on consumer deposit balances, so funds have had to be found elsewhere, mainly from the money markets at competitively neutral rates. Fourthly, as interest rates fall, then the value of the 'cheap' retail deposit balances to the banks falls. As they rise, their value to the bank rises too. After a cyclical period of high interest rates, banking is now in a period of historically low interest rates, which does change the economics of the business, particularly the value to the bank of 'free' current account balances.

Assets also include buildings that the bank may own, and goodwill, which is the difference between the amount the bank paid for an acquisition and the book value of the acquisition.

Liabilities are primarily customer deposits. Other banks will also place deposits with the bank. These two items account for more than 80 % of the liabilities. The remainder is in long-term debt, where investors have bought a debt instrument from the bank, and in shareholder equity.

Banks don't pay high interest rates on customer deposits, but they have to pay the higher market rates on the deposits of other banks, higher still on long-term debt, and, given a good profit, the highest rates of all on the shareholder equity, although this latter rate is not guaranteed and varies with the performance of the bank.

The primary role of treasury in a retail bank is to manage the bank's balance sheet, that is its assets and liabilities. The goal is to maximise margins, manage risk and provide the necessary liquidity of funds. There is a strong emphasis on managing interest rate risk. It is also responsible for the securitisation of assets to free up equity capital. This treasury function provides the pedals and steering by which the bank leadership will deploy the bank's capital into the various banking businesses.

The assets and liabilities constitute the majority of the value in the bank's balance sheet. Imbalances in the balance sheet require the bank to use the capital markets to acquire assets or liabilities of the right amounts and maturity characteristics to regain balance.

2.12   CAVEAT – DEFINITIONS

We have been a little loose with definitions. The entities of capital, shareholder equity, Tier I capital, spread, margin and ROE have precise definitions, the precision being necessary for accounting and regulatory purposes.

Our usage of all these terms is generally accurate because we are discussing comparative measures only, not absolute measures. As an example, when looking at a bank's balance sheet, the Tier I capital consists of several line items, of which shareholder equity is only one, but by far the largest at perhaps 90 % of the Tier I capital. In differing circumstances, returns are frequently given by analysts, authors and banks as either pre- or post-tax returns. The returns can be returns on this, that or the other. In dealing with absolute values it is imperative to compare not just like-for-like, but numbers that mean exactly the same. To derive such exactly-the-same numbers takes a great deal of effort because, while the reporting is similar bank to bank, it is not exactly the same, and there are many notes attached to bank accounts that unavoidably complicate accurate comparisons.

For our purposes the explanations and implications of usage of the terms are more than sufficient, and avoid the need for many pages of definitions and details that do not affect the discussion.

The largest caveat is that banks do not provide their detailed accounting, but rather summary accounts. Because of this we can only compare banks one to another if they have exactly the same business mix, and so on. This is never the case. The large banks have many businesses in many countries and there is complex accounting, which is not in the public domain. Specifically, we are unable to isolate the numbers that relate just to retail and small business banking in a single country.

Surprisingly, perhaps, this does not preclude a good evaluation of the important points.

2.13 TO REALLY UNDERSTAND IT WITHOUT IT HURTING

Our emphasis in this book is directed at the practical business of retail banking and the 'just enough' information that we give to support the practice may stimulate the reader to want to find out more. But the preceding discussion is accurate, and as far as it needs to go for this book.

Those readers with a deeper interest in bank capital, and it is a fascinating subject, should consider reading *Managing Bank Capital* by Chris Matten. The first thing they will realise is that bank capital is a complex study, and that regulations are in a state of change, with new ones coming into effect in 2006. Somehow, it's easier when Chris explains it all!

Those readers wanting to understand more of the financial markets and the intermediation process in total, should consider reading *The Bank Analyst's Handbook* by Stephen Frost. It provides the science and theory upon which banking is grounded, and in a highly readable form. Stephen likes charts, and these really help.

2.14 SOME FURTHER POINTS

In this chapter we have taken a look at the basic model of banking. The income is primarily net interest income, derived from the difference in interest rates paid to depositors and charged from lenders, and the non-interest income, derived from fees and commissions paid to the bank by customers and others.

We have seen that a bank needs capital to operate, which it attracts from investors wishing to make a competitive return on that investment in the form of dividends and equity appreciation.

As well as the healthy revenue coming into the bank through net interest income and non-interest fees and services, there are some unhealthy outgoings. The largest expense is the administrative costs of running the entire banking operation. This is mainly centred on the bank's staff and their associated costs. These costs in total, expressed as a percentage of the total revenues for the bank, are the cost/income ratio.

Since a bank is a business, its purpose is to make a return on the investment that its owners have in the bank equity. We spent a little time on relating examples of loan accounts to the returns on equity. Deposit accounts were only briefly touched upon because their primary importance is in setting the cost of funds, that is, the lower rate from which the lending spread is calculated. Banks will want to attract deposits from customers directly because the costs of such funds are less than if they pay money market rates on funds raised directly from the money markets. Even though deposits are cheaper for a bank to acquire directly, there are large costs associated with deposit gathering, especially with transactional accounts, specifically current accounts. Strictly speaking, capital is not a requirement for deposit gathering, but a banking licence is. And it is the banking licence that requires the bank to have a substantial amount of equity.

The market valuation of a bank is the price that investors are prepared to pay for the ownership rights to the shareholder capital in a bank. You cannot pay £1 to buy £1 of shareholder equity in an established bank; it will cost a good deal more than £1. The return on equity, ROE %, that the bank earns is a strong measure of a bank's overall performance as an investment, and heavily used to compare the performance of different banks. Although we have not directly addressed the subject, the sustainability of the ROE is as important as its size, because it generally doesn't change quickly, so it implicitly gives a good indicator of future performance if its past performance has been good. The profit that a bank makes is simply its operational profit after all the good and bad news has been absorbed. The capital is the amount that the bank has to hold at its own (its shareholders') risk in order to be able to provide banking services. The risk a bank assumes reflects management's appetite for risk and its ability to manage it. Well managed, the higher the risk, the greater the reward. Poorly managed, or poorly selected, it can be fatal to the bank's existence.

Pretty much all of this is the same for each bank, certainly the mechanics and the rules are the same. Credit risk, which migrates into loan losses, is vitally important. Put simply, if a bank makes a 2 % spread and has a loan loss of 2 % then it will make zero profit, even ignoring costs. That is, if just one in fifty of its average loans defaults, the bank makes no profit. If costs are taken into account, then a default rate of just one in eighty or so average loans will blow it. You can see why good credit management is critical.

A missing dimension, and an extremely important one, is the performance of the bank over a period of years, perhaps five years. It is possible to lend to high risk and high return activities in the belief that they will lead to higher returns, but the markets show that sustainability of performance over time is primarily dependent on strategies adopted, and the risk appetite and skills of the bank's management. This is particularly apparent over an economic cycle, which can extend over a period of seven years or more, and appears to be lengthening.

In summary, Figure 2.5 shows four scenarios, the first a no-risk scenario, whereby a bank can make a modest ROE for its investors at little risk. The second scenario is where management makes the right risks, handles them well, gets lucky that the environment doesn't lurch in a new direction, and wins. The third is where they assume the wrong risks, and lose. And the fourth is where they balance risks to make a healthy and sustainable ROE and a respectable return for their investors, even if events do hurt them a little along the way.

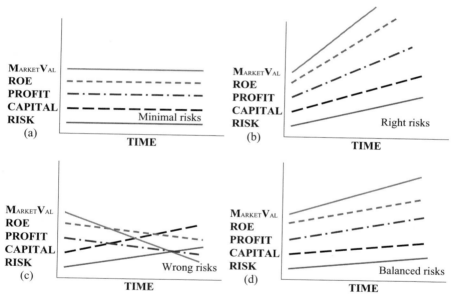

Figure 2.5 Four possible scenarios: (a) no-risk; (b) management chooses the right risks and wins; (c) management chooses the wrong risks and loses; (d) management balances risks for a sustainable ROE

In seeking to improve the returns for its investors, a bank may make a strategic departure from its normal business, not in a massive sense, but in a moderate and measured way. Only a portion of their business is usually affected. Even so, if that new initiative meets with less success than planned, because of unfortunate timing, some economic dislocation or other unforeseen events, then the negative impact can be severe. Not only did the bank incur costs to launch the new initiative, but also it will take time, often many years, to fully recover. Such 'misfortune' has a significant impact on earnings and, if it is a long-term problem, the market valuation of the bank.

We should emphasise that banks exist to take a certain level of risk in their lending activities. Not to do so leads to lacklustre results. In successful banks, calculated risks are taken, not foolish ones, and the credit approval process is highly important.

3
Accounts, Services and Channels

3.1 ACCOUNTS

3.1.1 Current accounts

Today, the current account is the pivotal piece in the customer/retail bank relationship. It is where the 50-year relationship begins if there is to be one. And, boy oh boy, do current accounts ever lead to internal discussions, operational complexity and cost. The value to the consumer is not the account itself, it is in its ability to support transactions that the account holds its power.

The current/checking/transacting account has a special place in a bank's armoury, especially relative to potential non-bank competitors. The current account is typically the central account of all banking relationships. It is hard for a consumer to function without a current account or, should we say, a transactional account. It's even harder for a bank to make money from the high number of retail current accounts with modest balances, typical transaction volumes, a debit card and a monthly mailed statement. An average balance of £1000 in such an account is certainly not profitable, and that's most of them.

Most employers pay earnings directly into their employees' current accounts. Many companies and organisations credit benefits payments, investment dividends, expenses and so on. When paying bills, current accounts can use standing orders (pushed by the paying account to the payee account, fixed amount, fixed dates), direct debits (pulled by the payee account from the paying account, variable amounts, variable dates) as they agree with their payee. Few cheques are written out for mortgages, loans, utilities and so forth.

Typically, the funds come in on payday and reduce over the month. Most of these funds go into large payments such as mortgages and life insurance policies shortly after receipt. Historically, current accounts have not paid interest, but the importance of the current account, its central point, has formed the basis of customers' relationships with the banking industry, and therefore become highly competitive. Time changes things, and building societies now offer current accounts, and current accounts now pay interest on the balances.

Once a customer has their current account they are reluctant to change it. There is 'stickiness' to the relationship, and therefore something to be built upon. In truth, customers are somewhat trapped in that particular relationship, it is just too much effort to change, and other banks' current accounts are mostly comparable in every way. If they are not, the differences are too small to get worked up over. It is also location independent; move town and you don't have to move your account.

Once a customer has their current account, that is pretty much all they need from their bank at this moment. The bank has a marketing advantage in that they have a right to insert sales blurbs into their monthly customer statements enticing them to other products, but that's about it.

But what an account it can be. At its full capability it allows money to be sent to you directly, as with payrolls; it enables the automatic initiation of payments to others on some calendar basis with standing orders; it allows utilities to directly debit money from your account for electricity or telephone usage; it pays interest on credit balances; and if you have insufficient funds it can allow you to overdraw at a short-term interest rate; it has a debit card attached to it so you can get cash from zillions of ATMs around the world; you can use the same card to purchase goods and services; you can get cashback at retailers when you go shopping; you can write out cheques; deposit and withdraw cash at branches; you can transfer funds automatically from your account into another account at the bank or another bank; you can watch it all on the Internet; you get a statement periodically mailed to your home; you can use a call centre to pass the time of day. It makes tea.

Quite remarkable, and expensive to operate, all things considered. You can also use your debit card in ATMs abroad; the bank will automatically retry direct debits if there were insufficient funds on the due date itself, and much more.

There are fees involved or minimum balance agreements for many, especially for small businesses. Other than fees, the only offset to the cost is the value of the account balance, net of any interest it pays out, and other revenue generated by a customer's other (more profitable) accounts held with the bank. Other than that, if you transgress the rules or arrangements you might get a nasty letter from the bank deducting £30 for bad behaviour, but that is not considered a genuine revenue source as much as a reasonable penalty by the bank, however unreasonable it is.

3.1.2 Savings accounts

Savings accounts are coming up strongly in importance since they too can have a debit card and support purchases and cashback, ATM access, transfers, direct debits, direct credits and what have you. But not cheques and standing orders, or other tiresome things. Savings accounts are becoming indistinguishable in many ways from current accounts. They may become the transactional account of choice for retail customers in time.

Although banks have an array of savings accounts, they are, in reality, all the same product, and the bank seeks to improve aspects of its business by fiddling with the rates, amounts and time commitments in order to optimise their income. But really, a savings account is a savings account is a savings account.

Savings accounts pay modest interest and the rates are typically tiered and banded up the ying yang to encourage customers to keep more in them for longer committed periods, and thus provide stable funding for the bank.

3.1.3 Loan accounts

Loans are the primary source of profit for a bank. Loans are also becoming a commodity, and come in two main types – secured and unsecured. A secured loan is where the bank has recourse to some security if the loan is not repaid. Mortgages, car loans and home equity lines of credit are examples. Unsecured loans are where the bank can chase the customer up and hound them if the loan is not repaid, but the bank is not guaranteed repayment because the loan is not secured. Examples are personal loans and credit card balances.

The differences between loans, mortgages, other secured loans, personal loans, and revolving credit (credit cards) are sufficient that they do warrant different product types, but probably not as many as most banks offer. Still, there are important variables – fixed rate or variable rate, interest only, fixed term, drawdown loans, buy-to-let and buy-to-share mortgages, and others. All of these were introduced to meet some market need at some point in time. There is more work involved in making loans than with deposit/savings accounts, and there are usually fees involved. And ... there is risk.

3.2 PAYMENTS

Payments can be initiated with cheques, credit cards, debit cards, Internet transfers and branch transactions. A customer can set up automated payments and can initiate a variety of other payments as and when they want. Customers take payments for granted, but they are complicated for a number of reasons. In fact, payments are one of the most necessary capabilities that a bank offers because they provide the ability to 'move money around'.

Customers see and care little about what happens in practice, it is now just a normal thing. Payment systems are the result of massive cooperation between all banks, and are a commodity. But they are a major cost and operational challenge for banks. Table 3.1 shows a snapshot of payment and cash acquisition volumes in the UK for 2003.

Now, anything that is done 14.3 billion times in a year must add up to a substantial cost. One penny 14.3 billion times is £143 million, and each of these transactions costs a great deal more than one penny.

Table 3.1   Payment and cash acquisition in the UK in 2003.

Transactions	Number (billions)
Debit card purchases	3.4
Credit and charge card purchases	1.8
Plastic card withdrawals at ATMs and branch counters	2.5
Direct debits, standing orders, direct credits and CHAPS	4.3
Cheques (for payment and cash acquisition)	2.3
Total non-cash	11.7
Total non-cash payments and cash acquisition	**14.3**

Source: APACS (the UK payments association)

Since 40 million consumers make use of these payment mechanisms, then, on average, we are each the cause of one bank transaction each day (14.3 billion/40 million = 358).

Table 3.2 shows some more detail of the trends in these payments over ten years and over one year. This chart gives transaction volumes, and clearly, cash is still king *in transaction volume terms*. Two-thirds of payments by volume use cash. A report from APACS in July 2004 gives the *values* of payment systems. Right now, the UK is on the cusp of plastic cards (credit, debit and store cards) overtaking cash *in terms of value*. The headlines of a recent APACS report (APACS, 2004) were:

- £243.9 billion of plastic card payments in 2003, expected to grow to £269 billion in 2004, overtaking cash payments of £268 billion.
- Debit cards lead the growth, accounting for 64.9 % of plastic card transactions in 2003, amounting to £130.5 billion.
- UK has invested £1.1 billion in chip and PIN anti-crime initiative.
- In 2003, plastic card fraud fell for the first time in eight years to £402.4 million.
- 160.6 million cards in use.
- £144 billion withdrawn from ATMs in 2003.
- 50 % growth in online purchases to 200 million transactions during 2003.

3.3   SERVICES – FEE-BASED AND COMMISSIONS

There was a time in banking, before the bank manager of myth became extinct, when you could buy a range of life event services from your bank. You could buy insurance, but your view of the product offered might have changed had you known that your bank manager was on commission from the insurance company, and that this went into his pocket and not the bank's. There were trustee, wills and personal taxation services and the like from the bank's trust company, and possibly property services,

Table 3.2 Total transaction volumes in the UK 1993/2003, figures in millions except for the number of ATMs.

	1993	2000	2001	2002	2003	Growth 1993/2003	Growth 2002/2003	% of total 03 trans
All plastic card purchases	1488	3914	4386	4819	5317	257%	10.3%	13.0%
Debit card	659	2337	2696	2994	3364	410%	12.4%	8.3%
Credit and charge card	748	1452	1562	1687	1822	144%	8.0%	4.5%
Store card (est)	82	125	128	133	130	59%	-2.3%	0.3%
Plastic card withdrawals – ATMs and counters	1277	2090	2250	2342	2457	92%	4.9%	6.0%
Direct debits, standing orders, direct credits, CHAPS	2047	3470	3705	3930	4272	109%	8.7%	10.5%
Cheques	3559	2699	2565	2393	2251	-37%	-5.9%	5.5%
For payment	3163	2515	2399	2246	2110	-33%	-6.1%	5.2%
For cash acquisition	396	185	166	147	141	-64%	-4.1%	0.3%
Total non-cash – plastic card, automated and paper	8371	12 185	12 907	13 483	14 297	71%	6.0%	35.1%
Cash payments (est)	27 273	27 910	27 684	26 662	25 859	-5%	-3.0%	63.5%
Post Office order book payments and passbook w/d	1444	880	791	687	690	-40%	0.4%	1.7%
Total transaction volumes	36 788	40 963	41 382	40 792	40 750	11%	-0.1%	100.0%
Number of ATMs – banks and building societies (units)	19 100	33 000	36 666	40 825	46 461	143%	13.8%	n/a
ATM withdrawals	1242	2027	2174	2268	2373	91%	4.6%	n/a
ATM cards	51	73	78	83	88	73%	6.0%	n/a

Source: APACS data and author calculations

and you could arrange a pension through the bank's specialist financial services arm.

As banks became profit conscious in the age of shareholder value, value-based management and other such techniques, some of these services fell into neglect, were discontinued, or sold off. Insurance remains, and is hugely profitable, as are pension products.

Our belief is that there is a need for these services, based on the old product set but broadened out to reflect people's increasingly complex life event needs. Should banks provide these? Certainly, the economic model has to change in order for it to be economically viable – but technology can help here, automating what were in the past labour-intensive paper-based processes. More importantly, primarily due to the appreciation of houses over the years, there is a lot more affluence to be managed. When it comes down to wills, trusts and estates, consumers will find that such things are no longer the preserve of high net worth bank customers, but that many of us mere mortals also have inheritance tax considerations and will welcome trusted advice, and pay a fee. Income tax advice is another area. Incomes are increasing, and more people will be required to undergo self-assessment, where banks could be useful.

Funny thing, all this. It's what banks did twenty years ago, but ditched when they did their compartmentalised sums on lines of business profitability. All change again. This time around, however, the asset sizes are proportionally larger and will sustain adequate fees.

We believe that such services are integral to the creation of firmer relationships with customers, which we discuss in the second part of this book. It may be a slog for banks to get moving, but these services all pass the big test – consumers will need them.

3.4   DELIVERY CHANNELS

There are six obvious channels, with four obvious purposes. This excludes partnerships and the more esoteric of both. They are shown in Figure 3.1 with an idea of their impact on helping the bank to perform. But overall, it is the individual customer's preference as to which channel to use. Some will never use the Internet to transact, or the ATM to get cash. Some will prefer phone access for as much as can be done on the phone. And so on. Customers A and B in the figure have distinctly different preferences.

Look at delivery channels from the customer's perspective. The so-called Internet customer may be happy to transact and communicate through this medium, but may prefer face-to-face when buying certain products. Equally, a dyed-in-the wool branch customer may be happy to be communicated with by mail, but wants a branch for transacting and buying. Figure 3.1 illustrates true usage and added value of and from delivery channels.

As with segmentation, the old adage that one size fits all could never be so wrong when talking about delivery channels. Banks have recognised this approach to delivery channels in their strategies and marketing. Some have transitioned away in their

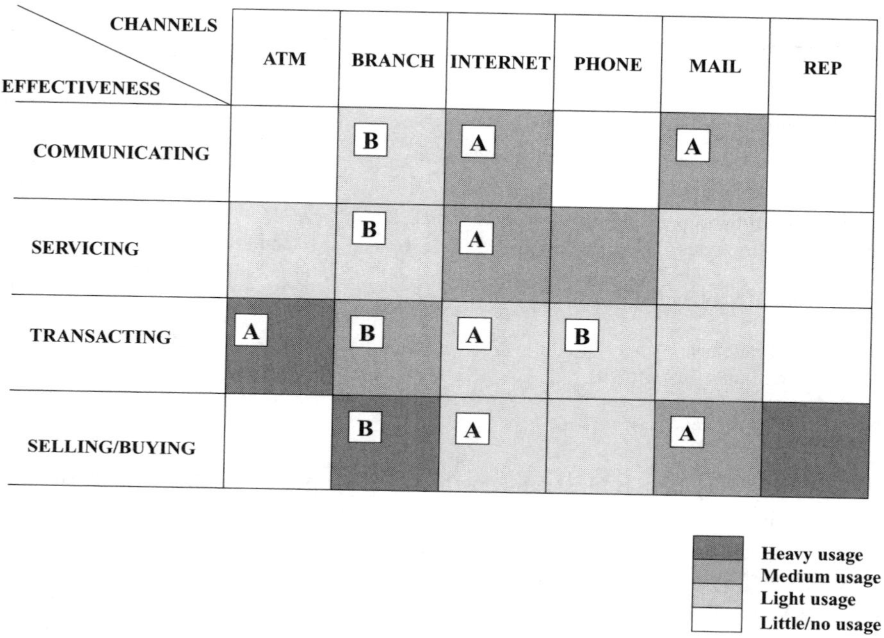

EFFECTIVENESS \ CHANNELS	ATM	BRANCH	INTERNET	PHONE	MAIL	REP
COMMUNICATING		B	A		A	
SERVICING		B	A			
TRANSACTING	A	B	A	B		
SELLING/BUYING		B	A		A	

Heavy usage
Medium usage
Light usage
Little/no usage

Figure 3.1 The six delivery channels and their purposes

customer segmentation strategies, recognising that one size does not fit all in terms of product needs for different customers. The same logic applies to delivery channels.

As some background, a predominantly retail bank gives the 2003 customer transacting channel usage of its 3.5 million customers as branch – 176 m, ATM – 152 m, Internet – 11.6 m, call centre – 5.4 m, phone IVR – 11.8 m. That's them, for that year, for a number of reasons, but it's still interesting.

3.4.1 Branches

Branches represent a seemingly simple problem, and yet what is there to say that hasn't been said many times before? It is not a simple problem, and it transcends science and engineering, although that is where the analytical effort is put. Branching is all about art. Our conclusion is that there is no right or wrong answer, absent a clear objective. Since banks are complex, and the distribution mechanisms and payment services are central to the bank functioning properly, it is probably best that branch populations are optimised rather than reduced dramatically, as has been happening over the last two decades (see Table 3.3). That is, until such time as the art is decided upon, in which case the decisions will become clearer.

Common sense suggests that a face-to-face dialogue is necessary as a part of a relationship, and that a branch is an obvious place to hold dialogues. For many of

Table 3.3   UK bank branches.

	1987	1992	1997	2002
Abbey National	677	680	816	766
Bank of Scotland	545	490	349	343
Barclays	2767	2281	1975	1685
Halifax			897	807
HSBC (inc Midland pre-1992)	2127	1716	1685	1615
Lloyds TSB (includes TSB after 1999)	2162	1884	1610	1871
NatWest	3101	2541	1754	1640
Royal Bank of Scotland	835	786	673	643
Total of all branches	13 813	11 751	12 200	10 754
(including banks not shown)				

Source: British Bankers' Association

us, Saturday may be the most convenient day to pop in for half an hour. But can we 'pop' into a high street branch with limited parking any longer? One issue for banks is where to locate branches – near work places or out of town – and what will they deliver? Where will banks put the balance between low-value (but sometimes necessary) regular transactions, and high-value (but infrequent) advice? As yet the patterns are not clear and banks will need to continue to rock 'n' roll with their branch networks until customer preferences and the bank operational models become clearer.

It is interesting that retailers are switching their marketing costs towards in-store promotions. It is estimated that 60 % of such costs will be in-store and only 40 % going to TV and media within a year or two, which is a reversal of last year. What is truly interesting is how retailers are moving towards the engineering and science of their businesses, having perfected the art. The engineering of bank systems is far from perfect, although it works, although perhaps not well enough.

3.4.2   ATMs

Much is spouted about ATMs. They have been around for forty years. They provide customers with the cash they want, when they want it, and more often than not, where they want it. Isn't it perverse that our cashless society is being held back by customers' adoption of these units, which the banks supply? Did this ever backfire or what? What was meant to be a cost reduction initiative has become a valued customer service run at great incremental cost to the banks to satisfy a competitive necessity, but is slowing down the rate of progress to electronic payment alternatives, which would favour the banks.

As Table 3.2 shows, cash is still king, and most of it originates out of ATMs. This chart is based on transaction volumes, but the value of cash taken out from ATMs (£144 billion in 2003) only just exceeds the amount spent using debit cards (£131 billion in 2003) – even though consumers make eight times as many cash purchases as they make debit card purchases.

In some way customers are paying for these ATMs. That will become more transparent as off-premises bank ATMs are sold to third party ATM companies, who do charge. In 2004 some £140 million will be collected in ATM fees and almost half of ATMs will be controlled/owned by third-parties, not banks. Many of these provide high convenience in less frequent locations, so the value of the service may well justify the fee to support the lower volumes of transactions. The banks do not pay fees to these third-parties.

3.4.3 Digital

Home banking, Internet banking, PC banking or whatever name you wish to attach to it was going to be the nemesis of branch banking as we know it. But the demand for the old banking war horses of cash, cheques and branches remains remarkably resilient and, on the face of it, retail banking looks much the same as it did 20 or 30 years ago.

However, the seeds of major change are already there now. The numbers of consumers switching to electronic access are starting to take off, encouraged by the increasing spread of PCs into the home and small business, and the rapid growth in the take up of dial-up, and now broadband. Virtually all banks now provide a secure Internet delivery channel and the technology is now there to provide a massive widening in the products and functionality, which can be delivered over the Internet. Sophisticated services are already available in the corporate and institutional markets – real time data feeds and financial analytics, cash management and securities management, portfolio valuations, aggregation of financial reporting from a pool of financial service providers and so on. And as retail banking customers' preferences become more demanding, we can expect to see a trickle down from the professional to the consumer market.

3.4.4 Postal banking

There has been major growth in postal banking as institutions extend their markets outside of their branch coverage, which is greatly enhanced by Internet access to the bank. This growth is largely led by high interest savings accounts and competitive mortgages. And like call centres, postal banking represents a staging post for customers who want to move on from traditional branch-based delivery but who are not yet ready for full-on Internet delivery. Northern Rock, for example, have established a successful postal channel that complements its others. Expect to see call centres and postal banking as useful aids to transitioning to the new Internet world, but both will probably have limited lifespans.

3.5 BANK COOPERATIVE CHANNELS

There are obvious opportunities, from time to time, for banks to cooperate. They do so regularly in their businesses, offering syndicated loans where several banks will fund a part of a large loan to a corporate client. Bank treasuries regularly borrow and lend from other banks. In engineering/operations terms they have cooperated on cheque handling, payments networks like SWIFT and EFT/POS, credit cards, clearing systems like BACS, and shared ATM networks. These were not all initially cooperative efforts. For instance, there were two competing credit cards originally in the UK, and there are still two competing shared ATM networks. Nevertheless, despite the implicit vulnerabilities, cooperation does promise lower risk, lower investment and achievable short-term objectives. But these risk-averse approaches do compromise the pursuit of unilateral, radical approaches that might generate substantial profits in the future; and they also slow down the pace of change and lower barriers to competitive entry.

Decisions to cooperate at industry level have been engineering in nature. It is usually from an agreement amongst some banks on the nature of the solution to a common problem, how it is to be managed and the distribution of costs and benefits amongst the participants. It often requires persuading others, such as retailers, and gaining consumer acceptance. There should be a competitive barrier through the participants' control of the system, which, in turn, should maximise the profit from the investment. That's what the founding four banks of BACS planned on. In the event, it created a monopoly that was offensive to the government and had to allow other banks to become members on the same terms as the founders. For such reasons there are unlikely to be many further quasi-monopolistic, profit-led cooperations in the future. Cooperation will become a tool for the industry's benefit, based mainly on cost or risk reduction, such as with the 100 million Chip and PIN cards now being issued by UK banks, and with shared credit history records. Such cooperation is competitively neutral and universally beneficial.

But of course, such decisions are pretty straightforward. We are really looking for competitively advantageous initiatives here. This really comes down to the formation of partnerships of distinctive competence. These will be more likely to protect participant interests and preclude participation by competitors. Of importance, large and small banks can play at this latter game since it does not create a monopoly by virtue simply of the formation of the partnership, so will not offend the government. The distribution of costs, benefits and transfer costs will be easier to agree, and the marketing can still be full-blooded in nature. Branch sharing is a case in point.

3.6   AND SOME OTHER POINTS

3.6.1   Account variations

There are several, not many, basic types of account. Each type has a number of variations. That is, a mortgage could have a fixed or variable interest rate, interest only or capital and interest, and be of varying duration. Savings accounts can have bands and tiers that offer higher rates for larger balances. In addition, there are many, many possible variables. In fact, a normal bank will have over 100 basic account variations, and to the extent that the attributes are allowable or supported by that particular account variation, dozens of attributes will be associated with that account. These range from attributes such as interest rates, bands, tiers, terms and conditions, limits, transaction counts, but also include statement options, alternative addresses, the ability to group accounts, automatic transfers from account to account based on some triggers, and so on. Many different accounts can be engineered by fiddling around with parameters and the like. Whether this is choice, which is good, or confusion, which is bad, is for others to judge. There are clearly cost implications with these infinite choices – it takes longer to explain, more mistakes are made and customer support is more difficult.

This approach is deeply associated with a bank's engineering, its IT systems in particular. The fundamental ways in which accounts are opened and closed, the way in which new capabilities are added and the ways in which new processes are developed all stem from the existing IT systems. After all, modifying something that is already there is obviously the quickest, least expensive and lowest risk way of providing a new product or service.

But in itself, this precludes new approaches to offering products and services, and it serves to increase complexity because the variations are so wide. It certainly increases operational costs because accounts become exceptions to the original basic products. It perpetuates expensive, old practices.

Another important point is that the customers themselves, possibly with limited help from bank staff, have to construct a solution to their own problem, rather than the bank offering a specific solution to a problem that has a variety of aspects. The point here is that bank staff are trying to sell, whereas the customers want them to help solve a problem. Given that the bank has thirty or more headline products, with what amounts to an infinite amount of variation within them, limited staff time, and much less newspaper print space to explain them, how does it all fit? It would be better to ask what the customer had as an objective, work out how to remove the obstacles, and then offer the capability that best addresses the problem.

The various products and services that a customer ends up amassing over the years are not integrated, integration being much different to interfacing. There is also the cross-subsidisation of other products and sectors, irrational pricing, uncompetitive rates and high costs. None of these are minor issues.

The public appears to like the simplicity of the ING Direct savings account model, and the unambiguity of the budget airlines' terms and conditions. If it leads to better rates and fares then that is a strong case. Being stupid about it, when a customer having three accounts with the bank phones up the call centre, the service person has to be able to resolve a situation that might involve any of 36 000 details. That's a lot of either staff training or bemused customers. The worst cases are the consequential ones. Say a customer's payroll credit was late. The knock-on effect of delayed payments and so on leads to instant dunning letters from all types of companies, penalties, and what have you. It takes many phone calls to sort it all out and make the customer whole again.

3.6.2   Bank cost allocation methodologies

There are many parts of a bank involved in supporting customers. To take the current account as the most complex example, customer usage involves cheques, branches, ATMs, funds transfers using BACS, computing, printing, mailing, and what have you. How much does it cost, where are the costs incurred, how much does that part of the service add to the value of the account, and so on? On the basis that if the bank doesn't measure these things then it cannot manage them, it has to have some methodology to do so.

Cost allocation is an art, a science and black magic, all rolled into one. There are several associated aspects to input into the cost allocations. ABC (activity-based costing) analysis seeks to break down activities into their component parts to understand where the costs are being incurred. Transfer pricing is a mechanism used to enable the various units of the bank to 'trade' the assets and liabilities generated from one business unit to another. Service level agreements are typically used to set operational standards between the business and support units within a bank.

The market segments that we used earlier may well be organised into different businesses, such as Private Banking, Retail, Consumer Finance and so on. The shared customers and shared costs need to be understood in order to know where the money is coming from and where it is going. The branch business may say that if a 'wealth' customer walks in and signs up for a credit card then they should get the sales credit to offset their costs. Alternatively, the wealth business might say that they themselves should get the sales credit and be charged for the branch costs of opening the account. So we have businesses wanting to minimise their cost allocations from the cost centres, and the cost centres trying to maximise their allocations to them. This makes for tension. Everyone wants to capture revenue since this is typically what bonuses are paid on.

All the sharing of revenues and costs has to be unshared and allocated into the right buckets for the businesses and cost centres to know how they are performing. A customer of whatever business invokes costs in many cost centres, and there are literally hundreds of these, so an equitable allocation methodology is needed. Now, quite understandably, each of these units has as its goal to improve its performance figures, by whatever means allowable, and that includes negotiating these allocations. Consider, if a million customers do a particular thing on a monthly basis then that is twelve million times they do it in a year. A cost of just 1p per time comes to £120 000 each year, and any business will try to see if it can negotiate that cost down, whereas the cost centre will try to negotiate it up. In these negotiations, nothing is the whole truth, and nothing is a lie.

Much cost accounting, horse-trading, negotiating and arm-twisting goes on before an accommodation is found between all parties, but it is inevitably imperfect in its relationship to the facts. Costs of cost centres fluctuate widely with volumes, some are high fixed/low variable cost models, some are the opposite, some accounts are simple and some are complex – there are many imperfections in this process. The status quo has been arrived at over the years and has been continuously pressured into its existing equilibrium, with a fair dose of internal politics as well.

How much does a cheque cost to deposit? What's the cost of an ATM withdrawal? How much does it cost to send a customer statement? So many simple questions. But the variations are immense in practice, and when multiplying a huge number, which is proportionate in some way to the numbers of accounts and transactions, by a second number, which is the cost, it is important that the sums are done as accurately as possible. The total of all these sums must add up to the operating expenses of running the bank after all, and that is about half the size of the total revenue. It is on the basis of these sums therefore that decisions are made on the profitability of branches, the success of businesses and much else. This impacts staff in job prospects and promotions, whether a branch is to be closed or a business sold.

This process and its various mechanisms are fundamental to customer, account, service and distribution strategies. If the resultant allocations are incorrect, then the businesses can reflect better or worse performance than is the fact. Important decisions are made on this basis – what to do with branches, which ones to close, where to direct marketing efforts, staffing requirements, and much else.

The process invites discussion of the benefits and problems of complex shared cost bases. This discussion is going to heat up as businesses in established banks, absorbing the allocated costs, see their new-model competitors with far lower cost bases performing better, and making better margins as a result. They also see outsourcers offering comparable services as their in-house operations at less cost than their internal cost allocations. If they decide to outsource that operation for their business, then that loss in volume will increase the unit costs for the business units remaining, thus exacerbating the issue.

3.6.3 And on product performances

What is the difference in the performance of different types of account? The performance of a bank account, in terms of the return on equity (ROE) is determined by seven factors, as discussed in the previous chapter. They are:

- The interest spread on the account balance % – **A**%;
- The monetary value of the account balance £ – **B£**;
- The fee income the bank receives as a result of the account (as a % balance) – **C**%;
- The costs incurred, using the cost/income ratio % – **D**%;
- The loan loss anticipated on the account % – **E**%;
- Corporate taxation % – **F**%;
- The amount of equity required % – **G**%.

The following spreadsheets show various values of these for five retail products, and the resulting product ROE. The asset size is fixed at £1000 so that we can calculate the fee income, but all other figures are in percentages.

Of the seven factors, we have chosen to highlight two in these charts – the spread earned and the cost/income ratio. This is to show the variation of ROE as these two values change. Why these two of the seven? Well, there is no choice in the equity requirements (regulations) or tax (government). Loan loss is a number that can be controlled. The fee income is set largely by the market. On the other hand, costs are under a bank's control, difficult to do anything about perhaps, but critical to everything. And the spreads (rates) are the consumers' headline issue. These costs and spreads are the two more interesting variables.

We have also focused on the loan losses for unsecured lending, because this is no less important by any means. Everything is important – you've got to watch them all, and all at the same time.

Don't forget, a 10 % ROE is poor, 15 % is a good average, and above 20 % is 'good and goodest' (if you can get there).

Mortgages

The first example is for mortgages. For a mortgage, the equity requirements are 2 % of the value of the loan. The fee income is taken as zero – while fees are made at mortgage origination, they are often associated with real expense (surveyors, solicitors) and for these purposes best ignored, because it is close to a pass through of fees to others. Also, they are not recurring. Loan losses in the mortgage business are low because the loan is secured against the value of the property. From these numbers, the ROE table is as shown in Figure 3.2.

Interest rates on mortgages are low and, as a consequence, so is the net interest spread, hovering around the 1 % mark. Mortgages do carry that low spread, but they have a low operating cost too. As a consequence, the target ROE should be in the mid to high teens. Figure 3.2 only deals with the capital, and takes no account of additional insurances that a bank might sell to boost its fee income, and therefore the product ROE.

Personal Loans and Credit Cards

Personal loan and credit card products have different values to mortgages for most of the seven factors. Equity will be (at least) 4 %, reflecting the risk. Again there are no fees on these examples, but the loan losses are (relatively) high. The upper area circled on Figure 3.3 relates to credit cards and the lower area to personal loans. Personal loans have lower operational costs than do credit cards.

The cost associated with credit cards is high, not least because of the marketing and sales spend, but the spread is high too. Loan losses aren't pretty either, in this example at 3 %. Personal loans range lower in spreads and costs. The loan losses are too high in this example, so the returns are low.

Let us repeat this chart with one single change – reducing the loan loss by half from 3 % to 1.50 % (Figure 3.4).

PRODUCT ROE %

MORTGAGE

Constant factors:
Asset size (fixed)	£1000
Equity	2.00%
Fee income (as % of assets)	0.00%
Loan loss	0.20%
Taxation	30.00%

Spread	Cost/income ratio							
	50%	45%	40%	35%	30%	25%	20%	15%
1.50	19.25%	21.88%	24.50%	27.13%	29.75%	32.38%	35.00%	37.63%
1.45	18.38%	20.91%	23.45%	25.99%	28.53%	31.06%	33.60%	36.14%
1.40	17.50%	19.95%	22.40%	24.85%	27.30%	29.75%	32.20%	34.65%
1.35	16.63%	18.99%	21.35%	23.71%	26.08%	28.44%	30.80%	33.16%
1.30	15.75%	18.03%	20.30%	22.58%	24.85%	27.13%	29.40%	31.68%
1.25	14.88%	17.06%	19.25%	21.44%	23.63%	25.81%	28.00%	30.19%
1.20	14.00%	16.10%	18.20%	20.30%	22.40%	24.50%	26.60%	28.70%
1.15	13.13%	15.14%	17.15%	19.16%	21.18%	23.19%	25.20%	27.21%
1.10	12.25%	14.18%	16.10%	18.03%	19.95%	21.88%	23.80%	25.73%
1.05	11.38%	13.21%	15.05%	16.89%	18.73%	20.56%	22.40%	24.24%
1.00	10.50%	12.25%	14.00%	15.75%	17.50%	19.25%	21.00%	22.75%
0.95	9.62%	11.29%	12.95%	14.61%	16.28%	17.94%	19.60%	21.26%
0.90	8.75%	10.33%	11.90%	13.48%	15.05%	16.63%	18.20%	19.78%
0.85	7.87%	9.36%	10.85%	12.34%	13.83%	15.31%	16.80%	18.29%
0.80	7.00%	8.40%	9.80%	11.20%	12.60%	14.00%	15.40%	16.80%
0.75	6.12%	7.44%	8.75%	10.06%	11.38%	12.69%	14.00%	15.31%
0.70	5.25%	6.47%	7.70%	8.92%	10.15%	11.38%	12.60%	13.83%
0.65	4.37%	5.51%	6.65%	7.79%	8.92%	10.06%	11.20%	12.34%
0.60	3.50%	4.55%	5.60%	6.65%	7.70%	8.75%	9.80%	10.85%
0.55	2.62%	3.59%	4.55%	5.51%	6.47%	7.44%	8.40%	9.36%

Figure 3.2 ROE figures for a mortgage

PRODUCT ROE %

CREDIT CARD
PERSONAL LOAN

Constant factors:
Asset size (fixed)	£1000
Equity	4.00%
Fee income (as % of assets)	0.00%
Loan loss	3.00%
Taxation	30.00%

Spread	Cost/income ratio							
	55%	50%	45%	40%	35%	30%	25%	20%
12.0	42.00%	52.50%	63.00%	73.50%	84.00%	94.50%	105.00%	115.50%
11.5	38.06%	48.13%	58.19%	68.25%	78.31%	88.38%	98.44%	108.50%
11.0	34.13%	43.75%	53.38%	63.00%	72.63%	82.25%	91.88%	101.50%
10.5	30.19%	39.38%	48.56%	57.75%	66.94%	76.13%	85.31%	94.50%
10.0	26.25%	35.00%	43.75%	52.50%	61.25%	70.00%	78.75%	87.50%
9.5	22.31%	30.63%	38.94%	47.25%	55.56%	63.88%	72.19%	80.50%
9.0	18.38%	26.25%	34.13%	42.00%	49.88%	57.75%	65.63%	73.50%
8.5	14.44%	21.88%	29.31%	36.75%	44.19%	51.63%	59.06%	66.50%
8.0	10.50%	17.50%	24.50%	31.50%	38.50%	45.50%	52.50%	59.50%
7.5	6.56%	13.13%	19.69%	26.25%	32.81%	39.38%	45.94%	52.50%
7.0	2.62%	8.75%	14.88%	21.00%	27.13%	33.25%	39.38%	45.50%
6.5	−1.31%	4.38%	10.06%	15.75%	21.44%	27.13%	32.81%	38.50%
6.0	−5.25%	0.00%	5.25%	10.50%	15.75%	21.00%	26.25%	31.50%
5.5	−9.19%	−4.38%	0.44%	5.25%	10.06%	14.88%	19.69%	24.50%
5.0	−13.13%	−8.75%	−4.37%	0.00%	4.37%	8.75%	13.13%	17.50%
4.5	−17.06%	−13.13%	−9.19%	−5.25%	−1.31%	2.62%	6.56%	10.50%
4.0	−21.00%	−17.50%	−14.00%	−10.50%	−7.00%	−3.50%	0.00%	3.50%
3.5	−24.94%	−21.88%	−18.81%	−15.75%	−12.69%	−9.63%	−6.56%	−3.50%
3.0	−28.88%	−26.25%	−23.63%	−21.00%	−18.38%	−15.75%	−13.13%	−10.50%
2.5	−32.81%	−30.63%	−28.44%	−26.25%	−24.06%	−21.88%	−19.69%	−17.50%

Figure 3.3 ROE figures for personal loans (lower circled area) and credit cards (upper circled area)

PRODUCT **ROE %**

CREDIT CARD
PERSONAL LOAN

Constant factors:	Asset size (fixed)	£1000
	Equity	4.00%
	Fee income (as % of assets)	0.00%
	Loan loss	1.50%
	Taxation	30.00%

Cost/income ratio

Spread	55%	50%	45%	40%	35%	30%	25%	20%
12.0	68.25%	78.75%	89.25%	99.75%	110.25%	120.75%	131.25%	141.75%
11.5	64.31%	74.38%	84.44%	94.50%	104.56%	114.63%	124.69%	134.75%
11.0	60.38%	70.00%	79.63%	89.25%	98.88%	108.50%	118.13%	127.75%
10.5	56.44%	65.63%	74.81%	84.00%	93.19%	102.38%	111.56%	120.75%
10.0	52.50%	61.25%	70.00%	78.75%	87.50%	96.25%	105.00%	113.75%
9.5	48.56%	56.88%	65.19%	73.50%	81.81%	90.13%	98.44%	106.75%
9.0	44.63%	52.50%	60.38%	68.25%	76.13%	84.00%	91.88%	99.75%
8.5	40.69%	48.13%	55.56%	63.00%	70.44%	77.88%	85.31%	92.75%
8.0	36.75%	43.75%	50.75%	57.75%	64.75%	71.75%	78.75%	85.75%
7.5	32.81%	39.38%	45.94%	52.50%	59.06%	65.63%	72.19%	78.75%
7.0	28.88%	35.00%	41.13%	47.25%	53.38%	59.50%	65.63%	71.75%
6.5	24.94%	30.63%	36.31%	42.00%	47.69%	53.38%	59.06%	64.75%
6.0	21.00%	26.25%	31.50%	36.75%	42.00%	47.25%	52.50%	57.75%
5.5	17.06%	21.88%	26.69%	31.50%	36.31%	41.13%	45.94%	50.75%
5.0	13.13%	17.50%	21.88%	26.25%	30.63%	35.00%	39.38%	43.75%
4.5	9.19%	13.13%	17.06%	21.00%	24.94%	28.88%	32.81%	36.75%
4.0	5.25%	8.75%	12.25%	15.75%	19.25%	22.75%	26.25%	29.75%
3.5	1.31%	4.38%	7.44%	10.50%	13.56%	16.63%	19.69%	22.75%
3.0	−2.63%	0.00%	2.63%	5.25%	7.87%	10.50%	13.13%	15.75%
2.5	−6.56%	−4.38%	−2.19%	0.00%	2.19%	4.38%	6.56%	8.75%

Figure 3.4 ROE figures for personal loans (lower circled area) and credit cards (upper circled area) with a loan loss of only 1.5 %

Bank happiness returns. There is a most dramatic improvement in performance. Profitability has doubled by halving the loan loss provision. If a bank wants to throw credit cards at consumers it must have a high spread. Otherwise it must 'know' its target consumers pretty well. Since we 'know' the customers and their propensity to default, then we have a better quality of unsecured loan, and the customer has a better rate. The returns are at the 50 % mark for credit cards and 35 % for unsecured personal loans.

Savings Accounts

Savings accounts are not lending accounts so we have to look at them slightly differently. The trick that we've used here is just to assume that we pass the funds to the bank's Treasury at a skinny spread – perhaps 0.5 %. This is therefore arithmetically the same as a loan to a bank. Bank loans are deemed in this book to have a 1 % equity requirement. There are no fees or loan losses. The operating costs of a savings account are low; they are not transaction intensive. The target ROE is therefore around the 30 % mark (Figure 3.5). There are clear opportunities for monolines.

PRODUCT **ROE** %			Constant factors:	Asset size (fixed)	£1000
SAVINGS ACCOUNT				Equity	1.00%
				Fee income (as % of assets)	0.00%
				Loan loss	0.00%
				Taxation	30.00%

	Cost/income ratio							
Spread	55%	50%	45%	40%	35%	30%	25%	20%
2.0	63.00%	70.00%	77.00%	84.00%	91.00%	98.00%	105.00%	112.00%
1.9	59.85%	66.50%	73.15%	79.80%	86.45%	93.10%	99.75%	106.40%
1.8	56.70%	63.00%	69.30%	75.60%	81.90%	88.20%	94.50%	100.80%
1.7	53.55%	59.50%	65.45%	71.40%	77.35%	83.30%	89.25%	95.20%
1.6	50.40%	56.00%	61.60%	67.20%	72.80%	78.40%	84.00%	89.60%
1.5	47.25%	52.50%	57.75%	63.00%	68.25%	73.50%	78.75%	84.00%
1.4	44.10%	49.00%	53.90%	58.80%	63.70%	68.60%	73.50%	78.40%
1.3	40.95%	45.50%	50.05%	54.60%	59.15%	63.70%	68.25%	72.80%
1.2	37.80%	42.00%	46.20%	50.40%	54.60%	58.80%	63.00%	67.20%
1.1	34.65%	38.50%	42.35%	46.20%	50.05%	53.90%	57.75%	61.60%
1.0	31.50%	35.00%	38.50%	42.00%	45.50%	49.00%	52.50%	56.00%
0.9	28.35%	31.50%	34.65%	37.80%	40.95%	44.10%	47.25%	50.40%
0.8	25.20%	28.00%	30.80%	33.60%	36.40%	39.20%	42.00%	44.80%
0.7	22.05%	24.50%	26.95%	29.40%	31.85%	34.30%	36.75%	39.20%
0.6	18.90%	21.00%	23.10%	25.20%	27.30%	29.40%	31.50%	33.60%
0.5	15.75%	17.50%	19.25%	21.00%	22.75%	24.50%	26.25%	28.00%
0.4	12.60%	14.00%	15.40%	16.80%	18.20%	19.60%	21.00%	22.40%
0.3	9.45%	10.50%	11.55%	12.60%	13.65%	14.70%	15.75%	16.80%
0.2	6.30%	7.00%	7.70%	8.40%	9.10%	9.80%	10.50%	11.20%
0.1	3.15%	3.50%	3.85%	4.20%	4.55%	4.90%	5.25%	5.60%

Figure 3.5   ROE figures for savings accounts

Current Accounts

The last example, shown in Figure 3.6, is for a current account. These differ from savings accounts in that they do attract fees and have higher spreads, and far higher costs. The reality may be that their cost income ratio exceeds 100 %. It is only relatively recently that interest has been widely paid on current accounts, but the rate is usually so low that the rate the bank's treasury pays should provide a reasonable spread of 1 % to 4 %. We have only used fee income in this one account. Current accounts have many fees attached to them, especially for small businesses. This could be a monthly maintenance charge, a per cheque charge, cash deposit charges, funds transfer charges and so on. There are fees associated with the other products such as cash advances on the credit card, but we omitted them. The spreadsheet requires these fees to be input as a percentage of the account size, and we have arbitrarily chosen that to be 5 %. The fees are the thing here.

Therefore, a target ROE, even for a current account, could be high, mainly dependent on the fees and costs. But really with current accounts, as you can see, pick a number, any number. We'd suggest that half of all consumer current accounts in a large bank make a loss.

	PRODUCT **ROE** %			Constant factors:	Asset size (fixed)	£1000
					Equity	1.00%
	RETAIL				Fee income (as % of assets)	5.00%
	CURRENT ACCOUNT				Loan loss	0.00%
					Taxation	30.00%

Cost/income ratio

Spread	115%	105%	95%	85%	75%	65%	55%	45%
4.0	−94.50%	−31.50%	31.50%	94.50%	157.50%	220.50%	283.50%	346.50%
3.8	−92.40%	−30.80%	30.80%	92.40%	154.00%	215.60%	277.20%	338.80%
3.6	−90.30%	−30.10%	30.10%	90.30%	150.50%	210.70%	270.90%	331.10%
3.4	−88.20%	−29.40%	29.40%	88.20%	147.00%	205.80%	264.60%	323.40%
3.2	−86.10%	−28.70%	28.70%	86.10%	143.50%	200.90%	258.30%	315.70%
3.0	−84.00%	−28.00%	28.00%	84.00%	140.00%	196.00%	252.00%	308.00%
2.8	−81.90%	−27.30%	27.30%	81.90%	136.50%	191.10%	245.70%	300.30%
2.6	−79.80%	−26.60%	26.60%	79.80%	133.00%	186.20%	239.40%	292.60%
2.4	−77.70%	−25.90%	25.90%	77.70%	129.50%	181.30%	233.10%	284.90%
2.2	−75.60%	−25.20%	25.20%	75.60%	126.00%	176.40%	226.80%	277.20%
2.0	−73.50%	−24.50%	24.50%	73.50%	122.50%	171.50%	220.50%	269.50%
1.8	−71.40%	−23.80%	23.80%	71.40%	119.00%	166.60%	214.20%	261.80%
1.6	−69.30%	−23.10%	23.10%	69.30%	115.50%	161.70%	207.90%	254.10%
1.4	−67.20%	−22.40%	22.40%	67.20%	112.00%	156.80%	201.60%	246.40%
1.2	−65.10%	−21.70%	21.70%	65.10%	108.50%	151.90%	195.30%	238.70%
1.0	−63.00%	−21.00%	21.00%	63.00%	105.00%	147.00%	189.00%	231.00%
0.8	−60.90%	−20.30%	20.30%	60.90%	101.50%	142.10%	182.70%	223.30%
0.6	−58.80%	−19.60%	19.60%	58.80%	98.00%	137.20%	176.40%	215.60%
0.4	−56.70%	−18.90%	18.90%	56.70%	94.50%	132.30%	170.10%	207.90%
0.2	−54.60%	−18.20%	18.20%	54.60%	91.00%	127.40%	163.80%	200.20%

Figure 3.6 ROE figures for current accounts

From these five product examples it can be seen that the power of each of the seven factors is strong, but that a 20 % or more ROE is a reasonable ambition in all cases. It is also clear that any lowering of costs has a great impact, as does the loan loss provision. These are the two variables that a bank has within its control. But competition, or the lack of it, does strongly influence fees and spreads, and a bank's ability to change either.

Since ROE is the primary goal for investors, and hence bank management, growth of business on an inadequate ROE is not really progress, unless that growth in the asset base leads to scale economies that will reduce the costs. A tougher credit policy, even if it leads to a reduced asset size, would increase the ROE by reducing the loan loss provision. In practice, these decisions are difficult to make.

WHERE DID THESE CALCULATIONS COME FROM?

For those interested, if you recreate and noodle around with these or similar spreadsheets, some things begin to scream out as you change the variables. The essence of the spreadsheet is:

- The interest spread on the account balance %   **A**
- The monetary value of the account balance (if ROA is to be calculated) £   **B**
- The fee income the bank receives as a result of the account %   **C**
- The costs incurred, using the cost/income ratio %   **D**
- The loan loss anticipated on the account %   **E**
- Corporate taxation %   **F**
- The amount of equity required %   **G**

The formula is as we used previously in the worked loan example in Chapter 2.
The values of the seven variables have been given a letter, A–F.
The values in the calculated spreadsheet cells are given by:

$$\text{ROE \%} = ((((A^*B) + C)^*(1 - D)) - E)^*(1 - F)/G$$

4
Real Banks and Challenges

4.1 SOME LISTS OF BANKS – INTERNATIONAL BANKS

Table 4.1 shows a small selection drawn from *The Banker* list of the top 1000 banks worldwide. The questions are – do banks differ, and does banking differ from country to country?

The table has three or four of the largest banks in each of eighteen countries. Because these are the largest in each country, retail banking may only account for 25 %–50 % of each bank's business. So their cost/income ratios in column 10 are higher than they would be for a pure retail operation. Column 2 shows the actual Tier I capital, which is primarily investors' equity. Percentages are useful for comparative purposes, but there is nothing in the table to alert us to mergers, or a disastrous previous year, both of which would distort the growth figures in columns 4 and 7. The numbers are normalised to $US, and the profit/Tier I capital in column 8 is pre-tax, so that national taxation is not a factor. That figure less 30 % gives a good approximation to the ROE %.

Zooming in on column 8, the pre-tax return on Tier I capital, the answers to the questions 'do banks differ, and does banking differ from country to country?' are yes and yes. While the process of banking is basically not different from bank to bank and country to country, there are wide disparities in this table that show that bank performances do indeed vary greatly from country to country, as indeed they do from bank to bank within a single country. Bank performance between countries varies primarily because of the different economic environments in each country; and within each country, the performance of banks differs based primarily on the strategies each bank has adopted in terms of, for example, the markets it serves and the effectiveness of its leadership. More banks from more countries only reinforce this point.

Banks domiciled in the same country are competing in the same set of national economic circumstances as each other. How well they can predict their economic environment, how quickly they can react to changes to minimise negative impacts or

Table 4.1 A selection of the top 1000 banks worldwide; figures in $US.

		1	2	3	4	5	6	7	8	9	10
Country	Bank	World rank	Tier one capital $m	Assets $m	Assets growth %	T1 capital/ assets	Profits $m pre-tax	% Profits growth	% Profits/ T1 capital pre-tax	ROA %	% Cost/ income
Australia	National Australia Bank	44	13 173	265 264	5.3 %	4.97 %	3756	29.6	28.9 %	1.42 %	49.98
	ANZ Banking Group	68	7835	121 739	7.7 %	6.44 %	2187	1.7	28.6 %	1.80 %	45.34
	Westpac Banking Corp	76	6899	147 717	15.9 %	4.67 %	1948	9.4	31.3 %	1.32 %	53.56
	Commonwealth Bank Group	78	6816	168 133	0.9 %	4.05 %	1986	−16.7	30.1 %	1.18 %	65.09
Brazil	Banco Bradesco	109	4695	60 976	23.3 %	7.70 %	939	8.7	22.1 %	1.54 %	70.68
	Banco Itau	114	4383	41 114	6.8 %	10.66 %	1942	33.6	46.9 %	4.72 %	46.10
	Banco do Brasil	117	4206	79 690	12.5 %	5.28 %	1635	40.5	44.3 %	2.05 %	62.05
Canada	Scotiabank	47	12 632	211 473	−3.1 %	5.97 %	2683	35.5	21.4 %	1.27 %	56.38
	Royal Bank of Canada	48	12 320	300 894	7.6 %	4.09 %	3480	8.4	29.0 %	1.16 %	59.76
	Canadian Imperial Bank	57	9494	206 114	2.1 %	4.61 %	1747	459.5	19.6 %	0.85 %	77.91
	Bank of Montreal	58	9348	190 106	2.0 %	4.92 %	1953	35.4	21.6 %	1.03 %	66.75
China	China Construction Bank	21	22 507	429 432	15.3 %	5.24 %	54	−89.6	0.3 %	0.01 %	46.23
	Industrial and Commercial	25	20 600	637 829	10.5 %	3.23 %	321	−61.5	1.5 %	0.05 %	66.41
	Bank of China	29	18 579	464 213	6.9 %	4.00 %	1215	−27.1	6.0 %	0.26 %	46.73
	Agricultural Bank of China	36	16 435	359 606	17.7 %	4.57 %	352	153.2	2.2 %	0.10 %	91.41
Czech Rep	Ceskoslovenska obchodni	fo(222)	1793	23 641	1.6 %	7.58 %	283	−22	16.5 %	1.20 %	67.20
	Ceska Sporitelna	fo(283)	1395	21 597	6.6 %	6.46 %	426	22.8	37.5 %	1.97 %	58.00
	Komercni Banka	fo(336)	1081	17 801	2.4 %	6.07 %	503	9.5	51.7 %	2.83 %	55.52

France	Credit Agricole	2	55 435	1 105 378	50.7%	5.02%	7416	35.3	15.1%	0.67%	64.34
	BNP Paribas	10	32 458	988 982	10.2%	3.28%	7997	18.3	26.0%	0.81%	62.90
	Societe Generale	23	21 396	681 216	7.6%	3.14%	5409	71.7	26.6%	0.79%	67.58
	Credit Mutuel	27	19 319	448 296	2.2%	4.31%	3123	27.0	17.8%	0.70%	64.30
Germany	Deutsche Bank	12	27 302	1 014 845	6.0%	2.69%	3481	−22.3	12.4%	0.34%	81.81
	HypoVereinsbank	32	18 142	605 525	−30.6%	3.00%	−2710	na	−12.8%	−0.45%	64.11
	Commerzbank	45	12 954	481 921	−9.6%	2.69%	−2501	na	−18.0%	−0.52%	73.30
	Bayerische Landesbank	50	12 141	395 846	−8.2%	3.07%	543	96.7	4.5%	0.14%	45.30
India	State Bank of India	82	6323	126 930	10.6%	4.98%	1894	31.6	32.4%	1.49%	46.07
	ICICI Bank	268	1469	28 861	17.2%	5.09%	442	−29.6	31.5%	1.53%	63.25
	Punjab National Bank	313	1184	24 127	21.4%	4.91%	448	102.2	44.0%	1.86%	42.04
	Canara Bank	405	846	17 282	13.8%	4.90%	277	na	35.2%	1.60%	46.67
Italy	Banca Intesa	34	18 050	328 637	−7.3%	5.49%	2469	761.2	14.1%	0.75%	65.84
	UniCredito Italiano	41	13 995	300 904	11.7%	4.65%	4390	6.0	31.8%	1.46%	54.50
	San Paolo IMI	46	12 677	255 847	−0.6%	4.95%	2107	63.9	16.8%	0.82%	61.90
	Capitalia Gruppo Bancario	70	7737	162 141	−8.9%	4.77%	172	78.1	2.2%	0.11%	70.03
Netherlands	Rabobank Nederland	15	24 830	509 532	7.6%	4.87%	3034	21.7	13.1%	0.60%	67.58
	ING Bank	17	24 089	684 004	13.5%	3.52%	2550	112.8	10.9%	0.37%	71.88
	ABN AMRO Bank	20	23 037	667 636	−4.9%	3.45%	6211	32.5	27.8%	0.93%	66.97

(Continued)

Table 4.1 A selection of the top 1000 banks worldwide; figures in $US (*Continued*)

		1	2	3	4	5	6	7	8	9	10
Country	Bank	World rank	Tier one capital $m	Assets $m	Assets growth %	T1 capital/ assets	Profits $m pre-tax	% Profits growth	% Profits/ T1 capital pre-tax	ROA %	% Cost/ income
New Zealand	Bank of New Zealand	fo(290)	1313	22 372	4.7 %	5.87 %	447	0.3	35.2 %	2.00 %	45.40
	National Bank of New Zealand	fo(296)	1277	27 704	8.8 %	4.61 %	287	−38.1	19.7 %	1.04 %	50.03
	ASB Bank	fo(436)	760	16 011	13.4 %	4.75 %	244	25.1	35.9 %	1.52 %	49.29
Poland	Bank Pekao	fo(253)	1580	16 845	−3.2 %	9.38 %	341	8.0	21.3 %	2.03 %	58.29
	Bank Handlowy w Warsawie	fo(258)	1519	8893	3.4 %	17.08 %	105	7.9	6.9 %	1.18 %	70.55
	PKO Bank Polski	292	1305	22 635	3.2 %	5.77 %	436	13.5	37.0 %	1.93 %	65.62
	Bank Przemyslowo-Handlowy	fo(298)	1256	12 936	13.7 %	9.71 %	161	214.0	12.5 %	1.25 %	66.87
South Africa	Standard Bank Group	116	4233	81 384	38.7 %	5.20 %	1332	20.0	32.9 %	1.64 %	56.17
	ABSA Group	145	3012	47 938	−16.8 %	6.28 %	977	36.3	38.0 %	2.04 %	57.05
	First Rand Banking Group	218	1851	40 238	7.9 %	4.60 %	755	13.6	42.6 %	1.88 %	58.77
	Nedcor	252	1595	47 076	14.2 %	3.39 %	−94	−137.0	−5.0 %	−20.00 %	74.56
Spain	Santander Central Hispano	22	21 408	444 012	8.4 %	4.82 %	5180	16.9	25.8 %	1.17 %	63.10
	Banco Bilbao Vizcaya	31	18 176	362 655	2.7 %	5.01 %	4814	22.2	27.2 %	1.33 %	56.77
	Caja de Ahorros – Barcelona	56	9557	146 637	12.7 %	6.52 %	1258	7290.0	13.8 %	0.86 %	64.97
	Caja de Ahorros – Madrid	98	5172	96 328	8.0 %	5.37 %	958	7.0	18.6 %	1.00 %	na
Sweden	Nordea Group	49	12 319	331 132	5.0 %	3.72 %	2141	28.7	17.5 %	0.65 %	63.00
	Svenska Handelsbanken	83	6302	173 258	−1.3 %	3.64 %	1575	11.2	26.4 %	0.91 %	44.57
	Skandaviska Enskilda Banken	88	5861	175 862	3.1 %	3.33 %	1095	5.4	19.3 %	0.62 %	66.99
	ForeningsSparbanken	89	5795	137 778	4.7 %	4.21 %	1315	37.1	23.2 %	0.95 %	57.27

Country	Bank										
Switzerland	UBS	18	24 064	1 120 543	17.3 %	2.15 %	6749	82.5	29.4 %	0.60 %	75.43
	Credit Suisse Group	33	18 105	777 849	0.7 %	2.33 %	4673	na	27.6 %	0.60 %	70.46
	Schweizer Verband	122	3885	82 577	10.2 %	4.70 %	479	12.6	13.0 %	0.58 %	55.14
	Zurcher Kantonalbank	123	3860	62 017	−4.7 %	6.22 %	485	200.4	13.2 %	0.78 %	65.30
United Kingdom	HSBC Holdings	3	54 863	1 034 216	36.2 %	5.30 %	12 816	32.8	27.3 %	1.24 %	47.93
	Royal Bank of Scotland	8	34 623	806 207	12.1 %	4.29 %	10 992	29.3	33.7 %	1.36 %	55.07
	HBOS	11	29 349	650 721	14.7 %	4.51 %	6721	29.5	24.1 %	1.03 %	45.69
	Barclays Bank	13	26 761	791 292	12.0 %	3.38 %	6862	20.0	26.3 %	0.87 %	58.44
	Lloyds TSB Group	26	20 030	449 780	21.5 %	4.45 %	7760	66.8	42.0 %	1.73 %	52.21
USA	Citigroup	1	66 871	1 264 032	15.2 %	5.29 %	26 333	15.6	41.8 %	2.08 %	52.50
	Bank of America	4	44 050	736 445	11.5 %	5.98 %	15 886	22.3	36.5 %	2.16 %	53.13
	JP Morgan Chase	5	43 167	770 912	1.6 %	5.60 %	10 037	298.5	24.9 %	1.30 %	68.03
	Wells Fargo	14	25 074	387 798	11.0 %	6.47 %	9588	7.8	41.2 %	2.47 %	60.16
	Bank One Corp	16	24 499	326 563	17.7 %	7.50 %	4390	−7.8	18.1 %	1.34 %	60.31

The notation 'fo' in the table means 'foreign owned', a subsidiary of a larger bank domiciled outside of the country. We have shown in brackets what their ranking would be if they were looked at as an independent bank. Where 'na' is shown, it means that the data in the cell is not applicable because of losses, or not available.

Source: Top 1000 banks in 2003, *The Banker*, July 2004

maximise opportunities, whether they can offer comparable or better products and services at a lower cost than their competitors, whether the strategic decisions of the last few years are paying off or not, and so on, all go to determining their performance relative to their domestic competitors. Taking a single snapshot at a point in time does not tell the whole story, but clearly there is a wide variance in performance within each country.

Comparing banks from different countries requires extracting the economic environment factors, which cannot be done without much more detail. Still, many countries are similar by nature of growth, income per capita, interest rates and so on, so some comparisons can be made as to the relative effectiveness of banks, and indeed the banking industry in a country. For instance, a comparison of banks in Italy, France, Germany and The Netherlands is meaningful to the extent that they have the same currency and central bank, and are all in developed countries in some process of harmonisation. However, even then there are significant inter-country disparities, as the figures for Germany relative to other countries show, and Italy's banks show a wide variation in intra-country performance.

The wide variance in the performance of banks in different countries, and in the performance of competing banks within a single country in providing comparable banking services seems to lead to the inevitable conclusion that the management strategies and their execution, coupled with an ability to manage the business at the detailed level, play the most distinctive and differentiating role in a bank's performance. We think that this is no different from other industries.

The fact is that the performance of individual banks is all over the place, indicating that something is missing. One important missing piece is their performance over a period of, say, five years. Some banks came into this year with an overhang of problems acquired previously. Some show growth/decline as the result of acquisitions/divestments. The practice of banking, or more particularly the management of banking, does vary greatly in certain countries. There are many things that need to be understood before a table such as this could be used to divine much useful observation. Five years of data would allow us to do that.

Most of these banks are large national and international banks, so this is not specifically indicative of retail banking. What we would say is that each of these banks is subject to exactly the same science of banking, and that the majority of the engineering is similar too. It's a bit of a stretch, we know, but this all suggests that the strategy and art of banking as exercised by the leadership, past and/or present, appears to be the most likely cause of the differences.

4.2   GLOBALISATION

It is de rigueur to address the globalisation of businesses. And if there is one business to which this applies in spades it must be banking, on the basis that trade and investment flows, and the associated money flows, are continuously swishing and swashing around the world. Against this backdrop, global banking has a real meaning to large corporate and capital markets customers who transact with banks across the world's major financial markets and also in emerging markets.

But in terms of retail banking from the customer perspective, globalisation is largely a marketing plus, not a factual plus. Retail customers have little need for 'global' capabilities over and above credit card usage, ATM usage and the occasional international funds transfer. All these are already provided without asking.

To be specific, HSBC has some 120 million accounts around the world, and has as extensive a global network as any. If each customer has more than one account, then they may have 60 million retail customers. In a world with a population of 6 billion people that is 1 % of the world population. Actually, that's impressive to us, but having a non-exclusive relationship with 1 % of a market is not the plan, a global retail bank seems pretty meaningless in fact. However, the HSBC claim to be 'the world's local bank' is a powerful and meaningful statement. Certainly, a frequent traveller probably derives some comfort from knowing that there are branches worldwide.

4.3 UK BANKS

Table 4.2 is from the same listing in *The Banker*, with the UK banks in the world top 1000 in terms of equity capital, whether they are in retail banking or not. The fifteen banks shown with *** by their name, something less than half of the total, have a large proportion of their revenue based in UK retail banking. The monetary values have been converted from $US to £UK using an exchange rate of £/$1.80.

There is a high degree of concentration in the UK banking industry, as can be seen from the rightmost column. The largest five banks account for 80 % of all assets, and the top eight for 95 %. There are plenty of other banks and near-banks in the UK, and they include some large institutions like Nationwide Building Society and the Government's National Savings & Investments (which itself attracted £7.5 billion into Premium Bonds alone in the year to March 2004), so the degree of concentration isn't quite this acute, but is still acute. Building societies are not listed here, because they are not classified as banks.

As well as building societies, which are an important part of UK retail banking, there are credit unions, which are insignificant in terms of size in the UK, but do have an interesting business model and enjoy market success in other countries.

Another set of players serves the sub-prime market. Companies like Kensington, Cattles and Paragon may not have wide name recognition, but they and others do service some of the modest needs of over eight million people in the UK. With the HSBC acquisition of Household Finance in the USA, the pejorative opinions towards serving this real market are being moderated.

Without going into a great deal more depth about the banks, it is inappropriate to comment on relative performances. Their annual reports range from a hundred to five hundred pages each. Some are global; some are regional within the UK. What can

Table 4.2 UK banks in the top 1000 in 2003, figures in £UK (£1 UK = $US 1.80).

	1	2	3	4	5	6	7	8	9	10	11	12
Bank	World rank	Tier one capital £	Assets £m	Assets growth %	T1 capital/ assets	Profits £m	% Profits growth	% Profits/ T1 capital pre-tax	ROA %	% Cost/ income	% of tot assets	% cum of tot assets
HSBC Holdings ***	3	30 479	574 564	36.20	5.30 %	7120	32.8	27.3 %	1.24 %	47.93	22.70 %	22.70 %
Royal Bank of Scotland ***	8	19 235	447 893	12.10	4.29 %	6107	29.3	33.7 %	1.36 %	55.07	17.70 %	40.40 %
HBOS ***	11	16 305	361 512	14.70	4.51 %	3734	29.5	24.1 %	1.03 %	45.69	14.28 %	54.68 %
Barclays Bank ***	13	14 867	439 607	12.00	3.38 %	3812	20.0	26.3 %	0.87 %	58.44	17.37 %	72.05 %
Lloyds TSB ***	26	11 128	249 878	21.50	4.45 %	4311	66.8	42.0 %	1.73 %	52.21	9.87 %	81.93 %
Abbey National ***	53	6151	175 278	0.30	3.51 %	−691	na	−10.2 %	−0.39 %	82.91	6.93 %	88.85 %
Standard Chartered	77	3807	66 823	6.40	5.70 %	857	22.2	23.2 %	1.28 %	56.05	2.64 %	91.49 %
Northern Rock ***	139	1817	36 846	13.80	4.93 %	383	18.6	22.4 %	1.04 %	33.77	1.46 %	92.95 %
Alliance & Leicester ***	146	1661	48 014	17.40	3.46 %	520	12.0	31.1 %	1.08 %	57.37	1.90 %	94.85 %
FCE Bank ****	157	1531	17 261	7.7	8.87 %	227	6	16.2 %	1.32 %	65.05	0.68 %	95.53 %
Bradford & Bingley ***	183	1276	31 918	26.80	4.00 %	261	9.3	20.6 %	0.82 %	63.48	1.26 %	96.79 %
Schroders	220	1008	2613	7.20	38.59 %	65	247.1	6.4 %	2.49 %	89.93	0.10 %	96.89 %
Merrill Lynch International	314	657	7808	10.70	8.42 %	76	−14.2	12.3 %	0.96 %	72.23	0.31 %	97.20 %
The Co-operative Bank ***	321	640	9536	9.10	6.71 %	131	6.2	21.9 %	1.37 %	61.54	0.38 %	97.58 %
Yorkshire Bank ***	fo(394)	561	7639	7.90	7.33 %	273	38.5	51.8 %	3.57 %	46.12	0.30 %	97.88 %
Clydesdale Bank ***	fo(390)	496	8146	−2.90	6.08 %	152	−9.5	30.4 %	1.86 %	56.60	0.32 %	98.20 %
Egg ***	427	432	11 596	10.70	3.73 %	−34	na	−7.7 %	−0.29 %	74.34	0.46 %	98.66 %
Investec Bank	fo(463)	386	5087	−26.40	7.58 %	4	−88.7	1.1 %	0.08 %	90.20	0.20 %	98.86 %
Close Brothers Group	503	346	3197	17.00	10.82 %	69	13.9	21.0 %	2.18 %	64.18	0.13 %	98.99 %
Singer & Friedlander Group	508	342	2186	2.90	15.63 %	92	124.9	28.4 %	4.22 %	72.11	0.09 %	99.07 %

Moscow Narodny Bank	584	272	1041	−8.70	26.11 %	18	8.1	6.6 %	1.72 %	68.34	0.04 %	99.12 %
Standard Bank London	fo(624)	239	4241	10.20	5.63 %	8	−64.7	3.4 %	0.19 %	70.40	0.17 %	99.28 %
Northern Bank ***	fo(625)	237	3396	0.70	6.99 %	96	13.1	39.2 %	2.84 %	54.19	0.13 %	99.42 %
ABC International Bank	fo(676)	208	1227	−2.40	16.98 %	8	na	3.9 %	0.65 %	85.38	0.05 %	99.47 %
N M Rothschild & Sons	691	202	4039	−0.50	5.01 %	17	−10.3	8.4 %	0.42 %	56.76	0.16 %	99.63 %
Gulf International Bank (UK)	fo(721)	189	1897	−16.80	10.00 %	−36	na	−18.1 %	−1.91 %	239.72	0.07 %	99.70 %
Nomura Bank International	758	169	409	−63.30	41.30 %	28	na	17.6 %	6.87 %	19.83	0.02 %	99.72 %
Daiwa Securities Bank	803	153	325	−7.40	47.14 %	4	139.7	3.0 %	1.38 %	91.42	0.01 %	99.73 %
Sabanci Bank	849	138	571	11.10	24.08 %	9	10.6	7.0 %	1.65 %	na	0.02 %	99.75 %
British Arab Commercial	852	136	1227	−7.90	11.10 %	21	97.0	15.4 %	1.71 %	52.49	0.05 %	99.80 %
EFG Private Bank	fo(865)	131	642	−9.30	20.39 %	1	−77.2	1.1 %	0.21 %	91.02	0.03 %	99.83 %
Melli Bank	fo(866)	131	1189	16.70	10.96 %	14	180.3	10.9 %	1.19 %	25.24	0.05 %	99.87 %
National Bank of Kuwait	fo(916)	116	888	−12.20	13.07 %	6	−44.3	3.7 %	0.61 %	59.40	0.04 %	99.91 %
Ahli United Bank	fo(923)	116	1306	2.60	8.85 %	14	6.1	11.8 %	1.06 %	54.95	0.05 %	99.96 %
Julian Hodge Bank	927	114	416	7.10	27.46 %	11	35.4	9.3 %	2.50 %	50.55	0.02 %	99.98 %
Bank Saderat	fo(931)	113	616	−14.20	18.44 %	8	48.1	7.1 %	1.32 %	37.15	0.02 %	100.00 %
Totals		115 788	2 530 830			27 696						100 %

Source: Top 1000 banks in 2003, The Banker, July 2004

be seen, however, is that there are few correlations with size, such as profitability or percentage asset growth, or cost/income ratios.

So that profits are normalised, for UK and international comparisons to be made, *The Banker* gives pre-tax figures. Thus, the nearest we can get to an ROE % figure would be to reduce column 8, pre-tax profit/Tier I capital, by the UK corporate tax rate of 30 %. From the last row with the totals, we see that the overall Tier I capital ratio is 4.55 % (115/2.53 billion), and that the overall pre-tax ROE is 23.9 % (27.7/116), which is about 16.7 % ROE after tax.

Here are some brief thumbnail sketches of the large banks in the UK. The intent is to highlight some differences in the hope of amplifying the opportunities to differentiate and excel.

4.3.1   HSBC

HSBC is a major success story, starting as a Hong Kong based regional bank, imbued with a strong Scottish ethos. Gradually it expanded into the Far East and US and then made a major leap by acquiring the ailing Midland Bank in the UK. Its strong retail bank continues to make acquisitions around the world and is now in the first division of global banks. Run by a tight international management cadre, its strength has been clear strategic vision, an emphasis on tight cost management and determination. The world's favourite local bank is a great description, but these local banks are well integrated, and can do anything required of them. HSBC continues to expand by acquisition in developed markets, with recent acquisitions in the US and France, and acquisitions in emerging markets such as Turkey and Mexico. First Direct lead the way in UK direct banking. It is a successful model, enjoying high customer loyalty after more than 15 years of operation.

4.3.2   Royal Bank of Scotland

RBS is a Scottish success that has grown mostly by acquisition outside of Scotland. Starting off as a regional Scottish bank, it grew by acquisition and organic growth in England, developing a focused, cost effective business model. When NatWest, a stodgy largely English domestic bank, lost its way, including a debilitating foray into investment banking, RBS mounted an effective takeover, kicked into play by BoS at the time, and the subsequent integration with NatWest created a first division UK retail bank. International expansion has been largely limited to retail banking acquisitions on the east coast of the USA and cross-shareholdings and collaboration with the Spanish bank BSCH. Major contributors to their success have been extremely strong, directed senior management and an obsession with cost management and the ability to execute change quickly and effectively. The NatWest integration was an object lesson. RBS has also had a huge success with its retail market insurance strategy.

4.3.3 HBOS

HBOS is the product of two UK banks – Bank of Scotland, the oldest and much admired Scottish bank, and Halifax, which had grown to be a top building society before converting to a bank. Halifax is the senior partner in this business, which is a major UK retail banking force. Both banks came with strong solid operations, but arguably the conservative Bank of Scotland had lost its way strategically and will gain from the exposure to Halifax's outward looking management.

4.3.4 Barclays Bank

A blue chip UK retail and international bank which lost its way for a time but now seems to be coming back with a commanding position in the corporate market and cards, and a strong position in retail banking. A major international presence was neglected and fell into decline and there were distracting diversions into investment banking, but international growth is now back on the agenda, particularly in Europe, and cards and investment banking have come good. A particular strength is Barclays' depth of business-as-usual management, but quick and effective change has not been its strong point.

4.3.5 Lloyds TSB

A bank with roots in three distinct businesses that have taken time to integrate. Lloyds Bank, an English retail bank first acquired Bank of London and South America, a largely South American retail bank, and Trustee Savings Bank, a UK savings bank. Bringing all of this together was a major struggle for Lloyds. Early on, Latin American debt was a major preoccupation, and the integration of TSB took far too long. On the plus side, Lloyds has managed to avoid the distractions of investment banking and has exercised tight cost and strategic management to create an efficient retail banking operation. In the process there has been a major withdrawal from international business. Lloyds TSB acquired Abbey Life and Scottish Widows, but has had its moments with its insurance activities. The major question is where Lloyds TSB goes from here.

4.3.6 Abbey National

Abbey was a successful and leading UK building society before demutualisation. It then went downhill, squandering its war chest on scattergun expansion in inappropriate or high-risk activities and running up major losses in the process. As we write, it has now been acquired by BSCH bank from Spain and has shed non-core businesses and got back to the knitting. Overall, Abbey is a sad story of a dash for growth outside of its competencies, which came off the rails. The lesson is that in banking, as in skiing, you go off piste at your peril.

4.3.7   Standard Chartered

Standard Chartered's roots go back to colonial banking in the Far East and Africa, particularly Hong Kong and South Africa. As the world changed, it found it tough going and for a period went through a rocky patch. It still remains an emerging market bank with a relatively small footprint in the developing world. The bank is battle-hardened through adversity, and is now reaping the benefits of economic boom time (relatively) in emerging markets. It was never able to find a developed market anchor, as HSBC did, and its future probably lies with an alignment to a developed market bank seeking international reach.

4.3.8   Alliance & Leicester

A steady top tier former building society, focused and cost conscious. It has an interesting Internet focus, a relationship with the Post Office and has made big moves into small business banking and cash handling. It is developing its own model, which appears to be well set to take it forward.

4.3.9   Northern Rock

Another top tier former building society, focused and cost conscious, but with a difference. It has developed a major position and capability in the mortgage securitisation market, and thereby has taken a major step towards what we believe is one of tomorrow's retail banking models.

4.3.10   Bradford & Bingley

Life has not been dull at Bradford & Bingley. A leading building society, which declared that it would never demutualise, then proceeded to demutualise. There was diversification into investment products, third party mortgages and a mortgage processing joint venture with a US software house. There is frequent bid talk. The trend has now reversed with a strategy to exit various of its newer businesses and concentrate on its core business. The lesson – in banking as in life – is that what goes round comes round.

4.3.11   Yorkshire Bank

A profitable, focused and cost conscious English retail bank. Under the ownership of National Australia Group for a number of years, it does what it does, with no apparent desire to break out. But at these levels of profitability and profits growth, who would want to? Well, it does/doesn't. It's about to be merged with Clydesdale by its owners, NAG.

4.3.12 The Co-operative Bank

The Co-operative Bank and its stable-mate, Co-operative Insurance Society (CIS) are undergoing integration to form a true banking to insurance group (Co-operative Financial Services), which also includes *smile*. This model of Bancassurance has every opportunity to be more successful than the first wave, where banks acquired insurers (Lloyds TSB + Scottish Widows, Abbey + Scottish Mutual, etc.) and 'integrated' them.

What also augurs well for Co-operative Bank is its ethical and environmental positioning and values. Such a difference, and we cannot call it differentiation because this is a genuinely held approach and not a simple strategic ploy, is envied by competitors and admired by customers. If trust, integrity and ethics count, then . . .

4.3.13 Clydesdale Bank

A profitable, focused and cost conscious Scottish retail bank. Under the ownership of National Australia Group for a number of years, it does what it does with no apparent desire to break out. Clydesdale is rather less profitable than its siblings, Yorkshire Bank and Northern Bank. With RBSG and HBOS as neighbours that comes as no surprise.

4.3.14 Egg

Egg is one of the original Internet banks, established by Prudential Insurance. The most significant problem was an over-enthusiastic expansion plan – first into France, and then, the plan went, into the world, starting with the USA of all places. It all met with unsurprising consequences. If only it had stuck to its UK knitting. Egg UK is a success in its own right, and its business model worked.

4.3.15 Northern Bank

A steady, top tier former building society, extremely focused and cost conscious. In fact, all the NAG banks (Clydesdale, Yorkshire and Northern) seem to have clear performance objectives, so we'll take that as read. NAG has indicated that it wishes to sell Northern, and that will attract HBOS and one or two others from the UK market, or more likely, a European bank which has no UK competition regulation constraints.

4.4 A LITTLE MORE DETAIL ON SOME UK BANKS

We want to link these banks to the equity market, since bank performance in the equity market is a sine qua non of capitalism.

Table 4.3 shows selected line items from the twelve banks in the FTSE 200, giving their high-level performances. This selection covers a wide range of size and activity.

Table 4.3 Selected income/expense figures for FTSE 200 banks in 2003; monetary values in £UK millions (£1 UK = $ US 1.85).

	Abbey	Alliance & Leicester	Barclays	Bradford & Bingley	Close Brothers	Egg	HBOS	HSBC	Lloyds TSB	Northern Rock	RBSG	Standard Chartered
Net interest income	2148	738	6604	436	126	269	5459	13 936	5255	451	8301	2968
Non-interest income	519	635	5807	303	196	155	3487	8364	4619	209	10 928	1785
Operating income	2432	1373	12 411	738	322	424	8946	22 201	9808	660	19 229	4753
Operating expense	2014	696	7253	440	207	288	3363	10 640	4476	203	8389	2283
Profit before charges	n/a	586	5158	263	116	105	3766	10 021	4735	436	8645	2089
Loan loss provision	474	61	1347	7	22	137	1025	3294	950	49	1494	536
Profit before tax	n/a	525	3845	263	78	n/a	3706	6927	4348	387	6159	1542
Tax	42	146	1076	49	25	n/a	1091	1686	1025	112	1910	495
Profit	n/a	379	2769	213	51	n/a	2675	5241	3323	275	4249	1047
Cost/income ratio %	56.50 %	50.70 %	59.00 %	63.50 %	64.20 %	51.00 %	41.60 %	51.30 %	52.20 %	29.80 %	42.00 %	48.03 %
Assets £ millions	176 775	48 424	443 361	32 191	3573	11 695	408 413	559 036	252 012	37 160	455 275	120 282
ROE %	n/a	22.1 %	17.0 %	16.7 %	15.0 %	n/a	17.7 %	13.0 %	27.4 %	21.1 %	18.7 %	15.3 %
ROA %	n/a	0.78 %	0.62 %	0.66 %	1.43 %	n/a	0.65 %	0.94 %	1.32 %	0.74 %	0.93 %	0.87 %
10 % of operating expense	201	70	725	44	21	29	336	1064	448	20	839	228
As a % of pre-tax profit	n/a	13 %	19 %	17 %	27 %	n/a	9 %	15 %	10 %	5 %	14 %	15 %
10 % of revenue	243	137	1241	74	32	42	895	2220	981	66	1923	475
As a % of pre-tax profit	n/a	26 %	32 %	28 %	41 %	n/a	24 %	32 %	23 %	17 %	31 %	31 %
10 % of loan loss	47	6	135	1	2	14	103	329	95	5	149	54
As a % of pre-tax profit	n/a	2 %	5 %	0 %	4 %	n/a	4 %	6 %	3 %	2 %	4 %	5 %
Full time equivalent staff (FTE)	27 000	6100	78 900	6745	1900	2660	67 400	219 200	71 600	4000	111 200	30 000
Market cap £ billions (17/10/04)	8948	4044	35 490	1854	944	748	29 578	99 525	24 272	3133	50 603	11 414
Stock 52 week - high	619	916	572	330	889	198	782	919	476	789	1764	1002
- low	420	796	443	252	632	91	663	784	392	669	1464	834
- %variation	47 %	15 %	29 %	31 %	41 %	118 %	18 %	17 %	21 %	18 %	20 %	20 %
- present	604	892	552	293	655	91	760	892	434	744	1610	970
P/E ratio	n/a	10.8	10.7	8.7	11.4	n/a	10.8	14.5	10.1	10.4	15.3	16.5

The numbers above are selected data items from, or derived from, the bank annual reports. Market information is added.
Sources: Bank 2003 Annual Reports. The Sunday Times Databank October 17th 2004

HSBC is the second largest bank in the world by market value with a total staff of 220 000 and 120 million accounts. RBSG is a world top ten bank that covers all activities. Lloyds TSB is large, with a bias to retail and small businesses in the UK. Close Brothers is a small private/merchant bank, Bradford & Bingley is a former building society and Egg is primarily an Internet bank. These twelve banks cover a wide range, with staff numbers from 2000 to 220 000, and assets from £4 billion to £560 billion. The Co-operative Bank is not included here because it is not a publicly traded company.

The banks shown cover a wide and varying range of activities and vary in their basic business mixes. Behind each column lies a great deal of complexity and difference. The sale of a unit, the failure of a large initiative and the benefits of a merger are not shown. Neither is there any history to indicate the sustainability or otherwise of this level of performance, or the value of the franchise other than the market capitalisation.

The line items of net interest income, non-interest income (primarily fees and commissions) and operating expense within a bank are comparable in size. Loan losses, mainly credit problems and highly dependent on the choice of the served markets, can be significant and can fluctuate widely from year to year. They are dependent on, or related to, the management's choice of the markets it serves and its 'appetite for risk' and credit policies.

The cost/income ratio shows that the costs of running a bank are not small; in our early little example they were 55 % of the total income, and this is borne out in these tables. The costs of running a bank are indeed not small. In practice, the operating costs for most banks are comparable in size to the amount of their net interest income, their largest single source of revenue. This surprises people, including all of the public and most bank staff. They assume that the spread between borrowers and lenders is quite large enough, thank you, for the bank to be comfortable. They know as customers what they pay for a loan (between 6 % and 18 %), and what they get paid for their savings (between 0 % and 5 %).

These numbers show that a reduction in cost of, say, 10 % would have the effect of increasing profit by about 15 %, assuming no service deterioration. Similarly, growing the revenue by 10 % would lead to a 30 % increase in profit if the costs remained constant. The market capitalisation would increase greatly with either improvement. But as attractive as the prospects of organic growth and reduced costs are, they prove to be difficult to achieve, despite being the two most obvious targets of the banks. Conversely, a reduction of revenue by 10 % on the same cost base would be mightily dangerous. The third performance improvement target is usually credit risk. Look at the provisions for loan loss – this is a risk business alright.

Note also the variance of stock price for each bank, and this 52-week variance is not historically unusual, not the result of any particularly peculiar year. Sustainable performance is hard to achieve. The leverage of capital in banking is high enough that blips in performance become blurps in equity value. A deposit in a bank is safe; an investment in one is an entirely different matter.

The banks in Table 4.3 are only the twelve listed in the FTSE top 200 companies. They show the concentration of banking into a few institutions. The ratio between the largest and smallest is 100:1 by asset and staff size, yet their ROEs do not correlate to size. This indicates that big is not necessarily beautiful or ugly. It says that either scale economies aren't difficult to achieve, or scale diseconomies are easy to achieve, or both. When a bank is large it is more difficult to find a market to be served that is large or potentially large enough to make a material impact on performance. Overall, there are probably more difficulties in seeking performance improvements in a large bank than a small one. The comfort for the large bank is that it can buy out any emerging new idea at any time if it so chooses. This could hinder innovation and competition, but that's the same in all industries. On the other hand, competition for the markets may be more serious for the large banks. As good as a 10 % increase in business would be, a 10 % decrease would be seriously threatening.

To be put into the previous tables in *The Banker* requires the institution to be listed as a 'Bank'. There is another FTSE classification 'Specialty & Diversified Financials'. There are six companies listed in this sector which derive at least half their profits from lending to non-prime customers. They are Provident Financial, Cattles, Paragon, Kensington Group, London Scottish Bank and S & U. As a group, these six companies have outperformed the FTSE All Share, FTSE 250 and FTSE Banks over one, three, five and ten year horizons (Source: Clear Capital Limited, 2004). The first two of these companies are in the FTSE 250 with market capitalisations of £1532 and £1058 million respectively, making them larger than Egg as at September 12th 2004. In all, Clear Capital estimates in its research note that there are 24 significant players in the UK non-prime lending space, and that the market has around eight million customers (20 % of the adult population).

Another instance of so-called niche players are the large car manufacturers – GM, Ford, Volkswagen, Renault and others – who have huge finance subsidiaries which would comfortably place them into the Top 1000 banks, some in the Top 100, were their finance subsidiaries classified as banks. In fact, FCE Bank in the earlier *The Banker* UK listing is Ford Credit Europe.

Should a competitor, or several competitors, hit upon some formula attractive to retail banking customers, then anything could happen in the market.

Much can be gleaned and discussed about the banks and the numbers, but the table is included primarily to support the case that in a highly leveraged business, an improvement in revenue and cost would be widely welcome. And that's where the book is heading. Based on these numbers, the banks have a combined staff of some 500 000. Not all of these work in retail banking. If half overall work in retail banking, and we add the 40 000 from building societies and guess at the rest of the retail banking industry (which is another 100 smaller banks, but also The Co-operative Bank and GE Capital), then the retail banking industry in the UK alone employs some 400 000 staff directly. There are possibly (a guess) 100 000 indirect employees comprising vendors from property management, office cleaners, security, catering staff, IT, media, training and all the rest. Make of that what you will.

May we reinforce an earlier comment – it would be wrong to use any comparison between banks based on this table, because it is just a point in time. A bank, and a large bank at that as many of them are, can be in dozens of different businesses and in many countries. They are operating in multiple market segments, different geographies and have different specialisations. Nevertheless, money is the common thread, and money has its price. Investors want a return on their money, consistent with risk and stability, so the equity market tries to normalise performances, and that is based on the levers of customer revenues and investor returns, and an enormous amount of other analysis. The time dimension is absolutely critical because that is an important indicator of leadership competence, which is the master key to everything.

4.5 BUILDING SOCIETIES

The Building Societies movement, for that's what it is, took a big hit in the 1990s when a number of the larger ones demutualised and became banks. As a grouping, their market share fell by over half as these societies transferred lock, stock and barrel into the banking industry. It started with the de-mutualisation of Abbey National and the Lloyds TSB acquisition of Cheltenham & Gloucester.

The nature of the movement is that there are no shareholders/investors requiring a return on their investments, but rather that the society shares their income between depositors and borrowers in the form of better rates. Essentially, they operate to serve their members, not to provide returns to investors. Building societies, therefore, can pay higher rates on savings and charge lower rates on mortgages and loans than can banks. And indeed, that is what they do, and their spread between interest paid and interest earned is lower than for banks as a result.

Building societies were the mass market banks, and because they had a simple savings and mortgage business model they were simpler to manage and operate, and were seen as less sophisticated than banks. Along with the other changes of the last ten years or more, the societies became far more efficient and polished than they were, and have successfully repositioned themselves in the competitive market of retail banking. For example, where the mortgage market share had fallen from 50 % to 15 % with the defections of Halifax, Abbey, Northern Rock, Alliance & Leicester, and Bradford & Bingley, the last quarter of 2003 saw them win 26.7 % of the net mortgage lending. Staff numbers grew by 14 % in 2003, and sector asset totals are now £225 billion. A snapshot of the UK building society movement in 2003 is given in Table 4.4.

In terms of performance, none of the bank performance measures are applicable. ROE means nothing since there is no equity. The cost/income ratio is meaningless because the intention is not to maximise income. ROA means nothing because the goal is not to maximise returns. They therefore have their own set of measures.

The quality of management in building societies is strengthening, their sound knowledge of the capital markets is increasing and they have a 'local' feel to them. Building societies could be on a roll again.

Table 4.4 Building societies snapshot 2003.

	Assets £ millions				
Nationwide	85 418				
Britannia	20 929				
Yorkshire	14 437				
Portman	14 112		2001	2002	2003
Coventry	8937	Average cost per £100 of assets managed £	—	0.90	0.85
Chelsea	7851	Net interest income spread %	1.42	1.26	1.24
Skipton	7347	Capital (solvency ratio) %	12.42	12.37	12.35
Leeds & Holbeck	5343	Market share of net mortgage lending %	14.4	16.5	21.9
West Bromwich	4296	Largest 10 share of society assets %	81.9	81.7	83.1
Cheshire	4026	Total number of branches	2081	2103	2126
Derbyshire	3921				
Principality	3578	Total assets		£225 billion	
Newcastle	3079	Number of mortgages		2.5 million	
Norwich & Peterborough	2837	Mortgage assets		£160 billion	
Stroud and Swindon	2090	Number of savings accounts		15 million	
Nottingham	1912	Savings balances		£155 billion	
Dunfermline	1869	Full-time staff		32 502	
Scarborough	1282	Part-time staff		11 440	
Progressive	1014				

43 others with assets of less than £1 billion
totalling less than £15 billion

Source: Building Societies Association – August 2004

4.6 THE CHALLENGES FOR BANKS

If the banking model is straightforward, the management of a bank is not. It is complex, and in principle it revolves around the science of rates, risks and durations; the economics of its served markets; the aspirations of its customers.

Neither are we overly concerned about the existing engineering inside the banks. The engineering should properly follow the needs of the business, it is the mechanism by which products and services are transformed into stable, controlled operations at an appropriate cost. Our criticisms of engineering stem from its tendency to push 'solutions' at the businesses, rather than allowing the businesses to pull the engineering into the solution that the business wants to see. A corollary to this is that engineering has developed the habit of imposing rigid standards around what businesses can and cannot do. This is especially true of matters around information technology. Yes, it is preferable and tidier not to have a proliferation of engineering solutions, in order to maximise efficiencies (minimise costs) and to retain tight operational controls. But that is no more powerful an argument, perhaps a good deal weaker an argument, than is the need to have the most effective solutions for the markets served.

We are concerned more with the 'art' of banking. The science tells us what will happen if we were to do something according to some predictions, it doesn't tell us what to do. If it did tell us what to do, there would be far less variation in performances and growth between banks than there is. Even as it is, Darwinian evolution has already effectively removed many a leadership team from the field of play. Surprisingly, over only ten years or so some huge banks have come unglued – Abbey, NatWest, Midland. The UK hasn't got that many banks to welcome any more such events. Engineering is capable of achieving anything reasonable or unreasonable that is asked of it, although usually at a stiff cost. In practice, engineers produce what they think we should have at the lowest cost they can deliver it, which is not necessarily quite what we wanted. The 'quite' in this sense is a small word with a big impact.

Placing the emphasis on the art has the major consequence that the bank no longer imposes a take-it-or-leave-it decision on the customer, but rather allows the customer to positively choose the products and services they want, based on their own criteria. As stated before, the art is all that the customer sees, and in the main we have concentrated on pushing engineering on them as some kind of substitute.

The previous tables showing facts and figures for banks indicate the real difficulties and opportunities that come about because of market appeal and growing the business. In those tables, in some complex way, the impact of the leadership and their art is writ large.

The art must be applied to the three major areas shown in Figure 4.1. Market appeal, attracting and retaining customers, comes from customers needing and wanting what the bank is providing. The ability to differentiate banking products is limited today when so many banks are offering similar products and services. This homogeneity

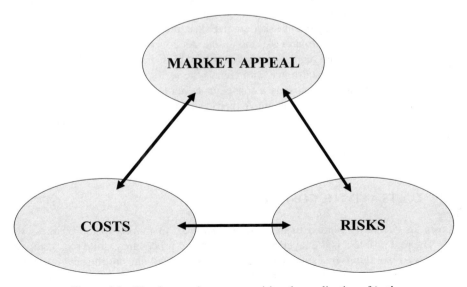

Figure 4.1   The three major areas requiring the application of 'art'

of the industry is because engineering has assumed a dominating role throughout the banking industry. Given that, growth is then primarily a function of the expansion of the served market, both in population and wealth terms, rather than through competition between products and services. All the banks enjoy this organic growth proportionally. So that seems to leave merger and acquisition (M&A) as the key strategic growth mechanism.

The costs are incurred because customers, regulators and bank management need service, awareness, accountability and support. The bank needs to provide access, payment mechanisms, documentation, controls and many other capabilities, and these functions do have a real cost. This cost is dominated directly and indirectly by the number of staff required.

Aside from credit risk, other risks come about for a number of reasons, but the core risks stem from the mismatching of assets (loans) and liabilities (deposits). Customers' low-value current accounts, where the customer can withdraw their funds at any time, are, in effect, grouped together to provide a committed five-year, £10 million loan to a company. Similarly, many variable rate deposits made for a short committed period are used to fund a 25-year fixed rate mortgage, which itself will probably only last for seven or eight years as the borrower moves house. The UK average is 7.5 years. And rates may change at any time, often on only one side of the commitment. Property may boom or bust. A borrower's creditworthiness may deteriorate; depositors may need access to their funds at short notice. These inherent mismatches and uncertainties of amounts, durations, conditions and interest rates are the norm, and this is where a bank comes in.

The bank functions as an intermediary between customers with surplus funds and customers needing funds. The bank is, in fact, a risk engine, pure and complex.

The business incurs far more risks than credit risk. These include interest rate risk, country risk, currency risk, event risk, default risk, equity risk, insurance risk, liquidity risk, systemic risk, operational risk, and so on. As concerning as all this might be, practices, procedures and regulations have evolved to manage these risks effectively. A bank failure is a rare occurrence, and always the result of a breach of the internal or external 'rules', and it is usually a conscious rather than an inadvertent breach.

In respect of these risks, the income/expense statement only singles out credit risk in the form of the loan loss provision, the other risks being implicitly absorbed into other line items. For instance, interest rate risk is absorbed into net interest income, and operational risk into the cost and revenue lines.

4.7   COSTS AND THE COST/INCOME RATIO

Costs are primarily related to the way we evolved operations to the business we do. The real problem is the layering of practices and procedures, quite reasonably to capitalise on previous investment and capabilities. It's a bit like putting new wallpaper over the old paper to spruce a room up. After a few times you have to bite the bullet and take it all off. The layering of our capabilities is quite extraordinary, starting off with data processing systems from the 1960s and 1970s, which are still handling the majority of the accounting data processing. We have layers upon layers of additional capabilities now, and have rarely had, or taken, the opportunity to see just what it is that we have and whether it makes sense. In any event, what we have works to today's definition of what we need. Each layer brought further processes and procedures with it, compounding forms, manual exceptions and so on.

As we have seen, the largest offset to the revenue generated from net interest income and fees and commissions is the cost of operations and administration. It can account for between 30 % and 70 % or more of total income. This percentage is basically the cost/income ratio. The costs are mainly staff and their associated costs, which, in round figures for a large bank, are in the region of 55 % of total expense. Occupancy costs are relatively modest at about 10 % of the total (banks close branches to reduce the cost of having staff inside them, not to reduce their rents). 'Other' costs account for about 20 % and this will include IT equipment, telecommunications, furniture and transportation. And the remaining 15 % is depreciation and amortisation. Most of the costs are in some way related to the numbers of staff, so the direct and indirect staff driven proportion of costs is closer to 70 %.

The cost/income ratio is only a relative measure, not an absolute. It is relative to the business model. The more labour intensive businesses, such as private banking and trading, will have higher cost/income ratios than those like retail banking, which will have lower cost/income ratios. Therefore, the main uses of the ratio are to compare similar businesses, and to monitor efficiency progress over time in a single business. A trading business could have a ratio of 70 % and make terrific returns on the capital it employs. The absolute measure of performance is indeed the return on the capital employed in each business. Still, to see the cost/income ratio decline where the business mix is stable is generally a good indicator, unless the customer experiences suffer too much.

The cost/income ratio represents operating expenses expressed as a percentage of total income. It excludes loan losses, goodwill amortisation and extraordinary costs, such as acquisition integrations. In the retail banking businesses, the top performing large retail banks will have a cost/income ratio of about 40 %, the average is perhaps 55 %, and under-performers are at 70 %. That is to say that for each £10 of operational income, the costs are £4, £5.50 or £7 respectively. So, at a cost/income ratio of 50 %, there goes half the potential ROE.

However, using a 50 % cost/income ratio, if we are making the 75 % pre-everything return from net interest income and fees, that still gives 37.5 % after costs. That is still huge.

If you have capital, why would you not start up a bank?

4.8 RISKS

In the same way as we addressed capital and intermediation in the second chapter with the objective of explaining some of the important basics as they apply to retail banking, here we go again with risk. Risk as a subject is huge, and still quite early on in terms of being understood. Fortunately, the risks in retail banking are well established and do have a limit. For instance, we're not involved with country risk, currency risk and a number of other risks that concern other parts of a bank.

The following list of risks is from the introduction to the *Royal Bank of Scotland Annual Report*, so that's good enough for us:

- general economic conditions;
- borrower credit quality – provisions for bad and doubtful debts;
- changes in interest rates;
- operational risks;
- regulatory requirements developments;
- strategic decisions regarding organic growth and potential acquisitions.

It is circular to generalise on the relative importance or suggest the predictability of each of the above. It is self-evident that in booms, business volumes go up, and they come down with busts. When times get tough, credit losses rise. Changes in interest rates impact demand and cash flows. The business is also dependent on the operational ability to process a large number of transactions efficiently and accurately.

But other than for costs and strategic decisions, most influences or difficulties are tidal, in that they affect every boat in the same way. The article on the two Irish banks previously given shows that. Costs and the ROE are mainly determined by the businesses the bank chooses to be in and the way it chooses to operate. That is, what they do and how they do it determines their performance. The opportunities to distinguish their performance from competitors are themselves offset by the constant migration of staff and ideas between banks, a wall of advice (some good, some not so good) and observations of the market. These all promote homogeneity in the banking industry, they promote a sameness of expectation and performance. Indeed, it makes for a commodity business. The point remains that it is only what a bank chooses to do, and how it does it, that can provide significant positive differentiation, and the many good things that flow from that.

After seventeen UK parliamentary reviews of banking since 1997, and with the EU regulations, the regulatory burden is becoming a real risk. Over-regulation has great impact on banks and the customers, as does under-regulation.

Risk and the need to understand, measure and manage risk in its many different guises is a thread running through all retail banking activities. It also gives the business a split personality. The public face of banking is all about giving customers easy access to convenient payment products, such as cards, allowing them easy access to their funds and about helping them to buy consumer durables, cars and housing through easily obtainable loans. But underlying all these activities is a complex web of risks. Banking, even retail banking, is a risky business with a history that includes failures and disasters. And, although the nature of the risks changes over time, there are core risks intrinsic to the business, often complex and hidden from view, they can come back and bite you if taken for granted. Also, what goes round comes round, and today's bankers would be foolish to ignore the hard lessons learned by previous generations of bankers. Career bankers would almost certainly regard this as a statement of the obvious, but as the industry undergoes transformation and an infusion of new blood, it is perhaps not so obvious to someone coming from IBM, Tesco, Mars (bars, that is) or Proctor & Gamble.

4.8.1   Credit risk

The obvious risk in banking is credit risk – the bank lends money which the borrower does not repay, leaving the bank with a loss. Previous generations of bankers knew their customers and were shrewd judges of character and of business, they took lending decisions personally. Most personal and small business decisions are largely automated now, with sophisticated computer-based business information systems feeding highly mathematical risk analytical systems to evaluate creditworthiness and monitor whether borrowers are getting into financial trouble. Believe that if you want to, but that's what they say. Decisions are fast and consistent, creditworthy borrowers have no problems in obtaining credit. The real issues are at the margins. If the criteria are set too tight, you lose good customers and business; but if you relax them too much, you lose. If the credit policy is relaxed too far, then the shareholders take the hit, big time. The balance is fine, and large amounts of complex computer-based analysis are used to establish exactly where this fine line is. Consumer credit pricing tends to be one-size-fits-all. One way of managing around this line is to raise the price for less creditworthy borrowers to cover the increased risk of non-repayment. This is a slippery slope to go down, because creditworthy borrowers would then not unnaturally expect to receive a discount reflecting their higher credit rating. This already happens in corporate banking (the chip shop pays a lot more for their loan than BP does). This individual pricing, perhaps risk-based, is probably the way of the future for retail, but banks will first need to sort out their customer information files and clunky high-cost systems. While they are doing this, there is a first mover advantage here for an agile player.

Banks are in business to lose some money. That's the consequence of risk. Banks plan on having some losses. But lose too little and they have no customers because they will be excluding vast swathes of the population to whom they could lend. But lend to everyone and they will break the bank. Like everything else in banking, there is a balance. Banks build into their pricing a margin that covers the cost of people not repaying. This averages around 1 % to 2 % of loans, with far less for mortgages, and far more for riskier borrowers such as small businesses. In the jargon, this is known as *expected loss*. Profits are normally more than adequate to cover the loan loss provisions arising from these types of loss.

Very occasionally, a bank incurs an unexpected disaster where the normal level of provisions and profit margin built into their plans are insufficient to cover the losses. This is called, you've guessed, *unexpected loss*, and the capital of the bank is used to cover this – first out of profits, then from the issued share capital and reserves, and then the loan capital. If these are used up by the losses, depositors' money is at risk. This is where the deposit protection scheme kicks in, guaranteeing 90 % of a deposit up to £30 000. Nobody wants a bank to get into this position, which is why the regulators spend a lot of time analysing the riskiness of a bank's loans book and the adequacy of the bank's capital to sustain both expected and unexpected loss.

4.8.2   Treasury risks

The changing nature of bank balance sheets brings increasingly more complex treasury-related risks. The oldest of them all is liquidity risk, where the golden rule of banking is that you should not borrow short and lend long . . . in theory. Surprise, banks do this all the time – using call and notice deposits to fund, say, twenty-five year mortgages. The devil is in the detail here. Whilst many deposits are nominally repayable on demand, they are, by their nature, 'sticky' and unlikely to fly out at the first whiff of competition or trouble. Equally, although a mortgage may have a nominal life of twenty-five years, it is typically repaid after eight, and then refinanced when people move house. Banks also hold liquid assets such as treasury bills, deposits with other banks and securities that they can borrow against if needed (repos or repurchase agreements in the jargon).

Another risk is interest rate risk where, for example, the interest rate paid on deposits may be out of step with the interest rate charged on loans. To take a simple example, a bank with a fixed rate loan book at, say, 7 %, funded by variable rate short-term deposits paying 4 %, will make an interest spread of 3 %. But if short-term interest rates rise to, say, 8 %, the bank is obliged to continue charging the 7 % on the loans in line with the loan agreement, but the depositors now have to be paid more for their deposits, so the interest spread goes down, perhaps to 2 % or less. Because some loans can have a long duration, and deposit rates could rise several times during the life of the loan, the spread can get squeezed rotten, and even become negative, where the bank is paying more for the deposits than it receives for the loans. That is interest rate risk. By the way, if the interest rate falls, the bank doesn't clean up by increasing its spread (by paying less for the deposits than originally). The borrower pays off their loan and takes out a new one, possibly with a different bank, at the new lower level.

These examples are simple to see, but banks do run complex asset and liability structures, with combinations of fixed and variable rates with varying interest rate time periods on both sides of the balance sheet, all of which requires careful and detailed management. As with credit and asset liability management, there are complex computer-based analytical techniques to measure the overall interest risk and test how this might change under differing scenarios. This is called stress testing and looks at different ways interest rates may move over different time periods, and in differing economic scenarios.

To evaluate all of this, most banks have computer-based asset and liability analytical black boxes, supervised by the treasurer and an asset liability committee, to decide how safely the balance sheet can be mismatched. The regulator will have a view on this and agree prudential limits so that in the event of a liquidity crunch (say a run caused by major credit losses), a bank has sufficient funds to pay out depositors until the situation has stabilised.

If a bank's balance sheet structure is tight, it can obtain liquidity by raising a medium-term loan or standby funding lines from other banks, but like everything else in banking, there is a balance. Banks that have a natural flow of liquidity, typically those that are long established with large stable deposit bases, are better placed than banks that do not. Newer, fast growing banks will not necessarily have the same degree of natural liquidity. Liquidity can be bought, at a cost, but there can come a point beyond which it is not feasible to buy in liquidity, which will then be a constraint on growth.

All this brings us onto derivatives, a major growth area in banking, but still little understood by most of us. This explanation won't help much, but it'll move you along. Retail banks use derivatives mainly to manage their interest rate risk. Think of a derivative as a bet. With an interest rate derivative (interest rate swap, or swap in the jargon) one bank bets another bank that if interest rates for a period in the future go up, one bank pays the other bank a certain sum of money, and vice versa. Basically, if banks face a potential loss if rates move, they can insure against this loss through taking out a derivative. Some want to bet against a rate rise, and others against a rate fall. Because each bank's position is different, there is always a large pool of banks that are, within reason, prepared to write any number of differing derivatives. Also, if banks want to speculate on future interest rate movements, derivatives are an easy way of doing this, but alas, also of incurring major losses. The regulators take a close interest in the interest rate structure of a bank's balance sheet and its use of, and controls over, derivatives. Banks have already had their fair share of derivatives disasters, and the smart money is on there being more, but probably not in interest rate derivatives, where most of the hard lessons have been learned, but rather in more arcane and less transparent areas, such as securities or credit.

4.8.3 Operational risk

There are other risks, more hidden from view, but nevertheless significant. Operational risk is the loss resulting from an operational failure, such as paying money to the wrong person and not getting it back, or the cost of a computer crash. Once the Cinderella of risks, the regulators are now requiring that banks give due regard to operational risk under the new Basel II regulations, to be implemented by 2006. As dependence on systems grows, so does operational risk as more and more eggs are put operationally into single baskets. There is a parallel need for new risk management controls reflecting the changed operational environment.

4.8.4 Other risks

Other, less direct but nevertheless potentially painful, risks include reputational, regulatory and model risk.

Reputational risk is fairly self-explanatory. It is the risk of damage to a bank's reputation. Examples are mis-selling, mistreatment of customers or some kind of dishonesty. We've all seen the stories. Banks are fair game and cannot afford to take too many hits. Midland Bank's disclosure of some high profile account details caused their slogan 'The listening bank' rapidly to degenerate to 'The whispering bank'. This was all part of a downwards trend which, together with a bad acquisition in the US and generally poor management, led to them being taken over by HSBC, then a Scottish managed Hong Kong based former colonial bank – now in the world's premier league. In itself, reputational risk will not ditch a bank, but too many incidents and a bank will get a reputation for being accident prone and for having a management that has lost the plot. Like buses, disasters tend to come in threes. NatWest suffered similar incidents before falling prey to RBSG, then a large Scottish regional bank, and now also into the premier league. An aside here – are the Scots the best bankers in the world because they manage everything prudently and tightly, to the point of being parsimonious? As a nation they are surely punching well above their weight.

Regulatory risk is the risk of falling foul of the regulators, big time. As regulation becomes more broad, further reaching and intrusive, it is increasing as a risk. More particularly as the regulators flex their muscles and are prepared to make examples of major banks 'pour encourager les autres'. It is not just the bad publicity and fines arising from a regulatory breach – mis-selling, inadequate customer and transaction vetting, failure to implement anti-money laundering legislation, poor risk management, inadequate internal controls – the list is endless. It is also the management time taken up with containing the problem, cooperating with the auditors put in by the FSA to bottom it out, and the major management distraction in making sure it never happens again. Regulatory risk is a big issue and management ignores compliance at its peril.

There are other more arcane risks, amongst which we would single out *model risk*. As has been implied already, risk management is heavily dependent on heavy-duty computer-based analytics – on which many 'bets' are riding. Whilst senior managers will understand the inputs to and outputs from these models, how many understand the maths and data structures within the models? There is the potential of accidents waiting to happen. When a model is misconfigured, misused or whatever and blows up, it will leave the bank with a major black hole.

4.8.5   The risk about risks

There are two classes of risk. One is where two sides to the risk exist and where a market is established, such as with liquidity and interest rates – somebody has the liquid funds a bank may unexpectedly need to provide, or somebody will benefit from the rate going up or down. Basically, there is a deal to be made prior to any event that might happen. The other is where there is no market. An operational risk is such a risk. There is no market in operational risk. Such risks lead to hugely defensive behaviours and expense because nobody is prepared to say when enough is enough. Add in reputational risk, auditing risk, personnel risk, compliance risk, and the many other dynamics within retail banking, which are one-sided, and empires sprout up all over the place.

4.9   DIFFERENTIATORS

Banks differentiate themselves from each other through the effectiveness of their strategic decisions. This implicitly includes their cost of operations and containment of risks.

In addition, marketing, sales, product development, service quality, branch and ATM distribution and many other activities impact performance. Banks are continuously chipping away at their costs. However, most such activities are not fundamental in nature. They do not address the long-term legacy of a deeply embedded cost structure in operations and administration. The activities can become tactics that have moderate impact on the growth and/or performance improvement strategies, that can be implemented quickly. By contrast, the fundamentals are much less responsive.

All this is clear. Fundamental differentiators are more powerful than tactical differentiators, they are more difficult to create, and more difficult for competitors to compete against.

Fortunately for retail and small business banks, the customers are supposedly lethargic to change, and feel that the bank places some value on the time that they've had their account with the bank. That is the keel to the boat – we are still more likely to get a divorce than change our current account. Do many people change their bank account because it didn't have the largest ATM network? Because they liked the advertising? Because of a new product? It is rare that a new product launch has much impact on the market at large. In any event, competitors can most often rapidly replicate such products should they so choose, so that is not too threatening a concern. What are called new products are generally just variations on an already established theme. The CMA and offset accounts are two of the more memorable new products over the last twenty years that had appeal and were difficult to replicate. But even if a product is successful and can be replicated, it doesn't mean it will be followed. Nobody followed First Direct, Ryanair or ING Direct. Banks have a lot to consider, especially damage to their existing models.

Differentiators that would light up the market, or propel a bank into a higher level of performance are few and far between, pricing being the most obvious. In particular, it is hard to see how secondary differentiators can lead to a sustainable competitive advantage since they are relatively easy to replicate, even if that does require buying the other bank, or buying staff jazzy uniforms. Evidence of such successes must be in market share, which varies little each year other than through M&A activities.

There have historically been extraordinary differentiators, as in size, or lack of size, and the value of the brand as perceived by customers. But these differentiators are becoming less important as scale economies kick in at lower volumes, and companies give more attention to their brands. Bank brands in general have also taken a knock as they sail closer to the limits to compete. What are regulators for if they don't also give comfort and trust to the public? So regulation also conveys comfort and trust to customers, which is the main benefit of a banking brand, and the brand differentiator in banking is diminishing, especially in lending activities. 'Trust us because we're big' means nothing in this regard, irrespective of which actor says it in the commercials. Avis did better with its 'we try harder' pitch.

While the year-to-year change in a bank's market share is small, tiny, it is still a fact that the most successful banks also play a long game. An organic growth of one percent in market share each year has been a key tactic – looking back for even just five years confirms this. There is much merit in continuing to look for secondary differentiation opportunities, but do not expect any step function results. There have been precious few strategies unleashed outside M&A.

Most often, 'strategies' are dressed up tactics, and tactics are easily copied. Winning strategies take time to prepare and execute, and it is precisely for this reason that they have power, because they cannot necessarily be emulated quickly, easily and safely.

4.10   ACQUAINTANCESHIPS

Of course, the affinity that a customer feels towards their bank must be of some impor-tance. Service and customer experiences are important differentiators. The problem is that the customer does not feel that they have a relationship. They have a polygamous relationship with the industry – bank A for current account, bank B for savings, C for mortgage, D for more savings, E for their small business account, F for their credit card, C again for their house insurance, G for their PEP/ISA, A again for the other credit card, H for their car finance, and so on. They need the banking industry, but they do not necessarily need a particular bank. The average household has a relation-ship with the banking industry, but this in turn is made up of acquaintanceships with individual banks, insurance and investment companies, and the deepest 'relationship' with a bank extends to an average of less than two accounts. The customer obviously feels no real belonging. There is no friendly, influential, omnipotent bank manager. Each bank is a rigid institution, set in its ways. This is hardly the stuff of a friendship, let alone a relationship. To achieve their goals, customers pick and choose a number of acquaintanceships to meet their needs, and in so doing they construct their own relationship with the banking industry. For fun, consider that a person will want to open eight accounts of different types over the next ten or twenty years, and that they have a shortlist of the same ten banks to choose from for each new account. All other things being equal, there are ten to the power of eight possibilities on the outcome, that is 100 000 000 to 1. Spooky. A bank would be lucky, as things stand, to get the first four accounts, at odds of 10 000 to one. Perhaps 2.0 accounts per customer at 100 to 1 isn't too shabby. And how did we do even that? It used to be done through the convenience of the branch, a trusted and respected manager, and whatever else. The first two are history. It is statistically possible, if improbable, that no two people in the UK have the same eight types of account with the same institutions.

Adults in their twenties are frequently afraid of 'their' bank. Any phone call from their bank, even under the guise of 'customer care', concerns them. They see it as the adult equivalent of being called to the head teacher's office at school.

Businesses don't feel they have anything like a relationship with their banks either. Do they feel that they have a relationship with a person who really understands them and their business? In the absence of that, it might stretch as far as a partnership of convenience, for the moment anyway. A fair proportion of consumers and businesses are regularly 'robbing Peter to pay Paul' by manipulating one acquaintanceship against another.

A result of this situation is that the growth in market size, driven by an increasing affluence, often finds its way into further acquaintanceships outside of the normal banking circle. That is to say, the securities and insurance industries, foreign banks, retailers and a variety of other companies are competing for market share. A bank is not competing against only eight other banks.

In terms of assets, banks are growing at a solid rate as customer needs and wealth grow, but they are declining in terms of their share of the expanding market. They are undoubtedly missing opportunities.

4.11   TRENDS

The sky is not about to fall in on the banks. Whichever way retail and small business banking go, it will take some time to get there. This is because of the huge size of the industry, customer confusion, but most importantly because of customer behaviour. Most accounts are opened and closed because of some event or change in the customer's life. There is little competitive churn within bank accounts. Note that 30 % of mobile network customers change their network each year, but as differentiators reduce and choice confusion grows, so will that churn.

It is true that the banking industry grows assets at about 5–10 % year on year, as it does its profit. The first comparisons banks are interested in are peer performances, and how well they are doing relative to their competitors. That is understandable, and investors want to know. However, the wealth and debt of the nation may be growing at 20 %, so the market share is, in fact, shrinking. It is reminiscent of BA comparing itself to KLM, Lufthansa and Air France, rather than to Ryanair or easyJet. BT compared itself to France Telecom, Cable & Wireless and Deutsche Telecom, rather than the mobile network operators and the new fixed line competitors who were threatening to eat their lunch, such as Centrica with OneTel, Carphone Warehouse with Talk Talk, Sainsbury's and Tesco. Uncomfortable comparisons are ultimately more important than the comfortable ones. Tesco has three million insurance accounts and one million banking accounts at the moment with its Personal Finance arm. We think that a good proportion of this is brand new business to financial services.

It is likely that the dangerous competition will not be from the general banking industry, although there will be some banks that execute a successful strategy well. It will more likely come from supermarkets, the securities industry, retailers, the insurance industry, and perhaps telephone companies. There is no large business that can offer the size and quality of the returns on a large amount of equity that banking can provide. The only significant technical barrier is the regulatory process that ensures that starting up a bank is made difficult, primarily to do with deposit taking. But even that can be overcome through partnerships with banks, as the supermarkets have done, and with a concentration on lending and insurance, which does not require a banking licence.

De novo banks are of particular interest. While many have tried, few have really succeeded. It is of interest that *de novo* situations often actively recruit from the banking industry. It is no surprise that existing bank practices and products are replicated, costs and all, and the resultant bank fails to perform. It is certainly true in the UK that it was individuals with no background in the airline or network businesses that started successful budget airlines and mobile networks. They really had little idea of what could *not* be done, a point to ponder.

Especially in banking, where there are a large number of established competitors, a new entrant will not succeed by doing the same or similar things better. It will succeed by achieving the same or similar things differently. It is not about working harder, faster or smarter; it is about working differently. Banks do have room to work harder, faster and smarter within their departmental freedoms. But the limits to this are pretty obvious.

Now that the first wave of wannabe banks have come and either succeeded in getting established, or foundered, we can look to the next wave, which will approach the opportunity somewhat differently. Virgin Atlantic, Ryanair and easyJet took the 30-year-old lessons of Laker Airways and its Skytrain on board. The next wave in banking will include established banks seeking a new strategic path from their existing model, and this could take any of a number of forms. A few might see it as a way of transforming their existing bank into a new model. It will also see highly focused, specialised entrants. Some of the models will be inherently unsustainable in the face of annoyed incumbents and swift copycats. It's difficult to see the big banks changing their models, except for clear cost problems or real and present danger from competition.

Interestingly, this could see a point of departure as banks follow significantly different strategies. The what, why, who, how and when may lead to more uniqueness and less conformance to tradition. But many will strike a chord with customers and provide a good and sustainable return for investors. And the key will be to deploy information technology as the key competence, as befits an information processing company centred on retail financial products and services.

It is not clear quite how many horses a bank can ride at the same time, and it must make sure it picks a winning strategy. This presents a real threat, since it is customers and investors who will decide upon the success of any chosen strategy or strategies, and they tend to act in unison.

A bank may decide to focus on a tightly defined area of the market with the view of excelling at one or a few products and services. At the other extreme, some, especially the largest banks, will want to be all things to all people. As the range of products and services grows in a bank it is important that the major mission does not become obscured. For instance, Tesco has the consistent line that price and value are attached to everything it sells. It does not have low prices on some items and high prices on others. Indeed, as some supermarkets have expanded their ranges to include electrical goods, clothing, petrol, financial services, phones, medicines, and what have you, there is a strong consistency across the pricing regime and value policy. In the UK we have now got to the point where 50p in every £1 of household spending (excluding mortgages, utilities, and the other big items) is spent in supermarkets.

To establish a relationship, banks will have to establish their mantras. It cannot be best for savings, worst for mortgages, and average for checking accounts and loans, and absolutely the worst for insurance rates. It can't keep changing rates at will, otherwise customers will constantly be re-evaluating their deals with the bank, and thus their relationships. A bank has to promote 'always in the best quartile' for rates, or 'always the best service', or 'always the best quality' or some such on which customers can rely. Waitrose makes little attempt to be the cheapest supermarket and has a clear quality strategy which works.

People do 'shop around' for their financial products, so getting them to make more use of a single bank requires this consistency of mission. As long as the bank, or supermarket, retains its mission, their selection remains more assured. However, if each purchase raises a decision for the customer, then it will be more difficult to build the desire (by both customer and bank) for a relationship.

Figure 4.2 is only to show that the chances of getting a deeper relationship, which by the very nature of the customer's life events could be over many years, are difficult,

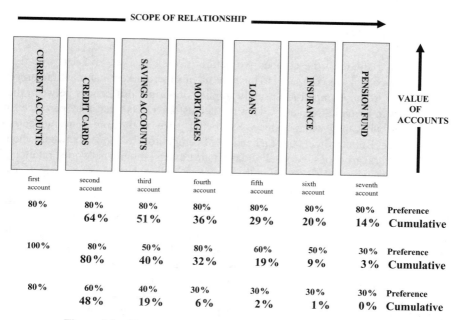

Figure 4.2 How easy is it to gain more accounts with a customer?

even when a customer has a high level of preference for a particular bank. Just how easy is it to get a second, third and fourth account with a customer, and does cross-selling without a relationship value, such as relationship pricing, hold much hope?

This shows the difficulty of deepening product sales with each customer – the going gets tough after two or three products. To which, aggressive promotional product pricing from competitors also seeks to snag business away. The logic that screams out is to make products competitively better through pricing – risk based on the strength of the relationship. This to boost both balances in the various accounts and the number of products used by the customer. There is a need for a trustworthy advisory service, and what else?

So, to improve the odds of gaining a deeper relationship, why not offer a better deal to a customer who already has one product relationship with you if he buys another, and so on? After all, there is no 'acquisition cost', rather an 'opportunity income' by attracting the customer in with another product. *smile*, the Internet bank from the Co-operative Bank, was possibly the first real strategic proponent of 'relationship pricing'. Their core current account gave a competitive rate on credit balances to attract customers, then offered better rates on other products (savings and loans) to those customers who had the current account than if someone just bought the *smile* loan or deposit product. Some six years after launch, *smile* is recognized as one of the successful Internet banks, and this sensible approach was a distinguishing feature. Tesco and Sainsbury's also already give discounts on some financial products if you have others with them. It's a form of relationship pricing.

4.12 COMPETITION

Banks always allude to the competitive nature of their market, and it is true that there are many banks as compared to the handful of supermarkets, car manufacturers, airlines, and so on. Competition usually implies important differences between the competitors in a qualitative sense. That is, the customer gets what they perceive to be closer to what they want, better value, better price, with more convenience or better service. But customers have a handful of competitors to choose between when it comes to cars, groceries, goods, holidays, hairdressers, mobile networks, retailers, and so on. The nature of competition is fairly clear in these businesses – competitors are similar but markedly differentiated.

Something is different with banking. There are dozens, if not a hundred competing institutions for deposit and lending products. There is fine print attached. There is scope for misunderstanding and confusion. The products, at first sight anyway, are all pretty much the same. Promotional deals, and deals that have a lower rate for the first years, and so on, muddy the comparisons. The supermarket flyers on their financial products are noticeably more clear than the bank ones. The primary deciding factor is the rate, especially for long-term accounts. Whether the faith is warranted or not, customers feel safer with a name they recognise. Is that what differentiation is all about?

Although there are many banks, the year-on-year change in market share amongst banks (excluding mergers and acquisitions) is small, suggesting that interbank competition is fairly benign, that customers do not have frequent events that trigger a need, that banks are not easily able to differentiate their products, that customers cannot see clear and sustainable advantage by a more positive, active, selection.

But in fact, the market size for financial products is growing faster than the combined growth of all banks. The securities, investment, supermarket and insurance sectors are increasing their share of customer finance business that might otherwise be with the banks, as they have been doing inexorably for many years. New competitors are appearing. It is not so much that institutional barriers are disappearing, because these were removed some time ago. There is simply growing competition in most of the banking market segments.

Other than legal barriers, the barriers to entry for new entrants into retail and commercial banking are mainly to do with the customers' perception of what they want from a bank. That is to say, no new entrant could afford to establish the hundreds of local offices, if that is what a customer would expect. Yes, the capital required to get a bank up and going is substantial, but that is not, prima facie, a barrier.

A new entrant would have to establish a trust and comfort level based on a brand value (M&S, Sainsbury's, Tesco) or a strong set of credentials (ING, Zurich). They would have to establish a satisfactory service plan, and be competitive in price, which means paying more or charging less. Above all, they would have to be able to more closely align their products to market needs that are not as well served today as they could be. A strong brand is no guarantee of success, but it does remove one possible cause for failure.

Many have tried, including units from within existing banks. The results are widely mixed with more a likelihood of disappointment than success. For every PayPal or ING Direct success there are many others such as B2, Evolve, Zurich, Egg, which are less successful than planned. Many others never even get to the point of public awareness. None had a problem with getting the capital.

If this record of repelling invaders gives comfort to banks, it will be short-lived comfort. Perhaps the credit card product was the first to emerge as a competitive product, notably MBNA, but the pace will accelerate from here. Just as many men 'proved' that man couldn't fly by jumping off the Eiffel Tower, flapping their gadgets and dying, it was subsequently proven that man could fly. It is safer to take off from the ground than jump from a high structure or cliff – you get more chances. Tesco, Sainsbury's, ING and PayPal have proved that competition against banks for their traditional mainline business is possible, just as others have captured a good slab of the wealth sector at the higher end of the banks' traditional market. There will be an inevitable long-term consequence. Many bank activities could be vulnerable, and not just to large players in the major areas. An example would be Currencies Direct, a new and growing company that specialises in converting currencies for consumers and small businesses who are buying/selling property or trading abroad. Basically, wholesale FX rates for middling amounts.

Banks have a mobility problem whereby, because of the long and heavy investment in their existing ways of working, they have erected huge mobility barriers for themselves. The dominant reaction to ideas, opportunities or threats is to adjust, modify or enhance what is there already. The effect of this is to reinforce the fundamental problems.

The following three examples illustrate the problem.

4.12.1   The Y2K experience

So pervasive are systems that banks had to spend serious amounts of money to prepare for the year 2000. Many of the systems were unable to process correctly, and this mobility barrier was only overcome over a five-year period with many IT staff. These staff were therefore unavailable for progressive tasks to move their banks forward.

4.12.2   Competitive business models

Spurred by the Internet, or rather the climate that the Internet created towards new ideas, a range of business initiatives was rushed out. These were typified by brand names with single words such as Go, Buzz, IF, *smile*, Cahoot, Marbles, Goldfish, Evolve, B2; or by tagging an 'e-' or '.com' or 'Direct' onto something. Many banks experienced mobility barriers in their developments, even though the essence of the new business models had been 'proven' over many years by initiatives such as First Direct, Direct Line, Ryanair and easyJet.

There were many discussions over the degree of separation of the new initiative from the parent. There was often a muted commitment to the initiatives from senior management. Within the organisation there were a number of compromises, some of which damaged the business model. No two followed identical paths. The threat was that there was to be a competitive tidal wave. In the event, in banking there was no tidal wave. Perhaps that was because banks were primarily playing a competitive pattacake pattacake amongst themselves.

4.12.3   Offset accounts

The offset account presents two problems to established banks. First, it would be grim for banks if all customers that had a mortgage decided to offset all loans against their mortgages. Margins would fall overall. Secondly, cobbling together existing legacy systems to support offsetting is not an easy job for most bank IT systems.

4.12.4   Super retailers

This is just a 'suppose' discussion around the subject of retailer banks as opposed to retail banks. We have Tesco and Sainsbury's in mind. Let's also consider mobile network operators for a little too.

Figure 4.3 is meant to be a possible sequence of events, not the sky at night! In the first case, we have the old customer–bank relationship. Then, we have the

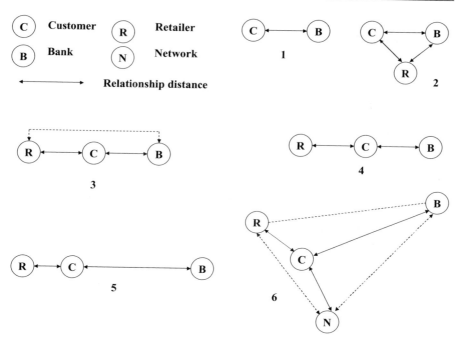

Figure 4.3 A possible sequence of events showing the changing relationship between the customer and suppliers of banking services

nice relationship of recent years where customers, banks and retailers co-exist quite happily. Then, the retailers decide to get into financial services – as they have now done – but with banks as partners for capital and operations. Then, perhaps, the retailers, having learned the ropes, use their own capital and implement more efficient operations. Then, the customer–retailer relationship gets stronger and the customer–bank relationship weakens. And then, in the last of the sequence, in come the network operators with mobile payments. They have tried, with and without banks.

Well, it's possible. What is this all about? It is about customer ownership. Banks, retailers and others are selfish when it comes to 'owning' their customers. Customers themselves want to know precisely who they are dealing with and not get pushed from pillar to post to get explanations or to resolve concerns. So each bank or retailer will want 'control'.

Such a process will marginalise the banks. The retailers and others, such as network operators, have a competence and a closer relationship with their customers than banks do with theirs – and it's the same people. It is a fact that 50p in every pound spent in the UK is spent at a supermarket. It is a fact that the majority of the population would rather forget to take their wallet than forget to take their mobile – they can always borrow some cash from a friend. It may not be fair, but that's the way it is. The supermarkets captured 42 % of petrol sales, 54 % of newspapers and magazines and 38 % of toiletries and pharmacy business in short order. Clearly, they are not to be underestimated. Still, it's a safe prediction that they'll not get this kind of market share in retail financial services . . . isn't it?

4.13   PRICING

Pricing is a key component to a retail banking strategy. Pricing in banking has always been viewed mainly as a marketing tool. The result of this is that the accepted pricing methodologies compromise the functional and strategic roles of what pricing should be about. The served markets are increasingly price driven, so there is a growing need for accurate and specific pricing to ensure profitability and to establish a long-term market position. The way it exists at present is a difficult compromise between the legacy from the pricing methods going back to the big bank oligopoly and the preferred ways of pricing. The result of this is to under-price the smaller relationships, and whilst large customer bases have their advantages, these are offset by lower unit profitability, because the handling costs and the offsetting value of the deposits is lower. Figure 4.4 shows the actual pricing situation, as compared to the ideal.

The customers may well expect that the flurry of words towards relationships – relationship officers, we value your relationship with us – will lead to some visible

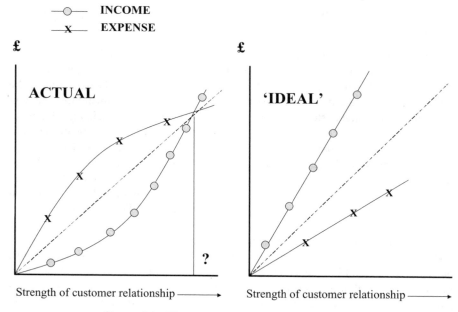

Figure 4.4   The actual and 'ideal' pricing structures

proof of the actions behind the words. Pricing, relationship pricing, would be one strong piece of evidence. Certainly, an ability to price a relationship profitably would enable a bank not to have to compete on price/rate for every banking product and service. Inevitably, specialists in a particular product line who achieve an adequate level of scale will always be able to compete heavily on price for their specialist products, and their staff will be knowledgeable.

4.14 ROUNDUP

A bank is a data- and process- and information-dominated organisation. As data processors, banks are impressive and hugely reliable. A large bank will process 1000 or more transactions per second at its peak, from perhaps 50 000 terminals. The less glamorous but more impressive fact is that in the early hours of the morning it will batch-process in-clearings, other transactions and internally generated transactions, processing over 500 million transactions in a two-hour processing time slot. Saving you the arithmetic, that is about 70 000 transactions per second. This is done night in and night out. Such is the reliability of bank systems that an ATM outage for a large bank, even if it is only for 30 minutes, makes the national press. Therefore, at doing what it does, the bank IT operation is supremely efficient and reliable. Given the volumes of accounts and transactions, the unit costs for processing are low, so the processing is efficient – and impossible to match at low volumes. The facts are that the direct and indirect IT-related processing costs are less than 10 % of the total costs in the large banks, some 5 % at RBSG for example. By the way, it is always amusing that IT equipment is lumped together with furniture in the annual reports, or do the accountants know something that the IT people don't? The totality of IT costs, to include IT staff, equipment, communications, networks, terminal devices, maintenance, training and so on, is difficult to give, but ranges from 10–20 % of operating expense.

The first fact is therefore that the bank exists, it is reliable, it is growing and it is profitable. That's a fair set of reasons to suggest that improvement is best made through safe, incremental changes. There must be no disruption to service, and no operational risk.

The second fact is that more than 70 % of all costs are incurred around the human side of processes and procedures, deeply ingrained into the bank and difficult to change. These are, in part, due to the products and services offered, both the quantity and complexity, and in the mechanisms to manage risks. But the IT systems have a great say in what staff have to do, as we shall discuss later.

A third fact is that because of the complexity of vertical and horizontal integration of a bank's operations, the knock-on effect of changes, or the problems that changes may cause, can be significant. The bank has many lines of business that are managed and measured independently, yet they share staff and systems resources to a high degree. There are phenomenal interdependencies. The positives of this situation are many and mostly economic, but the negatives include inflexibility, even as short lead times are increasingly important for market success. Cost allocation methodologies usually distort the truth.

A fourth fact is that the role of the IT groups in banks has needed to metamorphose over the last twenty years, as much as, or more than, any other function, but it hasn't. This is in order to move from automation, through data processing into information processing. Perhaps because of the first two problems, this metamorphosis has been extremely slow in banking. Banks have got stuck in the data processing stage. Whilst they have all the information technology that is available, it is not being applied to the core of the problems. While some businesses and departments have been able to adapt to the opportunities that information technology has presented, the majority of a bank has been practically, if not religiously, precluded from benefiting from these changes. To have allowed each business and department to follow its own IT path would have invited systems anarchy that would have damaged economics, controls, efficiencies and effectiveness. Not to have allowed it to happen at all would have seriously disadvantaged the business. Banking IT groups have sought a middle path, which has met with mixed success. This has been, and remains, an acute problem.

The major problems for a bank are those that would put customer 'loyalty' at risk, or negatively influence a decision to open an account or increase account usage. To the extent that loyalty is equivalent to lethargy, the threat is small. But the flipside to this is the difficulty of getting customers to move accounts from one bank to another. The critical thing is that at an 'event' point for the customer, the customer makes a choice of bank to provide the necessary product or service. Those choice points can increasingly lead to a positive, non-lethargic selection if the bank was preferred for some reason or reasons. There may be only ten, twenty or thirty such event points in a customer's life. A failure to satisfy such event points has serious consequences, and there are many lost opportunities.

4.14.1   The realisations

The systems in place, implicitly including practices, processes and procedures, determine the majority of the cost of operations because they ultimately determine what type of, and how many, staff are required to achieve the necessary functions of the bank. They determine who does what, how often, how much it costs, the service levels, and so on. By extension, the systems in place go a long way to determining the performance of the businesses, customer acquisition, retention and satisfaction, and the rates and fees charged and paid – which is just about as fundamental as it can get.

This is a dilemma – the existing status quo cannot take the bank to where it will need to be within acceptable time and cost constraints, but the risks and costs associated with any major changes are unacceptable.

The sky is not falling in. We may not be going forwards as fast as we'd like, but we're doing OK relative to our peers. We are not really feeling threatened. Banks will rationalise their performance in the market with all kinds of claims as to their advantages or disadvantages.

It seems that just four aspects dominate customer behaviour, however. They are:

- *Customer service.* This is the other side of the customer experience of using a bank. How convenient, how easy, how quick, how helpful, how clear, how flexible is the bank towards its customers?
- *Brand.* This translates in the customer's mind to trust and comfort. It is not clear that banks have retained the brand influence that they had in the past, but it is still powerful, especially for deposits. Increasing regulation moderates these fears.
- *Products and services.* These are still seen as commodities, and still have their roots in the past. There is still little effort to create different products and services that relate to today's needs in market segments or to customer events. It is still one-size-fits-all.
- *Price.* Costs for the bank are the price for the customer, most obviously in rates earned or paid, but increasingly in niggling charges.

The development of strategy around these four aspects will determine the relative and absolute success of a bank. Again, these aspects are little different to other industries. Banking is not a special case that defies normal commercial and marketing rules.

A bank today is the result of a hard-earned legacy of trust, presence, capability and competence at intermediating between borrowers and lenders and providing payment services. Banks remove the risk from an important part of their customers' lives. People and companies have ebbs and flows of funding requirements, usually triggered by events in their own situations. But in truth, banks provide no more than was available fifty years ago, except for some pretty basic electronic tricks, mainly in the area of payments, like ATMs, credit and debit cards. We should recall that cheques came in 1890, credit cards in 1955, direct debits in 1962, debit cards in 1980. Not a searing pace. We have current accounts, savings accounts, investment accounts, revolving credit, secured and unsecured loans, and mortgages – just like our parents. The major difference between accounts then and now is in the flavours. There are many tiers of rate, bands of investment, terms and conditions, penalties, bonuses, levels of service, and what have you, as opposed to the vanilla of the past. Note, however, that vanilla is still the favourite flavour for ice cream, and cheddar still the favourite cheese.

The bank collects business through standard sales efforts, different from other industries only in its flairless sameness. It enters the appropriate data. It processes the data. It keeps its management and customers informed of that processing using management reports and customer statements. It provides ancillary services such as payments. It provides explanations to customers when they need some help. That's about it. Yes, they manage the bank and monitor controls, but that is not onerous and is highly prescriptive. *How difficult can this business be?*

The nub of the bank is data processing. Let us not confuse this with information technology, which is something else. Banks have a massive amount of data today, basically accounts and transactions, which need to be processed.

Generalising, a large retail banking operation may have about 2000 branches and 50 000 FTE (full time equivalent) staff. Some 20 000 FTE staff of the total are in branches, perhaps half of them directly customer facing. Breaking out where the 30 000 FTE staff who are not in the branches are, and what it is that they do, is interesting – to say the least. There are 3000 sitting in call centres, 2000 in central IT, more in operations. Each regional processing centre has its staff. A trip around the bank's internal directory gives an idea of how labyrinthine the organisation is. This piece of analysis can be expanded on, but there are hundreds of departments all doing serious work. For every one FTE worker obviously doing something for a customer, there are more than two other FTE staff in the bank doing the unseen and unobvious, and perhaps unnecessary. *Can this be smart work?*

There is no doubt that banking should be an information processing activity, as Walter Wriston of Citibank pointed out 25 years ago. But the evidence shows it still to be hugely labour intensive. If 20 000 of the staff are directly customer facing and 30 000 are in support, it is unclear that data processing, let alone information technology, has been as effectively deployed as it could be. Alternatively, what it is that has to be done cannot perhaps be effectively automated. The manufacturing equivalent of such a situation would predate Henry Ford.

4.15 KEY OBSERVATIONS

- Consumers make few financial product and service decisions, and they are mainly spurred by life events, life-stage points and lifestyle decisions.
- Banks have difficulty in focusing their energies towards an increasingly complex and volatile market. Sometimes one wonders whether it's all too complicated to make proactive, competitive decisions, rather than being driven reactively.
- The totality of factors and their complexity that universal banks have to consider is becoming unfathomable. It's a tough enough business anyway. By the time you've worked out the politics, it is even more difficult.
- Regulatory conformance has become a major burden. Banks have to produce more 'products' for regulators than they do for their customers.
- The mix of factors and interactions within banks is so extensive that each organisational unit needs its own strategic decision-making matrix. It is not allowed it in practice.
- Banks are placing a great deal of faith in their relationship strategies, when in fact, the customers do not necessarily value a single, one-sided relationship over the most appropriate and/or better priced competitor products and services. Relationship management is in danger of becoming a

tactical sales activity, not a strategy; of becoming a lip service, not a true belief.

- With account aggregation, a customer can view all their acquaintanceships with the banking industry, as well as from the insurance and securities industries, on a single screen. PC software will develop to analyse the whole set of acquaintanceships. A 'single view' does not require using a single bank. The threat to banks is enormous.

- High promise technologies, such as imaging, are being considered once again, only if the benefit is to the bank. We remain driven by engineering, not pulled by art.

- From where a bank stands, there is even further need for increased 'sophistication' in policies and organisational structures to carry out those policies. That is true. But for sophistication we might read confusion, for organisational structures we might read overheads. Thin them down.

- Intuition and insight are disappearing. Fat and happy cats do not easily change.

- Just how much analysis is enough? Sooner or later decisions are needed.

- Shared cost bases can bring economies, and they can bring diseconomies. We cannot dismember it all, so we'll live with it. Are we certain about these scale economies?

- There are increasing numbers of logjams, and the logs are not being pulled away. Ask any customer, or any member of the ground level staff.

- Much business is being conducted, not at the optimal business level, but rather at sector level, or corporate level. Governments do that. It leads to poor cost allocations and undermines initiatives. An employee couldn't make a difference if they wanted to.

- Society is evolving faster than banks. As service institutions in an increasingly service-oriented society, banks will have to evolve at the same speed as the society in which they operate.

- Retail banking was once a mature industry, and the behaviours appropriate for a mature industry do not suit those for the growth industry that banking now is.

- The impetus for the adoption of technology is almost wholly driven by engineering considerations. Much more should be driven by its advantage to customers, even most of it.

- Cost structures are dominated by the efficiency of the organisation in its distribution of products and services and use of resources. Effectiveness is given second billing.

- Cooperation makes eminent sense in many situations, but is increasingly being used to avoid competitive decision-making because it plays well to risk-averse, conservative organisations. What could be better than a unique customer proposition that is difficult to copy?

- Technology is used in a supporting role, whereas its potential in a competitive role is unrealised. It is not only unrealised, it has never been done.

- Cross-subsidisation of businesses precludes rational pricing. What does it really cost? The cost allocation methodologies are highly questionable.
- Reflexive responses to the market and organisation tend to reinforce old errors, do they ever!
- Actions should be market-led – not product-led, technology-led or organisation-led. And there is nothing wrong in preparation for likely, or even possible, trends.
- Radical strategies are needed to build strong market positions. That's where HSBC and RBSG came from.
- The retention of customer business is becoming more difficult. Although customers may still keep their accounts, their funds are becoming more widely dispersed.
- The market is fragmenting faster than is thought. Established banks have erected their own mobility and exit barriers that competition can capitalise upon.

5
Systems and Information Technology (IT)

After four chapters, primarily on banking, all of a sudden we do a right turn into systems and IT? Well, forget the IT for a minute. The reason is that almost everything a bank does is dominated by 'systems'. A system is about orderliness, control, a set of connected things, procedures, practices and loads of other words. A system doesn't necessarily have anything to do with IT. When a bank recruits staff, it has a system to do so. This includes advertising the opportunity, arranging interviews, establishing qualifications, negotiating the employment and so on. That process is an orderly, joined up system with inbuilt procedures and mandated practices.

In order to have millions of customers doing many millions of things, the bank's thousands of staff have to know what's going on, and keep everything up to snuff. It was so for banks in 1750, 1850, 1950, and will be in 2050. The design of systems has been part of banking from 1750. The system design, introduction, redesign, replacement, obsolescence, change, improvement and all else goes on continuously. But imagine the impact of electricity, light bulbs, ballpoint pens, typewriters, photocopiers, fax machines and computers over the years. Each of these had their impacts. They were used to improve on the systems in place by speeding up things, reducing the labour in tasks, improving service, strengthening controls, providing information – indeed, even making things possible.

Whatever the systems in place today, it is these systems that determine the work content and the quality and cost of that work. Where information technology (IT) comes in is that it is without doubt the most powerful tool that banks can bring to bear on their systems. As a result, the expectation is that the bank systems will be redesigned to capitalise on IT. Well, computers and data processing are certainly not new, banks have had them for over forty years. Data telecommunications is not new, that's over 35 years old. Information technology is not new, perhaps it's about five years old in its current guise.

It was, is, and will be the systems that dictate most things in a bank, and certainly its market and financial performances. So what has happened to the systems, and what is going to happen to the systems as a result of today's information technology?

We really don't want to get deeply into IT. In fact, the precise problem with IT is that discussions get driven far too quickly down into the detail. Whatever are the right or wrong things to be doing with information technology, they are apparent at the higher levels of bank management. Their awareness of the subject of IT is, or is becoming, at the same level as their awareness in other subjects such as product management, marketing, treasury, HR and operations – IT is not a special subject (any more). Each of these is equally complex. Discussions on any of them do not need obscure acronyms and dense technological terms.

But systems, the way things get done around here, are a special subject. A bank's systems dominate what the bank can do, and the costs of doing it. Systems today are prickling with IT components and capabilities. And IT itself, as an integral part of the systems, helping to improve them, is now a large cost item, several times the cost of marketing for example.

IT projects take time to deliver, so the decisions taken about IT had best be right the first time – a bank can't spend the same money twice. Above all, in the short term, how well banks capitalise on IT capabilities to improve their systems will help determine the bank's success. The way IT is used will provide both differentiation in the market and operational efficiencies.

5.1   LEGACY SYSTEMS

As we've said, we use the word 'system' to mean the entire system, not just the IT piece. The retail banking systems that a bank has in place are inherited from the past, and hence they are known as *legacy systems*. These are the root cause of many of the problems that banks have in being able to create products and to service customers. To a large extent these retail banking systems determine costs.

Let us take somewhere in the late 1950s or early 1960s as the moment that data processing entered into banks. This was a pivotal moment, and a point that retail banks are still, believe it or not, pivoting around.

Up to that time, banking was achieved at the branch. Probably 80 % of the FTE staff were in branches, with 20 % in central or local Head Office support. Bank clerks used manual ledger cards or electromechanical devices with magnetic stripes to process data. Bank cards had not yet arrived. Direct debits and credits were just beginning. Customer statements were typed. A branch was almost a bank in its own right. There were no telecommunications networks or terminals as we know them today. If the banks had been in the car business, they'd have been building the cars in the back of the showroom.

Enter the computer. A handful of computer buffs (in those days from the Management Services Department) developed programs to establish a sequential account file, against which transactions would be centrally posted and statements would be centrally printed. Each branch was visited by a van every afternoon to pick up the transactions on paper tape, and every morning to deliver reports and customer statements. The goal, the only goal, was to reduce costs. After the initial blip, it did.

This started with savings accounts, and then current accounts, and then loan accounts, and then all the rest. It took about ten years to automate the posting, processing and printing of all the accounts across the entire bank. There were huge benefits to be had, too much demand for the data processing staff to handle, and too little time. There was no time to look back, it was all eyes forward, and great fun and satisfaction it gave. The benefits could be seen and were measurable.

After that initial period of ten years, during which the automation of many previously manual methods had been achieved, the bank had its data processing system in place. As it has turned out, it was in concrete. This now being in the early 1970s, data communications evolved and terminals, including ATMs, began to proliferate. A customer could use any branch of the bank for some services.

Still more requirements appeared, still new opportunities to automate were taken, and still we never could look back. In parallel, new technologies appeared with databases, computers, terminals and software. It was a fabulous ride. Automation became data processing became information processing became information technology. Increasingly, effort was needed to make the systems appear integrated, which led to many interfaces between practically independent applications. This brought operational complexities in terms of the sequencing of processing, and technical difficulties as the interdependencies grew rapidly. We became dependent on the automation.

The outcome was that the core bank processing systems were cast in stone by the 1980s. And these systems, and their thinking, are still central to a bank's IT systems today. There never has been the time or the funds to change. The Y2K pain and cost that came in the 1990s was simply about these old computer systems. In 1965, Y2K was not even considered. The designs, assumptions, programs, practices and procedures were formed way back, and the many subsequent changes and additions have not been able to break the grip of this legacy.

What bank staff actually did at work in the branches or in operations centres was largely dictated by their interactions with these systems, they entered data, enquired on data, checked reports, and so on. They manually checked, double checked and plugged holes in processes and procedures.

The same continues. The IT groups have only been able to make incremental improvements to the core systems and the emphasis has been on new channels and the integration/interfacing of new applications with the core systems. Business management, in the name of cost reduction, continues to look at how to automate out staff activity, creating further demand for IT. This is all stuff around the edges.

This is all hugely understandable, and there is no rogue in the story.

What banks now have is a complex and brittle collection of systems and their associated processes and procedures. Unlike an aeroplane, where 20 % of the energy keeps it in the air and 80 % pushes it forwards, bank systems use 80 % of the energy (and expense) to keep the systems up in the air and only 20 % of the energy to drive the bank forwards. The most effective use of information technologies is definitely yet to come.

But the worst part of all this is that these systems, whose basic designs go back 10/20/30/40 years, largely dictate staff costs. The systems assume interaction with staff, originally based on the processes and procedures in place at the time of the initial automation. Many improvements have been made over the years in the nature of further automation, streamlining processes, improving reporting and controls and delivering them on screens rather than paper, but the original outline remains clearly visible.

In most other industries, similarly inherited ways of doing business have encouraged fresh thinking to deliver superior products and services at lower costs than before. Entire buildings or factories are closed down, and new ones are built, capitalising on all the advances. Whether in steel, cars, shipbuilding, holidays, airlines, communications, transportation, IT, agriculture, building, fisheries, clothing, retailing, groceries, cruises, entertainment, cinemas, hotels or almost any field, there are new approaches now taken for granted. Customers, staff and shareholders have shared in these improvements. Their 'systems' were changed, big time.

Banks have not undergone such a change. In theory, banking is particularly vulnerable to new approaches, but it has been able to be resistant in practice because, as was said earlier, customers are not deserting banks (they need them) and neither are investors (they like them). There has been an inadequate stimulus to cause real change. Plus or minus, all established banks have the same situation.

The IT component, with IT staff and associated services included, accounts for between 15 % and 20 % of the cost base of a bank. Of that, some 80 % is spent on maintaining the systems – that is, keeping them going and implementing 'must have' capabilities as established by management and regulators. So, maintaining the systems and keeping them going accounts for between 10 % and 20 % of the costs in a bank. That's around £1 billion each year for the larger banks – 'just' to keep things going.

If your car only got five miles per gallon you'd know something was wrong and you'd do something about it.

5.2 BANKS ARE DEPENDENT ON DATA AND INFORMATION PROCESSING

A retail bank doesn't 'make' anything. It is a retailer selling and supporting a growing range of financially oriented products and services. Its core business is in its abilities to manage risk and process large numbers of accounts and huge numbers of transactions, and to sell.

As a financial intermediary, a retail bank removes customer risks by assuming them for itself, and it provides payment mechanisms. Like it or not, in pursuit of lower costs, banks have chosen to turn their products into commodity products. The tasks then become creating customer interest in their products and services, getting data into the organisation, processing the data, using that data to develop information to be better at selling their products and services, and to support the management, and to get information out to their customers.

In fact, a bank should be a retailer using data and information processing to provide the appropriate levels and types of service to customers, staff and management. Without an effective way of processing information and using that information to service its customers, the management and staff of a bank cannot realise the bank's retailing potential. The challenge increases with size.

Data processing will always be a required competence of a bank, but the need for an approach to information processing is the real challenge. New technologies, staggering price/performance improvements in technology, the easy availability of third party applications software and the ability to outsource data processing, business processes and communications networks, have all contributed to change the landscape of information processing in general.

What is the difference between data processing and information processing? Is it just a label introduced by the technology industries? Where does data end and information start? To our minds, information processing adds value, data processing just does a job. Put the line where you like, but there really isn't a lot of information coming out for the amount spent on IT. There's not much value being added.

It is the ability, freedom rather, to incorporate the information technologies into the design of the bank systems that constitutes the difference. If technology is designed into the processes, then the unit costs of the processes will be lower and the value able to be added will be higher. As things stand, most of the banks' processes within their systems were not designed to be handled by technology, rather by clerks with pens. If banks emulate legacy processes and procedures, or if these legacy processes and procedures have to be accommodated in any new design or operation, then the unit costs cannot be optimal, and much of the value cannot be added. The rationale for the existence of the processes and procedures in the first place is never seriously questioned, but that is where it all starts from.

When a poor process or procedure is optimised or streamlined, perhaps by the addition of some technology, you still end up with a poor process or procedure, but optimised or streamlined. Such actions may well reduce the labour content by one, two, five or ten percent. But, except in a conveyor belt factory environment, such as cheque encoding, a 10 % reduction in labour content does not lead to a 10 % reduction in labour. For example, you can lop off six seconds of every minute a cashier in a branch takes to serve a customer, but that doesn't mean that you can reduce the number of cashiers by 10 %. Banks have continued with their traditional approach of chasing these one, two, five, ten percent improvements, and this is no surprise. At the operating unit level that is all that can be hoped for. There is little that can be done to impact the pervasive inefficiencies of a process or procedure that can extend over many units. Pervasive improvements involve many areas of a bank, and bring friction.

Various technologies have given many major lifts to banks, as Figure 5.1 illustrates. Each of these technologies, and others, have helped business progress. But the received benefits have not been as large as is possible, for the bank or for the customers. In

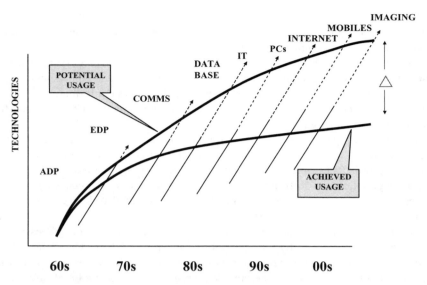

Figure 5.1 Diminishing contribution from additional technology

particular, bank customers, from their perspectives, have not benefited from the heavy technology spend of the last decade or more. Don't cite Internet banking – it is the customer's PC and network access – all the bank had to do was provide systems access, just like other companies were already doing. Don't mention CRM – customers have yet to see much evidence of a relationship. The promise of these technologies has not yet been realised in practice. What could have been achieved with each technology, and there is no shortage of good ideas, has been constrained by an inability to capitalise on it. This is because it couldn't be retro-fitted into the legacy situation. The technologies were grafted onto the status quo, not designed into it.

Consider the latest examples. Mobile phones are limited to balance enquiries, alerts and the like. That is not ambitious thinking. PCs and broadband enable us to see account statements and accomplish elementary transactions. No customer is aware that a bank has a database – after all, if it did then they wouldn't have to repeat all the information on every account application form, would they? Imaging? Forget it. And not many banks win awards for their Internet sites when compared to retailers.

There are a lot of technologies out there to be used, and capitalised on. Tremendous opportunities are being passed over because banks cannot include and integrate them – they don't integrate into the legacy situation, at best they interface.

Because of the restrictions imposed by the legacy systems, the IT industry has frequently presented technologies as magic bullets for banks. This hasn't helped the cause. Simply put, no-risk solutions that offer benefits without disruption, at modest cost, are few and far between. There will always be a procession of these enticements, and they will have some value, but they will not resolve the situation. For example, can a data warehouse containing what little we know of our customers add much? Can we apply relationship management to an acquaintanceship? And can we mine incomplete data?

Banks will have to get qualitatively better at making use of information technology because it must become a core competence, and it is a key enabler for market growth through better products and services, improved marketing and sales, reduced costs and improved risk management. It is a matter of how fast this will happen. Unlike the manufacturing and distribution sectors, where the true change from data processing to information technologies was forced upon companies by violent competition, banking was faced with the elective choice to change, which is a far more difficult decision. The basic business needs better applied information technology, the choice will not remain elective for much longer.

The reason that it takes three working days to make a non-urgent payment in the UK is simply because the processes and procedures and systems dictate it. All the banking systems are computerised, as are the employer payrolls and the utility companies' billing mechanisms. However, it still takes three days. It doesn't much matter what the clearing organisation might do with the existing status quo. The three days is designed and built into the BACS process. Improvement can only come from a redesign, and a total replacement system, which is being done by BACS. In several countries they already have real time clearing systems – because they were designed and built that way. IT has been used to 'improve' on many aspects of the existing clearing system, but cannot address the fundamental problems. Credit card payments are another case. You can order a book from Amazon.com and receive it in a day or two. This means packaging, shipping, mail and postal delivery. All this physical effort takes a lot less time than the time Amazon waits to receive its money from the card companies, which is all 'computerised'. Such delays, as with clearing and card payments, present a real threat for bank payment systems. Improvements here are now becoming mandatory because others might enter into the payments business with real time solutions.

We are now in a difficult chicken-and-egg situation, and have been for some years. Everybody knows it. The crux is that the concrete foundations of the early adoption of computers are difficult to move. The retail banking businesses themselves may be keen to move on, but unless the 'system' can accommodate new ideas then there is an impasse.

Banks are spending much money on IT, but they are not realising many of the cost improvements, productivity improvements and value-adding opportunities. And they will not until they change the bank systems to capitalise on the information technology.

5.3　INFORMATION TECHNOLOGY *WILL* BECOME A MAJOR DIFFERENTIATOR

We are now drifting towards more suitable products for the market, better customer service and lower costs. That does mean a powerful role for information technology – quite possibly more of it, but definitely better use of it. Banks have a powerful ally in IT and how well they make use of it is the opportunity.

Banks are a huge user of what is called information technology as measured by money spent, internally and externally. But the amount of money spent on IT has no correlation to its contribution – that's related to 'smarts', not to money. IT has now become a significant part of the cost structure of banking, especially if the true costs are added up – there are many staff around the bank that 'support' IT in one way or another, they are not classified as IT staff, but are doing jobs where their acquired knowledge of IT has become a sought-after skill. The official bank IT areas do not contain all the IT expense. This 'formal' expense, as we said earlier, is between 15 % and 20 % of the total operational expense. Nobody knows how much 'informal' IT expense is incurred. Few of us in banks have not burned up hours of our own and our colleagues' time trying to resolve what we might see as IT issues. Every department seems to have its own IT paramedics to give first aid for IT situations. And there is the cost of all those IT meetings with non-IT staff.

So that's OK then? No it isn't. Generalising, this expense doesn't produce the returns to justify the investments being made in IT. More obviously, IT is not enabling the bank staff – the majority of the cost base – to add value and thereby increase bank productivity. A great deal has changed from the gung ho days when computer investment decisions were waved through. There is no lack of belief that IT can and should contribute more, and the investments will surely be made – but only on the basis of a hard-nosed evaluation of the returns. The scepticism is not on the various technologies; it's on the abilities to leverage their use, and the lead time before the returns are apparent and worthwhile.

It is true that a bank can take newer information technology and make some use of it. For instance, the data warehouse is a common approach to addressing a number of issues in marketing and to generating information, not data, from the many pools of data available in the bank and its myriad computer systems. But this is still the second prize, in that the original data should have been fed immediately into an IT-based business information management system itself, from where this information would have been immediately available anyway.

The conundrum is that IT is good for a bank, and the technologies are inexpensive these days, but bank managements are trying to reduce IT costs. That is, the bank management feels that the returns on IT investments, and the speed with which the returns are realised, are inadequate to make the investments. Perhaps they feel that the risk of changing from their data processing systems to IT systems is too great. Perhaps they feel that it will take too long, cost too much, and be uncertain. Perhaps they've heard it all before. Whatever the reason, they don't choose to invest in IT as freely as they did in the past.

As the effective use of IT is able to be introduced, but only after the removal of the legacy systems constraints, then a bank will unleash significant potential power, and how the bank chooses to harness this can be expected to provide major differentiators between banks. There are few differentiation opportunities today that we can identify as having their basis in technology. With lower costs, the pricing can be keener. With better information, decisions can be automated and made immediately to authorise loans. With better information, the customer's sense of urgency can be addressed, the complexity reduced, the aggravation removed, the frequency of transactions can be increased, the convenience can be improved upon and the staff skills maximised. All of these are differentiators for customers.

5.4 IT AND THE RETAIL BANKING INDUSTRY

Estimates of IT expense in banks worldwide cluster around something like £200 billion, of which about half is spent internally and half is to IT vendors of one sort or another. UK retail banks, and this is an out and out guesstimate, probably spend in the region of £5–8 billion with the IT industry. This will include hardware, communications, professional services (development, consulting, systems integration, training, and so on), systems software, banking applications software and ERM/CRM software. Thus, a large bank may well be spending £500 million annually on its internal costs, and another £500 million with IT vendors.

This level of expenditure attracts a great deal of attention from all quarters, and it is not always of the helpful variety. The absolute level of cost, and the important nature of IT within a bank lead to immense amounts of, shall we say, discussion. Nobody is short of an opinion, least of all outside consultants and the IT vendors themselves. These discussions often lead to confusion and heavily compromised decision making. Bank managements are often asking simple questions and wanting simple answers, but get enmeshed in convoluted debates. Decisions frequently turn out to be wrong, or at least fail on delivery. It is all very imperfect. If choices are limited to what seems possible or reasonable, then there is a disconnect from what is wanted, and all that is left is a compromise.

The IT industry is complex, with many participants. IT, technology in general, can clearly be a good thing to have when used well. We can all see technology improving aspects of living all around us. But it is true that the technology businesses do try hard to push their products into situations where their benefit is highly suspect. The problems occur when technologies are used for the sake of using the technology, rather than because it allows significant value to be designed into the processes. At that point, no plug is large enough for the plughole. Unfortunately, computers make it easier to do a lot of things that don't need to be done.

Technology companies go up and down like yo-yos; companies float, companies fold, companies thrive, most struggle. This situation cannot be because the world necessarily needs them in all circumstances. So the selection of technologies and vendors plays an important role, as do the ongoing relationships with the vendors.

The technology industry has many players and types of player. In the same way that banks are focused on attracting customers to their products and services, so are these companies pushing hard for sales of their products and services.

Banks provide a large opportunity for IT vendors based on the huge amounts of IT power, capacity, bandwidth and whatever other metrics can be applied to the technologies themselves. But that is not what the real challenge is about. The real challenge is how banks make the best use of the information technology in the banking business.

This has been the IT industry's challenge for some years now. IT is all fast, and all wonderful, but how do we really make use of it? The IT industry has functionally fragmented to better provide these answers. There are many more companies in each of these areas than are shown in Figure 5.2, and there are many more areas of expertise than shown. We have given a rough estimate of the percentage of spend made in each of these areas.

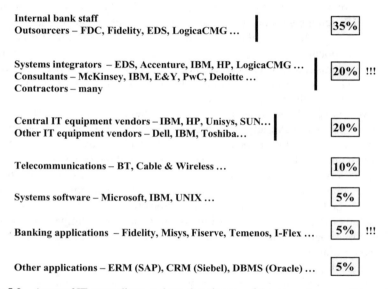

Figure 5.2   Areas of IT expenditure and rough estimates of the percentage spend in each area

Banks rely on much of what the IT industry has, and they need to make far better use of some of those things. The differences between banks, going forward, will not be in their application of science, but in their strategies, the financial engineering, the research and development that follows from these strategies, the translation of this into systems and the use of IT to deliver their services.

Banks typically have an unusually large proportion of staff in their IT departments/groups as compared to most other industries. The largest banks have a comparable number of development staff to Microsoft, Oracle or SAP, several thousands across all their businesses and functions, several hundreds in pure retail banking. The need to maintain and enhance bespoke legacy systems is one cause. Another is the belief, held by many, that the bank systems provide a competitive advantage relative to their banking competitors. A third factor is the wide range of technologies in use by banks, and a fourth is the acute need for speed, volume and reliability in banking, which sees them constantly needing the latest, greatest technologies and skills, some of which they may indeed have to pioneer to some extent.

Whatever the reality, the IT industry will claim to be up to the task, but many banks would rather not be totally reliant on them. So that situation continues.

In retail banking it has been many years since most banks' retail business management were able to dictate what they wanted from IT. This is because of the history of the retail IT systems – the infamous legacy systems problem. The conflicts of keeping the show on the road and progress cannot be reconciled easily. There are changing systems, keeping costs down, absorbing systems software upgrades, upgrading hardware, adding new delivery channels, developing essential new systems to support management (particularly in the financial management areas), recruiting and training staff, and so on. All these can only be prioritised and knocked off one by one. Throw in regulatory changes, the Internet, office automation, branch networks, continuous systems availability, disaster recovery and other zingers, and you have a real restriction.

The truth is that bank IT groups have done a remarkable job keeping it all going, and to high performance levels at that.

So, to our initial point that the retail banking business management had little say in it all – they have to queue up just like everybody else. This is a shared resource remember. It's also worth pointing out that if you have an exceedingly complex system which is mission critical plus, and it's working, a sensible thought is not to touch it if you can help it, or put in 'little' manual workarounds.

Was there a time when banks should have thoroughly invented or reinvented their retail banking systems? Maybe, and some tried. But even these new systems are now only younger legacy systems, although more flexible and so on than the older ones. The same basic problem exists, but less intensely. But even these changes over the last ten or fifteen years were replacing legacy systems with younger legacy systems, albeit better architected, better written and more stable. Information technology has now come of age. If banking is at some important inflexion point, so is IT, as it happens.

In Figure 5.2, we would point to the banking applications group as the key group. It may only be 5 % of the total, but that still amounts to a group with substantial revenues. Anyway, the point is that in here in some important ways, should lie the solution to the legacy systems problem. It is the smallest group, but it could hold massive capabilities for banks to exploit. It is not clear to us that it does, at the moment.

We implore the banking applications industry to stop investing in younger, better, faster, taller, cleverer, cheaper legacy systems – which is what most of them are doing. The objective is to get away from legacy systems and legacy thinking. Easy for us to say? We get there in the next chapter.

5.4.1 There are additional pressures now

Additional pressures? It's because all consumers and small businesses are well aware of just what IT is capable of through their own interactions with many companies and services. They also know when it is used well and when it is used poorly. They also increasingly know 'what it's about'. They are frequently interacting over the Internet themselves to find information, buy goods, or interact in some way. Broadband access at home is becoming commonplace. They are not impressed with bank systems. Consumer expectations are rising fast, and banks don't appear to be responding. They are responding of course, but it's slow. To ensure systems integrity within a highly complex and sensitive infrastructure dictates that the process of implementing change takes many months.

It's not just banks; it applies to any predominantly legacy system. The Y2K situation provided the clearest manifestation of the problem. The need to have four digits for the year instead of just two could be explained on the back of a postage stamp. There was nothing difficult to understand about the need – it could not be more simple or clear. And yet it took years to rectify, and huge amounts of resource. The net effect of all the expenditure was precisely nothing in terms of productivity, marketing, treasury, risk management or customer products and service. Newer systems have progressively fewer of these problems.

Meanwhile, the IT technology has exploded in its capabilities – it is no longer just computers as data processors, but computers as communications, office applications, databases, imaging, networks, information warehouses, and all manner of clever mousetraps that hide in banks.

Information technology is a great step on from data processing. For instance, if you have a medical check-up, the doctors and nurses prod, poke and spear you, and produce an informative, custom report within minutes of the last bloodletting. It can even relate you statistically to the population by age and so on. It is segmentation, no less, and CRM in action. You can see the world of airline schedules and prices ordered by date, price or whatever, having taken account of your preferences. Touch screen systems are in even the smallest businesses.

You yourself can do all sorts of things. Companies can do all sorts of things, like provide utility accounts that facilitate budgeting by flattening out summer and winter usage of gas bills and predicting usage.

All in all, customers know what can be done with IT. However, their experience of banking IT outside of Internet usage is that it is primitive. A staff member could no more swing their screen around 180º to explain something to you because the presentation is, what's the word, dated. Even within Internet usage it generally looks like a disjointed collection of capabilities, often requiring multiple codes for access. More importantly, the single most useful facility is to pay bills and transfer funds between their, or to other people's, accounts. The rest is usually not much more than providing Internet access to view accounts, that is, they are nice to have, but of limited value.

Customers want to be able to do all those things, and a lot more, using all their accounts from their multiple financial institutions. Aggregation services are a first step. Banks suck in their breath and explain the difficulties. Meanwhile, others will get on with it, and what with this and portal wars coming up it will be an interesting period.

The sheer number of bank staff in middle and back office functions in itself strongly implies inefficiencies, paper, errors, delays, exceptions, overhead and costs. It doesn't look automated, let alone look like information technology in action. Decisions that are in any way out of the ordinary, which means useful, cannot be given. It simply isn't impressive. When a customer phones up with a problem, it is usually a problem in that something has gone wrong or they are confused about the proliferation of choices. There are large numbers of call centre staff – why?

Bank management has its ear close to the ground. It realises that whilst it is logical and credible that IT can and should provide substantial benefits, there is little to convince them so to do. Their 14-year-old children are putting up their own websites and zooming and zapping things, producing clever things that a bank CEO would get an estimate in the hundreds of man days for. The various IT acolytes, vendors and consultants promote opportunities, but few of these have been realised in terms of returns on the investments made. IT is no longer a resource to be leveraged as much as it is a resource to be contained, or at the least approached with caution.

A good portion of bank IT seems to have a mission of its own, and has difficulty relating it to the business in practice. It's not true of course. Much of this is indeed due to the primary task of keeping the systems running through thick, thin and thinner. In a competitive sense, IT can offer important scale and scope economies. But this has not been clearly realised in retail and small business banking outside of mass data processing. A small bank appears to be able to offer the whole gamut of IT that is needed, even if it has a relatively small customer base and a handful of IT staff, while the big bank offers no more with a far larger contingent of IT staff. In fact, the proportion of expense spent on IT in small and mid-sized banks in their retail and small business areas is substantially smaller than that spent by the large banks to support comparable products and services. It is also the smaller banks that are pushing increases in scope. Neither of these realities are what economies of scale or scope were meant to be about.

Somehow, the bank retail business/IT dialogue has to be rethought. An ally as powerful and capable as IT should be utilised more fully. This doesn't, definitely doesn't, mean throwing more money at IT, but it does mean placing the money better. It just means 'you're not getting what you need, and we're not happy about not being able to give you better capabilities'. As they say – go figure.

5.5   THE IT INDUSTRY IS NOT WITHOUT BLAME

We can encourage banks to look more deeply into meeting their customers' needs, and help the banks to meet them at the right price. That's pretty much a message in this book. Is there any chance that we could ask the same of the IT industry in relation to its banking clients? If the banks are to provide better banking, it seems evident that IT should be called on to provide better banking systems, or systems that support better banking. Do IT companies know their client needs, or do they try to create needs? On the other hand, do the banks make honest use of IT companies, or do they try to manipulate them to achieve their own goals? We can hear the huffing and puffing coming up, but is the IT industry as a whole close enough to its banking clients as a whole? Do they know what problems they are trying to solve, or what opportunities they are trying to meet?

If we talk of the reinvention of an industry, the IT industry is an outstanding case. IBM itself has undergone an amazing transformation over the last ten years or so. Nearly 50 % of its 2003 revenues came from its Global Services Division (professional services of one kind or another), 31 % from hardware and 15 % from software. This is markedly different from the picture ten years ago, when hardware was the dominant revenue stream.

IBM is a leading IT vendor and services provider, with 320 000 staff worldwide – some 22 000 in the UK. Let's put some perspective on things, IBM has a worldwide revenue of about $ US90 billion (£50B) and makes a profit of about $ US8 billion (£4.5B). This profit is comparable in size to the profit of either HSBC or RBSG. That is, IBM is not quite as large in financial terms as most people would think. The banking industry towers above the IT industry. One large bank in the UK is 'worth as much' as the IBM Corporation. If Bill Gates of Microsoft cashed up, his premium bonds and passbook savings included, he could afford to buy one half of HSBC. Since less than a third of IBM's business is in the financial services industry, it is even smaller in banking industry terms.

Do the staff serving banks in the IT industry understand the banks' needs? Do the bank IT staff understand the width involved to provide better banking? The answer to both questions is that only a few do. Heinz understands its customers' customers. Airbus understands its customers' customers. But much of the IT industry sees its customers as the bank IT group. The fear is therefore that they may not know even their own customer, which is the bank, let alone their customers' customers. They have to have a far better feel for their customer's (IT department) customers' (retail bank management) customers' (bank staff) customers (consumers).

So, IT vendor to IT department talk about . . . IT. There's a surprise. They can and should do that, but only after they've talked about the banking and understand that.

Pushing customer relationship management systems (CRMs) and data warehouses, ATMs and card-based products, and so on is best – you hardly have to know anything about the business at all. Yes, there is a lot of common sense to it all, but common sense is a long way from being enough if you're to help the bank materially.

The net result of the IT situation is unsatisfactory, and at long last we are seeing it being questioned aggressively by bank managements. One day it was a crown jewel and the source of competitive advantage, but the next day it is being outsourced, with significant chunks going to strangers in India or Hungary. The IT industry has attracted far closer inspection than ever before as the 'mysteries' have been exposed as quite normal activities. Bank IT staff are unconsciously re-evaluating their loyalties – they weren't sure whether they were in the banking industry or the IT industry. They need to be in the banking industry. And frankly, so do those IT vendors serving banks.

To banking application vendors, processors, outsourcers we say – you are in the banking industry, you must get that straight. And renovation is not innovation. Get that straight too.

5.6 RESOLVING THE LEGACY SYSTEMS PROBLEM

Our guess is that out of the 1000 largest banks in the world, less than 30 of the established banks in developed countries embark on a major systems replacement of their core retail banking system in any year. It may be lower than that.

What that might mean is that banks may not have any pressing problem given the status quo in their markets. Within that, it might mean that they see no competitive edge (an IT industry favourite phrase that) in having 'better IT systems' in place. Within that, they're suspicious of the ROI suggestions. If all their competitors are plus/minus in the same IT situation then the bank leadership may decide to concentrate on competing with their banking skills. No bad thing.

It may mean that they are not convinced the new system will lead to a better financial performance than the existing one. It may be too disruptive. It may cost too much. It may not be executed on time and on budget, or even successfully.

The business of developing retail banking systems is complex. We venture to suggest that other than with simple monoline products, it may be that there will be no comprehensive new core banking systems to be written by any bank ever again! The risk, cost and difficulties are too great.

For certain, the larger banks are not looking for a younger legacy system. They are all heading in the direction of disentangling and simplifying their systems. This, for instance, may require separating out all delivery channel matters from the business matters; separating out customer matters; and separating out the generic processes from the factory processes.

But most importantly, banks need systems. IT is undoubtedly intimately embedded in the system, but it's not the IT banks are after – it's the systems. They need to replace their legacy systems, so they need new systems. Saying it another way, banks cannot replace their legacy systems without replacing their legacy systems. That may sound crazy, but it's not.

Pretty much, none of the banks are replacing their legacy systems. Based on current trends, the established banks will be providing products and services in five or ten years' time that will look much like they do today. They are addressing the problem of legacy systems in two steps. The first is to separate out the functions.

The legacy systems comprise hundreds, often thousands, of individual programs to handle the many products and services. These are often regarded as silos, in that they are end-to-end, individually self-contained systems that handle every aspect of the account – from delivery to processing. The need to share resource has led to a good deal of (complicated) interaction between these silos. Whether it impresses you or depresses you, this lot probably averages out at 20–40 million lines of programming code for a bank, and can go higher in a large complex bank. Except that it works, it's worthless.

Past efforts, with some success, have reduced the need to repeat customer information in the silos with the introduction of some kind of customer file. But we've never bitten the big bullet. In large banks, these legacy silos represent tens of thousands of man years of development and maintenance effort.

The separation process is a desk job to decide what goes where and so on. In Figure 5.3, we've shown four groupings for simplicity. Everything to do with delivery has a home, the same for customers, generic functions like credit scoring, pricing and General Ledger postings and the other agnostic and generic functions have a place. The product factories just concentrate on efficient processing and are unencumbered with non-product detail. With such an approach, the banks can replace a single component of the solution that will then be enabled across the bank. New channels can be added, which immediately support all appropriate products with no change to the products. Pricing can be introduced that is cognisant of the customer's entire relationship with the bank.

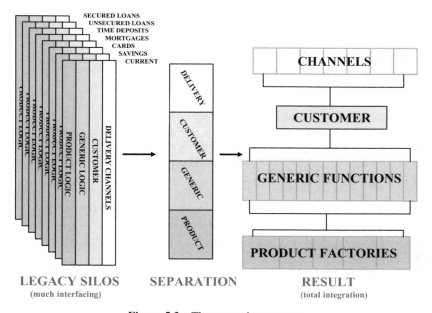

Figure 5.3   The separation process

Whereas each silo had to be checked, evaluated, changed and checked, which involved many resources, most enhancements, changes and additions will be able to be made within a component or two of the new architecture.

It's more complex than this suggests, and there are a number of important computer technology aspects. However, the goal of banks' IT groups is this 'simple'.

The IT industry has got to address these opportunities and problems. This particularly applies to the retail banking applications vendors and systems integrators.

There has to be a cocreation between the bank and the IT vendors, be they hardware, systems software, applications software or whatever. Only with a clearly shared vision of the target business model can a transition to the new, change management, low cost, and confident ROI model be achieved. Confidence, simplicity and speed again.

For our money, the large banks are not convinced that change is all in all a smart thing to undertake as things stand. They will only change their systems if competitively threatened or if their operational risk on legacy systems becomes too high (for them and the regulators). If the bank/IT 'discovered' or 'invented' a forward path, it would be listened to. The path outlined above is already the immediate direction for the large banks. If Y2K cost a tonne of time and money, then this will hurt more – but the results will be gratifying, and will substantially free up development resource in the future to work on go-forward projects instead of maintenance and so on.

This problem diminishes with the size of the bank, and more particularly with its scope of business. So the IT industry can prosper in smaller banks in the short term. But the banks' IT models are changing faster than the IT industry. That's new.

Frankly, much of the IT industry is trying to continue along some worn out paths, or cobble together some approximation of a solution from what they have. For large banks, this is getting to be an annoyance. The IT guys have got to come up with new architectures within which plug and play components can thrive and deliver real customer benefits, thus liberating banks from their legacy systems. Once banks have accomplished the separation step, then they will be looking for components/objects with which to improve functionality. That is the second step.

To pick up the theme at the beginning of this chapter, it's all about systems. We see the IT changing within five years, but we don't see the system changing. Since it is the system that dictates costs and the products and services, flexibility and pricing, then we may have another effort where much is promised and expected, and little delivered.

This has been the story of bank information technology, and its predecessor data processing, for almost twenty years now. Unless the systems are redesigned and redeveloped to capitalise on IT, then the benefits will not be realised. And this doesn't mean business process re-engineering (BPR). It means having a fundamental and unconstrained view of the opportunities in the banking industry.

It is at times like this that companies, banks and IT vendors included, have their opportunities to excel as others hold onto their old ideas and models. Most will renovate their products, and struggle. Some will innovate, and benefit.

5.7   A NEW APPROACH FROM THE IT INDUSTRY AND FROM BANKS

Given that it is the legacy systems that are inhibiting the banks' progress in many ways, and absorbing huge costs in doing so, then the IT industry has to choose between optimising/improving the status quo, or doing something differently. At the moment, most of the effort is trying to provide solutions that remove individual roadblocks by bolting on a capability here or there to ameliorate some tense requirement – but not in solving the underlying problem. Even outsourcing of development, testing and processing is aimed at solving problems that don't need to be solved, and shouldn't be there in the first place. When it does take hundreds, if not a thousand staff to keep something going, why wouldn't, shouldn't, a bank get the cheapest staff available consistent with meeting the goals? It's not solving the problem, but it is reducing the cost burden of the problem, which is second prize.

But it simply should not require such expense if the systems made use of the proven capabilities of the IT industry. We, the authors, are the last people to be proselytising the advances in information technology practices, but they are so real to us all. Even in writing a book, where we use spreadsheets, charts and word processing as the applications, we are enlisting the help of a vast amount of technology to put Excel spreadsheets into Powerpoint charts, which then go into the Word document. Any or all of these functions are performed by any of us sitting anywhere. In just a few years, the progress has been totally amazing, if we're honest. It is impossible to believe that the banking industry is not able to capitalise more on these and other technologies in its core functions.

If the IT industry has dreams, surely one would be to design and develop a banking system that capitalises on all these technologies resulting in an entirely flexible system where the appropriate business people can plug and play with intelligent objects to build the system that they need. Other than for a few pieces of arcane logic it seems inconceivable that there would be many programmers, as we know them today. It seems that testing should be confined to testing the workflow processes rather than programmer code. Retail banking hardly provides the same challenges to IT as some other industries, and it seems absurd that it is the legacy systems that are holding things back.

Most of the IT industry appears to believe this, that they could in fact develop a thoroughly modern solution which would give the business all the flexibilities that it wants, that would not need such cumbersome definition and development processes as there are today, where capabilities could be delivered in minutes, hours or days instead of weeks, months and years, and where the cost would be a fraction of today's costs.

But the IT industry isn't doing any such thing. It creeps along with incremental improvements, converts code from one computer language to another, it adds new/improved business functionality here, there and everywhere. It is not directly addressing the fundamental problem of removing the problems that the legacy systems bring.

There is a problem. But if everything IT has is so good, then what can the problem be? The problem is that the banking industry and the IT industry do not talk to each other except through their 'normal' channels, which are IT to IT. Neither knows what needs to be known (Figure 5.4).

There is a law, Putt's Law, that says that technology is dominated by two types of people – those who understand what they do not manage, and those that manage what

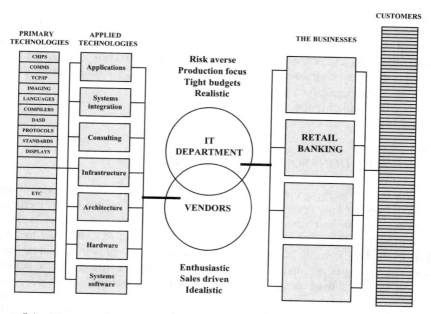

Figure 5.4   'The problem' – neither the banking industry nor the IT vendors know what needs to be known

they do not understand. Take a minute to think about this. IT vendors and bank IT staff are these people. It simply is not working. There is nothing that applied technologies cannot provide that the businesses need or should expect. The bit in the middle is the problem. Both the banks and the IT industry need to find a resolution to this.

IT in banking has become isolated from both the banking business and the technologies, and it's as true for IT staff inside the bank as it is for the vendors. The legacy systems, and the need to protect existing performance, are the root cause of this problem. But this has been exacerbated for the businesses by previous experiences with IT.

We have no wish to upset Mr. or Ms. Putt or their law, but perhaps there is a third type of person in IT – those who do understand and manage what they manage. The reason these are so rare is because of the difficulties in waltzing around in the goo of legacy systems. Many of the business people are capable, even eager, of using IT in a totally new opportunity, with some help. However, in a legacy IT environment they get 'you can't do that, you don't want to do this, you must do it this way' restrictions. The premium is on avoiding the rocks below, not on getting to where they want to go. The navigator is more important than the skipper. The skipper is smart enough to know that he cannot just order a straight line course from A to B without holing the boat. Of course, if we get rid of the rocks, then the navigator is less important by far – the skippers can navigate simple waters for themselves. This comes to a head during the ongoing debate about whether business people can run IT, or should IT people run IT. We think it far more appropriate that business people take charge, and the first step towards that in a major way will come with the removal of the rocks of the legacy systems. Then there is no need for the people who know where the rocks used to be! Only a few, very few, of these IT navigator people will graduate to captaincy, and run the business. The exceptions will be those who put as much effort into learning about banking as about rock formations.

There is a kind of limbo, standoff, barrier, stalemate, or what you will, which has slowed down change dramatically. Any ideas, anyone? Please?

5.8   APPLICATIONS SOLUTION/SOFTWARE LICENSING

The traditional licensing approach of the IT vendor applications solutions/software in retail banking uses a licence fee and a recurring annual payment. This method of licensing seeks to establish a basis for the licence price related to the size of the bank – be it number of accounts, number of customers, asset size or some other measure. This method of licensing initiates a large up-front investment with an annual recurring cost. Other pricing models exist elsewhere in banks, for instance 'price per seat' on trading/capital markets systems, and usage and/or subscription pricing for other areas. To the extent that the applications become commoditised, and their usage fluctuates with market changes, banks will increasingly wish to see a variable cost/pricing model, whereby the licence cost is more aligned to the benefits to be received from the solution/software. They will certainly wish to avoid large up-front licence costs, especially since there are additional large, up-front implementation costs, which means that changing applications brings a double cost whammy. Retail banks would also like to ensure that their chosen vendor displays ongoing commitment to such projects, and earning the reward up front, ahead of a successful implementation, does nothing to encourage this. There will be interesting new approaches to licensing which will join bank and vendor into some form of a risk/reward relationship from which both bank and their vendor could gain.

Part II
THE PROPOSITIONS

6
The Real World

For the next few pages we want to introduce some key observations on how most businesses work in practice and fact. The observations on which this is based are not academic or theoretical. They are based on solid facts. We are exposed to many pseudotheories on business, and sometimes they seem to gain a legitimacy that they do not deserve, based on the amount of talk they develop and the number of acolytes they collect. At first sight, they always seem obvious and easy.

So, before we rely on the previous observations on which to build a way forwards, let us first see what facts we can take from business in general. Banking does obey the same rules as other businesses, contrary to what many bankers still think. We can also say that about the IT industry.

6.1 BASIC FINDINGS ON BUSINESS STRATEGY

It was 25 years or so ago that Sidney Schoeffler of The Strategic Planning Institute in Cambridge, Massachusetts completed a study covering 1700 businesses, ranging across many industries and companies of all sizes, starting with General Electric. His approach was to take readings of companies – the many financial and operational numbers of their businesses – normalise them, and look for correlations. He then said it like he saw it, with integrity, and anonymity for the contributing businesses. The data was incorporated into the PIMS (Profit Impact of Market Strategy) database. The basic findings were extremely elegant. Unfortunately, they did not point the way to magic but rather to the sensible application of effort focused on the things that do matter, which were identified. So, whilst the work is widely respected and practised, it never made the headlines. The work has been continued to the point where 3500 companies, including many European companies, now participate in the PIMS programme to achieve a strategic edge based on evidence. The PIMS findings have remained remarkably constant through several business cycles and are included below with permission from the Strategic Planning Institute and PIMS Associates Ltd.

What is particularly nice about these findings is that only a few banks have participated, because, as we have been led to believe, banks are different. No, they're not. Certainly, some ideas date, or are found to be wanting, as time passes, but some stand the test of time well.

The original study arrived at nine basic findings, and subsequently, through the business cycles and shocks over 25 years, they have remained constant. We will go through these nine points, putting them into a banking context. It seems that not as much matters as we like to think. But what does matter, matters very much. We highlight with * the issues that we feel are most powerful in banking, and where answers and strategies are essential. The PIMS material is in italics.

I Business situations generally behave in a regular and predictable manner 'the laws of nature'

The operating results – profit, sales, growth, etc. – achieved by a particular business are determined in a rather regular and predictable fashion by the 'laws of nature' that operate in business situations. The business situation is the competitive interplay among the various buyers and sellers of the product or service in a particular served market. This means that it is possible to estimate the approximate results over a period of a few years on the basis of observable characteristics of the market and of the strategies employed by the particular business itself and its competitors.

Whereas we live with gravity, tides, leaves falling off trees, the growth of our fingernails, food chains, rain, sun, and so on, in banking we live with economies, governments, interest rates, wars, oil gluts and shortages that form the banking laws of nature. There's probably nothing we haven't experienced before, and we know more or less how to respond. These laws include some extremely powerful forces capable of moving the base rate from 1 % to 15 % and back based on nothing we can do much about. That's a 1500 % variance by the way. We can live with it, but we can't fight it. Banks help us through these storms if we use them right. Their core skill is risk management, and that is not easy.

II All business situations are alike in obeying the same 'laws of the marketplace'*

In the same way that all humans obey the same laws of physiology, despite differences in appearance, personality, religion, behaviour, state of health, etc., businesses obey the same laws of the marketplace. The first case makes possible the applied science of medicine, in which a medical doctor can usefully treat any human. The second makes possible the applied science of business strategy. Specialising in a certain business is a division of labour, it does not argue against the principle.

All other things being equal, which they usually are, the same product selling at a lower price or better rates sells more units. A more pleasant tasting version of the same food sells better. People prefer dealing with pleasant people than with unpleasant ones. People prefer the products from companies they trust. Many of us prefer prompt service and straight answers to straight questions. There are banks, and there are banks. Customers do have choices and they do respond to 'better banking' – be it products, rates, terms and conditions or service.

III   The laws of the marketplace determine about 80 % of the observed variance in operating results across different businesses*

Some lines of business are very profitable and have favourable business characteristics (fast food); others are much less profitable and have unfavourable business characteristics (coal mining). The laws of the marketplace account for 80 % of the variance in performance. This means that the characteristics of the served market, of the business itself and of its competitors constitute about 80 % of the reasons for success or failure, and the operating skill or luck of the management constitute about 20 %.

Another way of saying this is that doing the right thing is much more important than doing it well. Being in the right business in the right way is 80 % of the story; operating that business in a skilful or lucky way is 20 % of the story.

How banks meet customer needs, price products, provide service, ensure quality, handle paperwork, respond to problems, and what have you, materially forms their business models, and thus their performance. How well the business model translates into the market is the thing. Whether their operation is as good as it could be or not is less important, and the operation can be revisited and improved upon. Above all, we have got to serve our markets with the right things to serve their needs.

How well we do that internally is not as important in the grand scheme of things. This does not mean that the execution should be less than perfect. It does mean that choosing to do the wrong thing, where customers will not respond, is futile, irrespective of a brilliant execution. Doing the right thing is more important than doing the thing right.

IV   There are ten major strategic influences on performance*

(a) Investment intensity

Technology, and the chosen way of deploying it, governs how much fixed and working capital is required to produce a unit of sales or a unit of value added in the business. Investment intensity generally produces a negative *impact on percentage measures of profitability or net cash flow. That is, businesses that are mechanised or automated or inventory-intensive generally show lower returns on investment and sales than businesses that are not.*

No, you didn't misread or misunderstand what this says. This finding in particular gives pause for thought, especially in banking. Let's look first at the general point, irrespective of our interest in banking. Investment covers a wide range of subjects: buildings, processing centres, vehicle fleets, robots and IT, for example. These investments clearly govern the split between fixed and working capital, since money can only be spent on one or the other. The finding is that the higher the percentage of investment intensity (fixed and working capital) the lower the profit, and the evidence is common, clear and extremely powerful. But it is unexpected, and that is why you need an explanation, which is given in the section immediately following.

Superficially, banks are not investment intensive and banks lease and rent things rather than having capital tied up in owning. A bank wants as much of its capital as it can free up available to support asset generation. But, by our stretched definition of capital investment, to include human robots, banks are highly capital intensive.

(b)   Productivity*

Businesses producing higher value added per employee are more profitable than those with low value added per employee. Value added is the amount by which the business increases the market value of the raw materials and components it buys. Productivity is especially valuable to the extent that it does not require additional investment.

Productivity is one part of efficiency. The critical thing is the value that is added. Handmade goods can attract a higher price than machine made goods, simply because the customer perceives higher value added, so that adds to efficiency. A bank interaction that really addresses the customer need is adding value, and increasing productivity as a result. Productivity is best looked at as the achievement of the central business goal, which is to have customers borrow/lend/use services from the bank. The back office functions and the numbers of pieces of paper handled per hour do not add value in the customer's eyes, but the speed with which a loan is approved does add value.

Of 3500 companies, including most large household name companies that you and we know of, PIMS provides interesting statistics.

The effects of (a) and (b) are substantial in practice. Figure 6.1 says that if productivity can be achieved with less investment, then life is good. We know that, you know that.

These influences are immensely powerful. Think about this. If you were in charge, and you had £1M, would you invest it in customer-facing staff, non customer-facing staff, branches, IT systems, TV advertisements, sports sponsorship, community programmes, product development? Remember, the goal is to add higher value from the staff and the bank. Which would you not invest it in? Answers on a postcard please.

(c)   Market position

The served market is the specific segment of the total potential market – defined in terms of products, services, customers or areas – in which the business actually competes. A business's share of its served market, both absolute and relative to its competitors, has a positive performance impact, but tends to create a ceiling for growth.

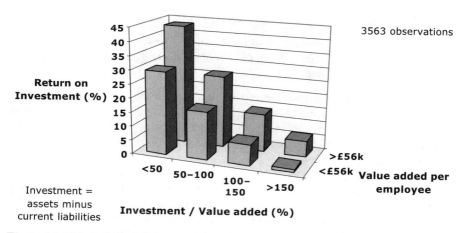

Figure 6.1 Maximising ROI by adding the most value for the least investment. Reproduced by permission of PIMS Europe Ltd

This can be as strong an influence in retail banking as it is in other industries, or indeed other banking sectors. The general point is that market share is of great strategic value and banks lose market share at their peril, particularly when there is a price war. Clearly, since a TV commercial costs the same to all banks, and one bank can reach five times as many of its customers with a commercial than a smaller bank, the large bank is advantaged, and we would expect to see that come through in its performance. It must be better to be bigger, but by how much? Certainly, small banks are able to compete effectively. The definition of the served market seems to be a key to this. It is better to be a big frog in a small pond than a small frog in a big pond. Banks have their choice of ponds, be it customer segment, geographic area, business speciality, distribution method, or some combination of these and other choices.

(d)   Growth of the served market

Growth is generally favourable to monetary measures of profit, indifferent to percent measures of profit, and negative to all measures of cash flow. Shareholders seek a combination of profits, cash flow and growth; so being in a growth market gives a further boost due to the growth dimension.

There are always growth parts within the served markets. Overall, the retail sector of banking is a growth market, and much influenced by the products and services that banks can offer to suit customer needs. Appropriate actions taken as the result of the early identification of both growth markets, and in predicting declining markets, gives a significant advantage. As a growth market, retail banking is an extremely attractive place to invest, and as a consequence, there is no shortage of capital available to invest – indeed, there is an excess of capital available relative to the opportunities.

(e)   Quality of the products and/or services offered

The customer's positive evaluation of the business's products/service package, as compared to that of competitors, has a favourable impact on all measures of financial performance, and on growth.

Banks concentrate on getting the product out of the door, usually in a 'me too' manner, rather than spending more thought on the quality differentiation that could give them a 'me better' posture, and arguing later. There are major opportunities to bring in fundamentally different customer propositions for those willing to break the banking mould.

Figure 6.2 brings points (c) and (e) together. This says that big players are advantaged. It has nothing whatsoever to do with their capabilities. It has a lot to do with the perceived value that the customers think they are receiving. A bank needs to be perceived as superior. And, in addition, it is best to have a large market share. Well, boyos, you get to define your market. Is your market universal banking, taking on all comers in all things? You have no chance. Looks good for monolines however.

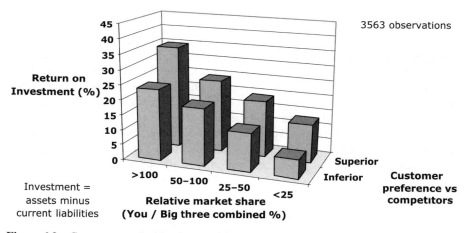

Figure 6.2   Customers prefer big players with a larger market share. Reproduced by permission of PIMS Europe Ltd

(f)   Innovation/differentiation*

Extensive actions taken by a business in the areas of new product introduction, R&D, marketing effort and so on, generally produce a positive effect on its performance if that business has a strong market position to begin with. Otherwise, while modest innovation is beneficial, beyond a fairly low threshold it damages profitability. Out-innovating competitors usually boosts growth.

The strength of this influence is yet to be realised in banking. This subject of innovation and differentiation is to imply significant new initiatives, not just variations on a product theme or marginal differences of terms and conditions or slight service improvements. We're talking about products that are new to the market, services that have not been undertaken before. The goal is to capture and retain significant market share before competitors can fully respond. We want to erect barriers for competitors. Market position is important when inviting customers to try something that is really new or different, but even then the risks remain high – for Barclays, often regarded as an innovator, it took years of strong nerves whilst Barclaycard lost money until it came good, whilst the much heralded B2 savings product sank without trace, as did the innovative B2B.com corporate Internet banking venture. Out-innovating competitors is fun, but it hurts profitability, while it may boost growth.

(g)   Vertical integration*

For leaders in mature and stable markets, vertical integration impacts favourably on performance. In markets that are rapidly growing, declining, or otherwise changing, or for followers, the opposite is true.

Are we seeing a move away from vertical integration? If this is a growth market, then we should be. If the market is to change at any pace, then the rigidity, and efficiencies, of vertical integration swings from being a good thing to being an inhibitor to action. There are some key elements within banks that probably should not be vertically integrated. Much of the vertical integration has been the result of relentless pressure to squeeze costs out. The undoubted efficiency gains may be at the expense of productivity and the ability to add value for the customers. Through the 1980s banks went relentlessly for vertical integration, gold plating everything they touched. Since the more cost conscious ways of the 1990s, there have been strong pointers towards outsourcing all but the most core functions, and this trend has some way to go before banks reach the degree of outsourcing of other businesses.

(h)   Cost push and complexity reduction

The rates of increase in costs such as salaries, wages and raw materials have complex impacts depending on how the business is positioned to pass along the increase to its customers and/or to absorb the higher costs internally. Many businesses have costing systems that flatter low volume, high margin products, which leads to ever higher complexity, more fixed costs, and worse performance.

It is doubtful that banks can push down much harder on costs than they do. There is always that point around the corner where service can suffer if costs are pushed too hard. Perhaps this point has already been reached. This has to be looked at closely. Staff costs account for the main pressure by far. On the other hand, if staff capabilities and skills are to be increased, then the individuals' costs will rise. Many costing systems underestimate the true costs of supplying small orders, so businesses unnecessarily proliferate products and customers, and this hurts performance.

(i)   Current strategic effort

The current direction of change of any of the above factors has effects on profit and cash flow that are frequently opposite to that of the factor itself. For example, having strong market share tends to increase net cash flow, but getting market share drains cash while the business is making the effort.

There are a number of ongoing efforts such as cross-selling, customer-for-life, customer retention, customer acquisition, and so on, which are using significant resource. Irrespective of the success or otherwise of these efforts, the resource is not available to be used on anything else. Is the current strategic effort giving paybacks? Are you sure? Indeed is it a strategy at all or is it just a mission statement plus a one-year budget plus two years' projections dressed up in business school speak? Additionally, banks can be clawing back from older strategic errors that can take years to put behind them. Banking is littered with them, especially dating from times when capital was particularly easy: free if in credit banking; buying banks or finance companies overseas, particularly in the US, or buying UK estate agents or surveyors; forays into corporate banking or pensions, and so on. Mostly, banks would have been better off sticking to their knitting.

(j)   Being a good/poor operator*

There is such a thing as being a good or poor 'operator'. A good operator can improve a strong strategic position or minimise the damage of a weak position. A poor operator does the opposite. A management team that functions as a good operator can produce results greater than one would expect from the strategic position of the business alone.

This is self-evident we believe. Some leadership individuals and teams have what it takes, and some don't. A little like the 'X' factor. This all becomes pretty obvious in action. This is a BIG thing. Businesses in periods of opportunity and change need adaptability, participation and incentives to thrive. In maturity, businesses need discipline and clear systems to perform well.

V   The operation of these major strategic influences is complex

Sometimes these forces tend to offset each other. For instance, greater investment intensity (which reduces profit) is intended to go along with greater productivity (which increases profit). The net effect is the thing. Sometimes they reinforce each other, such as a strong market share and high quality, to give a cumulative effect. Consider, a high R&D has a positive effect if done by a business with a strong market position, but will decrease earnings of a business with a weak market position.

Performance is a blend, a combination of the impacts of all these factors. It is not realistic to have no capital investment, and it is not affordable to provide the productivity of private banking to the mass market, since it will not pay the value. In many instances, a degree of vertical integration will be desirable. It is unlikely that banks have an optimal position on many or any of these influences.

VI Product/service characteristics don't matter

In making a strategic assessment of a business it doesn't matter if the product/service is chemical or electrical, edible or toxic, large or small, red or blue. What matters are the characteristics of the business, such as the ten listed above. Two businesses making entirely different products, but having similar investment intensity, productivity and market position will usually show similar operating results. And two businesses making the same products/services but differing in their investment intensity and so on, will generally show different operating results.

Whether the bank is selling accounts, mortgages, insurance, pensions or electricity, the same messages apply. The products are much the same across the marketplace and it is how they are delivered that determines the degree of success achieved.

VII The expected impacts of strategic business characteristics tend to assert themselves over time

This means basically two things. First, when the 'fundamentals' of a business change over time, for example if the quality rises or vertical integration declines, performance will move in the direction of the norm for the new position. Second, if the actually realised performance of a business deviates from the expected norm based on the laws of the marketplace, it will tend to move back toward that norm.

What is right is right and what is wrong is wrong. Results may not pop out immediately but they will tend to move to what is expected. Conversely, banks moving too far from the industry model put earnings at considerable risk, as did Abbey with its foray into corporate banking and junk bonds and TSB by buying Hill Samuel, or Midland when it bought Crocker. Many banks around the world, such as Abbey, Midland, Credit Lyonnais and a number of Scandinavian banks, to name a few, have been hit by dashes for growth in overheated markets such as US consumer credit, junk bonds, films, property, shipping and Russian bonds. A major danger in banking is the easy availability of capital enabling bankers to go off piste. A basic law of retail banking strategy is therefore to stick to the knitting.

VIII Business strategies are successful if their 'fundamentals' are good, unsuccessful if they are unsound

A good strategy is one that can confidently be expected to have good consequences; a poor strategy is one that can confidently be expected to have poor consequences. The laws of the marketplace are a reliable source of confidence in estimating both the cost of making a given strategic move and the benefit of having made it.

Banking is not gambling. It is a creative risk management business.

IX   Most clear strategy signals are robust

Where a particular strategic move for a business is clearly indicated to be a good idea, such as when the cost/benefit projections look clearly favourable, that signal is usually quite robust. This means that moderate-sized errors in the analysis don't render the signal invalid; and moderate-sized changes in the position of the business, such as its vertical integration or operating skill, don't either.

You'll know soon enough if you've got it wrong, or if you've got it right – even if the results have not yet filtered through. It is not always so easy to work out which of the bits are right and wrong, and whether retreat or attack is the best response. That's when it's necessary to have an honest talk with a mirror.

6.2   INVESTMENT INTENSITY – A BIG DIFFERENCE

Banking is different from other industries, but for all that, it is similar to other industries in its specifics. In general terms, banks are no more different to a retailer than an airline is to a TV network, or a coal mine is to a truck manufacturer. There is no evidence that any of these should behave differently at the level of corporate performance. Certainly, investors place their money in rational ways, as do customers en masse.

A bank has few capital investments as assets on its balance sheet. Fixed assets are less than 5 % of total assets and come from a grab bag of items. Banks typically lease most of the properties they occupy. The major capital investments for banks are in systems, in the wider sense of the word, of which information technology is but one component. Even this is not itemised in financial statements, and in itself is smallish, if measured in terms of computers, terminals, software and software development. In fact, IT is bigger than is admitted, or than is known.

As an example, a bank will lease a £100 million property for its use, rather than own it. Banks generally do not own those huge buildings with bank signs on top. With that capital a bank can generate £2 billion of loans on which it can make, say, a 2 % spread of £40 million, which will see it making a 20 % or better return on the capital after tax. The leasing cost is an expense that reduces tax, and the overall net effect is that the bank improves the returns on the shareholder equity. Had it owned the property, then it would not make the £40 million loan revenue, would not have the lease cost as an expense deduction, and would have to keep its fingers crossed that the value of the property increased substantially year on year. If the investors wished to invest in property, they would invest in British Land or other property companies. Previously, there was a widely held view in retail banking that freehold property provided a hedge share capital against inflation, but with the fall in inflation, greater property market volatility and increasing financial transparency and sophistication, the financial argument has moved conclusively in favour of leaseholds. Perversely, having made major switches away from freeholds to leaseholds, experience is now showing that, as banks reconfigure their branch networks and property portfolios to meet the changing needs of the business, freeholds are proving to be more flexible than long leaseholds – so you can't win.

6.2.1 Balance sheet differences

The differences in the balance sheet between a manufacturer and a bank are illustrated in Figure 6.3. The asset size is the same, and the return on equity is the same (more or less), but everything else is different. The bank is not investment intensive, and the high leverage of the bank equity is critical to achieving its performance. By contrast, a manufacturer needs expensive plant to operate efficiently, and may acquire large stockpiles of components to use, and finished cars to sell. Just-in-time techniques can reduce the size of inventories, but still, a large proportion of their assets, or rather the owners' equity, is tied up and cannot be used for other purposes. Retailers and airlines are closer to the bank model, telephone network operators to the manufacturing model, and others are in between.

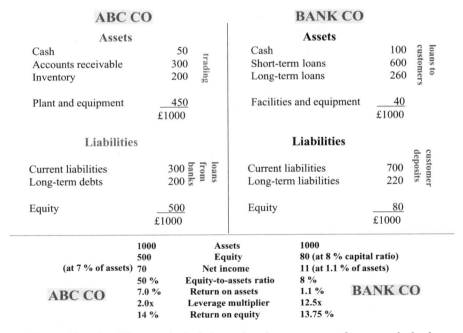

Figure 6.3 The differences in the balance sheet between a manufacturer and a bank

Operationally, banks are information processing companies. McDonald's, travel agencies or mobile telephone operators and retailers are, in large part, also information processing companies. It is clear that a large part of the value added by many companies like these stems directly from their prowess in information processing. Banks are at least similar. There are plenty of retailers to examine. As for the rest of what retail banks do, that all seems to be covered within a pretty rigid framework of procedures, processes, and so on. Much as it is with retailers. As such, we should expect banks to behave similarly to the behaviours associated with such businesses. Why not?

Conventional wisdom suggests that there is a strongly positive relationship between investment intensity and 'modernity' and 'progressiveness'. Consider car factories and their production lines. Everybody knows that technology is expensive, but that high labour productivity and efficiency follows from the extensive use of technology. And since modern technology and high labour productivity are judged to be 'good' things, they are expected to improve profitability rather than hurt it. But what happens in fact is that the commonly expected public benefits of investment-intensive businesses do indeed occur most of the time, but, alas, the expected private benefits to the bank of improved performance do not occur for the business owners.

The reason that profit declines as capital investments rise, and this happens in the world at large across all industries, is because competition is played in a different way in investment intensive industries than it is in others. When each of the firms competing in a particular industry has committed heavy investments on which a reasonable return needs to be earned, each becomes rather eager to keep its capacity loaded. In an investment-intensive facility, volume is commonly believed to be the key to profitability. This belief is as common in industries where the investment consists largely of working capital (supposedly variable, but always going up), such as with banks, as it is in those where the investment is largely fixed capital.

The competitive process in investment-intensive industries readily degenerates into a volume-grubbing contest, punctuated with frequent price wars, marketing wars and other over-intensive competitive measures that take most of the joy out of being modern, automated or otherwise investment-intensive. In particularly good years, when every company's capacity is loaded, this effect may not appear, but in average or bad years, the negative effect is pronounced. The rollercoaster followed by the microchip industry as it tracks the economic cycle is an almost pure example of this. The banking industry in particular has far more capacity than it uses. This is primarily because they can buy bigger processing boxes and more bandwidth at low prices, and have huge staff levels that absorb more volume.

A corollary to this is that since competitors engage in price wars, this more intensive price competition of investment-intensive industries reduces the market value of their product, and hence the value added by staff activities as perceived by the customers. To the extent that its suppliers accept retail banking as a commodity, then this has deep consequences. If the business is only about accepting and lending funds, then rates, fees and penalties are everything.

6.3 THE PEOPLE, PROCESSES AND TECHNOLOGY OF CAPITAL INVESTMENT

Capital investment comes as fixed capital and working capital.

First, it has to be said that a bank is about people (its staff), the processes in place and the technology used to enhance the effectiveness and efficiency of the operation. It is some combination of these three that dictates how fast the bank can run operationally.

As matters stand, it is the processes that are giving the problems (Figure 6.4), and to the extent that technology supports these processes, technology also becomes infected because it is inflexible in the main. However, it is the technology, and in particular the staff, that hold the promise of improvement – if only we could slay the process dragon and tame the technology.

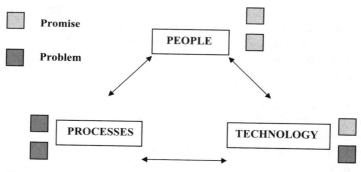

Figure 6.4 Current problems and the potential means of improvement

The processes are the most influential in the outcomes. The processes dictate the activities of staff and the usage of the various technologies more than the other way around. Clearly, the simpler the processes, the better it is for the staff and customers. Technology can be used to simplify and speed up processes. On the other hand, technology can dictate processes, and, in turn, impose procedures on staff. This seems undesirable, unless the technology is in itself so compelling that such an approach makes sense.

The people, the staff, are the most serious weapon that a bank has in order to add the value that customers see. No doubt, in time, technology will be able to 'replace' people with artificial intelligence, neural networks, heuristic self-teaching machines and what have you. We can all happily wait for those, and resist them when they arrive. In the meantime, we'll take the real thing. Does staff productivity really go up when you displace them with boxes? The reasons that staff are unable to add value to the extent that they are capable, is because the processes constrain them, and more boxes won't help much.

Technology seems to have become synonymous with computers, and this is quite wrong. There are dozens of technologies in everyday use. A computer is an extremely versatile thing, and is ubiquitous. We have them in washing machines, refrigerators, microwaves and mobile handsets. They are nothing particularly special any more. Most technology products have one or more computers (chips) embedded in them. The most common use of technology in banks is for processing data in a variety of scenarios. The area with most promise is the information processing technologies, capable of adding value to the data itself. Unfortunately, all these terms get bandied about loosely, and we end up with IT departments that actually attend to most of the things with three-pin plugs attached to a piece of wire, be they personal computers, fax and phone networks, broadband networks, data processing units, imaging systems, digital projectors, ATMs, branch terminals and whatever. All this 'stuff' has gravitated towards a single point, usually called IT or some such. It isn't IT really, but there's little point in pedantry, so we'll go with the flow and use IT as a catch-all word.

Consider, there are banks in much the same lines of business, which spend twice as much on IT as their competitor banks in proportion to their size. Their performances do not necessarily show any positive correlation with those investments (rather the opposite). Consider also the relatively low level of investment that IT represents as a proportion of a bank's total costs. It ranges from about 8 % to 20 %. The low figure is not necessarily good or bad, and neither is the high end. This variance is not due in the main to scale economies either, although that does account for a disproportionate share at the higher end of the range. Scale economies kick in at pretty low levels these days. The health warning on this 8 % to 20 % is to understand who is counting and what is being counted.

But with the IT spend at these levels, it is still only small in proportion to the entire spend, is it not? Well, no it's not. When a company builds a new, highly automated plant, the cost of staffing the plant is important. So the economics of this wonderful new production line must include the staff required to look after it. In manufacturing plants you see robots picking and bending and flailing their arms around. Weird, there are so few people, but those people that are there are part and parcel of the total system.

In a bank, taken as a whole, a large proportion of staff, certainly over 25 % and perhaps as high as 50 %, are in fact remote peripherals of the IT solution, insofar as their jobs are to feed it, understand its replies and take the appropriate action. These staff can therefore be looked at as part of the technology investment, albeit accounted for as expense not capital, and they are not part of the value-adding staff of the bank. They are the equivalent of the car manufacturer's staff bringing parts to the robots, and there are a lot of them. As we have said before, many staff 'serve' the systems – they are part and parcel of the systems. If there was an accounting category of human capital, then that's where they would fit. Robot humans accounted for as machine robots?

So, the bank IT capital investments, coupled with the staff required to serve them, become far higher than it appears. Banks are therefore far more investment intensive than is suggested from their balance sheets and income and expense statements.

We cannot talk about investment without a nod towards the return on the investment. Banks almost always question the returns on their IT investments. We have mentioned management confidence in strategies before, but with so much promise from IT how can it be that they resist the temptation to believe everything that they are told, and have historically been told, by IBM, Microsoft and dozens of IT vendors? That's easy. They have no confidence in the forecast returns on such investments – if they had they would do it in a flash. But at least you now know the answer. If the return on the investment is calculated with the numerator (benefits) overstated and the denominator (true costs) understated, then the calculation is not worth much. In this regard, management intuition has turned out to be correct, even though the reasons were perhaps not expressed.

Where IT is used as a simple displacement of more expensive staff, or staff not adding value, then decisions become no-brainers, even if anguish is still the accompaniment. So good old-fashioned automation is par for the course in banking. Putting in proper IT solutions, where the existing staff have access to further capabilities, necessarily increases the capital investment and can only be successful if the productivity of the staff, the value they add for the customer, is apparent. This is not usually the case. Simply adding another product to their repertoire does not of itself increase productivity. Bluntly, banks often chase their tails.

Where banks, particularly new or small banks, emulate established banking systems with all the attendant staff needed to run them, a debacle is sure to follow, since the returns on their systems will never be able to justify the investment, ever.

The investment intensity in the IT area does not have to be high to be good. There are many examples of inexpensive leverage from such technology. The low cost of sending inventory alerts to suppliers, sending fashion designs to clothing suppliers, paying invoices, and so on are not investment intensive. The IT staff in many businesses are small in size, and account for a small proportion of expense.

6.4 PRODUCT/SERVICE FITNESS-FOR-PURPOSE

There are many events in a personal or business life that may benefit from bank involvement. But banks typically concentrate on a limited set of products, which are really building blocks rather than solutions. That is to say, they proffer current accounts, savings accounts, mortgages, credit cards, loans and little else. It is for the customer to fulfil their needs using these basic blocks. Because customer expectations have been set rigidly by banks, this status quo is widely accepted. It was the same in airlines, leisure, telephones, TV, supermarkets, and so on. But it's not any longer.

A customer will have a current account, a debit card, a mortgage, a savings account or two, a credit card and a loan. These are all fit-for-purpose from the bank's point of view, but they are far from fit-for-purpose for the customer if the customer would just be more questioning. A customer might have a current account paying 0.25 %

interest on the balance, a savings account paying 3 %, a mortgage for which they are paying 7 % and a credit card balance on which they are paying 15 %.

The One account and the Woolwich Open Plan account seek to help by setting off current account balances with mortgage loans. Home equity lines of credit seek to give credit at mortgage rates. It is common with larger customer businesses to consider compensating balances. The CMA (cash management account) combines balances on a number of accounts to the benefit of the customer. But these products are isolated examples of what can be done, rather than general approaches. What is more, the benefits of changing to such an account accrue at a slow rate. Saving 2 % on £1000 over a year is but 6p per day. There are forms to fill in and visits to the bank. The switch is laborious. It is no surprise, therefore, that the majority of offset accounts are opened up at an event time, specifically at the time of getting a new mortgage.

There are no products generally available from the major banks that are truly designed to handle customer events. Even a mortgage is for a specific period of years. Most mortgages do not run to their full term – the average duration of property ownership is seven or eight years, whereas mortgages are usually for 10/15/20/25 years, and there can be a penalty for early termination.

Where is the product that enables parents to help their children into adulthood, to include savings by parent and child, and minimising educational debt? Where are the tax avoidance products/services? Where is the method to save up for the first property that links the history of saving to make the mortgage application process easier, and that includes household insurance at a competitive rate? Why is there so little fluidity between accounts, like investment funds have?

There are many opportunities to make products and services fit for the customer's purpose, over and above better rates, which are a sine qua non. An important opportunity is to 'package' products to include multiple integrated aspects, at lowest cost, rather than having separate offers that are contrary to the goal of a relationship.

In addition, there are occasional needs that come up where it is not immediately obvious to the customer that the bank can help. So off we go somewhere else. These are shown in Figure 6.5 as unfilled opportunities, and there would seem to be a number of such opportunities to fill by banks, directly related to consumer financial planning and management, that are not on offer. This seems a clear indicator towards the need for research and development (R&D) activities within banks. Perhaps these unfilled opportunities will turn out to be solutions.

A corollary to this is that there has to be bank staff to help in these cocreations, and be capable of helping. Knowing the products is not enough. Being judged on products sold is not the right way to assess staff performance. Somehow, we have to change radically to the cocreation of solutions, and measurements based on satisfied customers. Staff have to add value, and to do so they have to be skilled and empowered.

Are customers ever asked why they are opening an account, or more importantly why they are closing an account? That might be a good place to start.

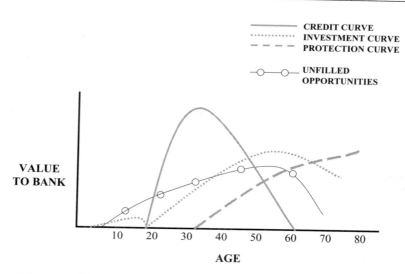

CREDIT CURVE
INVESTMENT CURVE
PROTECTION CURVE
UNFILLED
OPPORTUNITIES

VALUE TO BANK

10   20   30   40   50   60   70   80

AGE

Figure 6.5 A possible customer's financial history, showing currently untapped additional opportunities for banks

The products that banks offer consumers are the basic savings, lending and transacting products, with fairly inconsequential bells and whistles as options. The large corporates had requirements well in excess of these basics, and so corporate banking became more sophisticated – horror of horrors, they wanted netting and offsetting of balances, flexibility and other stuff. These capabilities have now worked their way down into private banking, wealth management, and now are even beginning to appear at the mass consumer level (Figure 6.6).

Where products were constrained into the different banking businesses, most often because of the engineering difficulties of making them widely available, it is now possible to extend these capabilities across all the businesses.

6.5 BRAND, SERVICE, FITNESS-FOR-PURPOSE, PRICE

Customer behaviour in terms of opening accounts is driven primarily by events in the customers' lives. Changing to a different product from another bank is driven by better rates and/or terms and conditions. Another driver is a change in the general economy that sees a significant opportunity to benefit financially by changing accounts – remortgaging for instance. Changes by customers to improve service, perhaps from annoyance or frustrations, are minimal. Retailers are more successful in setting their opening hours to suit customers than are banks. So, the drivers of customer behaviour are complex. The largest influencers of customer behaviour are, to our minds, the brand, service, the fitness-for-purpose of the product or service offered, and the price.

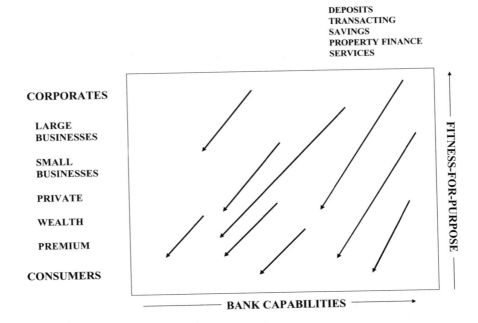

Figure 6.6 Services initially offered to the large corporates are now trickling down to consumers

The bank therefore has these four major competitive variables (Figure 6.7). Each of these has a customer equivalent, for example, what the customer sees as price has something to do with the bank's costs. The balance of these four variables determines the market success of the bank and its performance characteristics. It is not possible to excel on all variables since there are elements of mutual exclusivity between them. For instance, if service quality is proportional to the number of staff and locations, then costs must suffer. If brand awareness requires huge advertising, that similarly hurts costs. Quality is always put up as a variable between banks. They bang on about their quality being higher than that of their competitors. Whatever quality is, as seen by customers, it's within these four variables.

It is appropriate to suggest that a bank cannot excel on all four aspects, but it must still be credible on all four. The discussion that follows is necessarily somewhat subjective, because only with inside information can it be objective. The reader may not agree with the placement of all of the companies that has been made. In each placement, the two aspects that seem to be at the forefront are chosen.

Two of the aspects have been further qualified. In costs/price the promotional and introductory pricing has been ignored because it distorts the idea. Indeed, customers have been adept at flying into and out of accounts to enjoy, as an example, 0 % on

Figure 6.7   The largest influences on customer behaviour

transferred card balances for six months, only to move on to the next promotional offer from another bank when the six months is up. This churn raises costs and attracts unprofitable business. The other point is that in many cases, the convenience that a customer enjoys is not necessarily a service attribute of the bank, but a product attribute. As examples, ATM access and credit card acceptance are more an attribute of the products through the shared ATM and POS networks than they are of the bank.

There are many difficulties for a bank in defining its optimal balance of these forces, and huge problems in achieving the adjustments that would be necessary. For existing 'high street' banks, such as RBSG and Barclays for example, the freedoms they have in changing their cost structures and introducing new products are limited, as written about earlier. The result is that they capitalise strongly on their brands and the service that they can offer through their extensive branch and communications networks (Figure 6.8). There is no way that they could compete on price, even if they chose to.

The range of products and the rates, almost by definition because of their high market share, are 'average' in the industry. Their advertising is focused on their brand and their ability to spend time with the customer. They do not compete on rate, and their products are largely traditional or copycat. The same thinking could be expected to apply to most market leaders such as British Airways, Marks & Spencer, WHSmiths, Boots, BT, and so on. This is not to say that such companies are not addressing costs and products, but to say that because of who they are and what they have, the logical actions are to capitalise on their brands and service capabilities.

If a company has no strong brand, and no branches from which to provide services, then it has to think again.

There have been several attempts to enter the banking market with an emphasis on service and products (Figure 6.9), and there has been mixed success. Egg, Zurich,

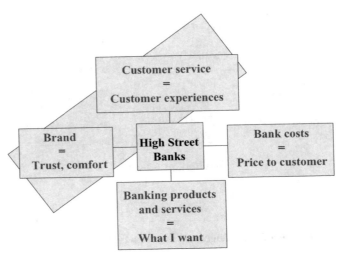

Figure 6.8 The high street banks concentrate on their brands and the service they can offer

Virgin and Goldfish are examples. They have what customers would see as strong parents, but it was decided not to capitalise on their parentage. All four sought to innovate with their products and service. Zurich failed, Virgin struggled. Egg is a success in the UK, and Goldfish jumped out of its bowl. It is debatable as to the reasons for the successes or disappointments, but the suggestion is that success stemmed from

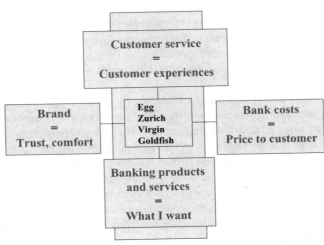

Figure 6.9 Some companies have attempted to enter the banking market by concentrating on service and products

the basic strategy of what markets to serve and how, rather than the execution of the plan itself. This fits with the strategic points made previously. Taking the Egg situation, it must be that what Egg chose to do in the UK was right, but what they chose to do in France was wrong. It was an issue of doing the right thing, not necessarily of execution.

And then there were the supermarkets moving into banking. The supermarkets, long expected to provide banking services, focused on price and customer service (Figure 6.10). Their success in attracting customers is now becoming clearer, but it has taken about six years since their launch, and their success in terms of investment and returns is not publicly available. Clearly, the supermarkets enjoy a low cost of operation, since the costs are largely incremental costs to their existing business, and they act as an agent for their products so that the revenue is largely based on fee income. A characteristic is that they partnered with high street banks for both capital and processing. In the event, they seem to have set their course towards commodity banking and cards, therefore avoiding the pain of cheques, standing orders and such manual effort. Insurance is an integral part of their business and value propositions. There seems to be a bias towards fee-earning products and arrangements, which minimises the capital required. One supermarket gives its account size as four million accounts, of which three million are insurance accounts. It does not appear that the depth of business is large in terms of asset size and banking products. There seems to be a lot more to come from the supermarkets, but we don't see it yet. They have been extremely cautious, and we can read that one of two ways. Without saying what those two ways are, we hope it's the second!

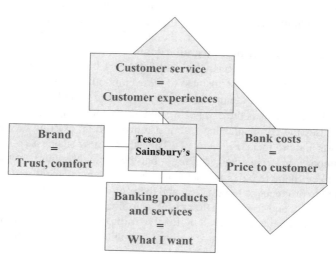

Figure 6.10 The supermarkets concentrate on price and customer service

Now consider a number of other businesses, just plucked out randomly from the top of our heads. Their strategies owe little to a pre-existing status quo. Few had an established brand or a service infrastructure to build upon. They had to define their markets, and the needs of their potential customers. There was significant R&D in many cases.

Arcadia/ Topshop-man	Tesco	Ryanair	easyJet	Vodafone
Orange	BurgerKing	Wetherspoons	Punch Taverns	Travel Inn
Budget Hotels	Direct Line	Churchill Insurance	IKEA	Renault
Saga	Radio 4	BskyB	Virgin Atlantic	Virgin Trains
Lastminute.com	Dixons	ASDA	Waterstones	e-Bookers
BUPA	William Hill	Federal Express	Borders	Starbucks
Pret A Manger	BHS	Classic FM	AA	Carphone Warehouse

These companies found gaps in the market, and some of the gaps were clearly huge. They all responded to the way we live today and kept up with societal changes. Each of these has invented or reinvented a mode. They have changed their industries. Fashion, travel, phones, supermarkets, insurance, books, electrical goods, broadcasting, food, retailing, healthcare, health clubs, holidays, cars, entertainment, broadcasting, road-side assistance, gambling, and so on. Supplying companies, even those whose names the public don't know, have done exactly the same. For instance, Brake Brothers have revolutionised good, affordable pub grub – don't be snobby, they have!

Some of these filled a previously unidentified need, but inevitably, the flipside is that a number of companies lost business to these competitors. Just how confident can any company be that some theme or other will not emerge and attract their existing customers? After all, this is the essence of capitalism and competition.

In these cases the companies have almost reinvented an existing business with a focus on costs and products (Figure 6.11). They are not new businesses – flights, beer and food, phones, insurance and banking – but they each brought new twists to old themes. The key characteristics are that what you see is what you get, and the business is engineered to produce the lowest cost, and therefore price. Of these examples, three are not in banking, and four are. Direct Line is in financial services (part of RBSG), and now provides insurance in the UK for five million cars and two million homes. ING Direct offers a single product – a savings account with one of the highest deposit rates (lowest cost). IF/HBOS (Intelligent Finance) focuses on mortgages but extends further.

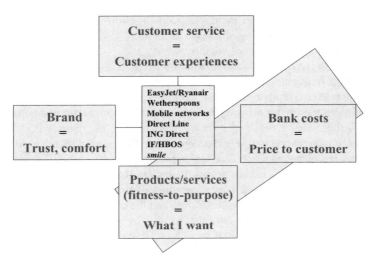

Figure 6.11 Newer companies have focused on costs and products

This sequence of figures suggests that no strategy is necessarily right or wrong, but not all strategies are available to all aspirants. The traditional banks, however, do have much less freedom. As previously alluded to, the strategy itself is more important than the quality of execution. It has to be said that within what they do, banks and supermarkets are extremely thorough in execution. However, the de novo implementations indicate that the absence of a legacy situation, and a tightly focused strategy, do give a clear opportunity to succeed.

To varying degrees, the examples of Egg, Zurich, Virgin and Goldfish show that a legacy mentality can damage a de novo opportunity. This is salutary to established banks. There have been many attempts, across the world, where banks have initiated strategies. The drag of legacy thinking, politics and systems have doomed most of these efforts into footnotes. The Co-operative Bank's *smile* is one of the exceptions, and it also introduced relationship pricing.

Doing the right thing is the prerequisite for success. Doing it well only adds a cherry on to the top of the cake. Not doing it well doesn't usually doom an initiative. The true cause of most failures is at the business model and business plan stage, usually only realised in retrospect. There are many implications to all this, but the challenge is to select the markets to be served, decide how to serve them and establish a strong business model and business plan.

6.6 PRODUCTS AND PRICE

From this cursory overview, we gain another view of the difficulties that established banks have, in that they are most comfortable using brand and service as their key strategic components, and size by implication. In some banking sectors, such as trading and commercial banking, these are immensely valuable. But both brand and service are vulnerable in the retail banking sector.

Brand is coming to mean less and less in this sector. It is the largest banks that have been fined most frequently for improper representations, or whatever. The regulatory authorities are, at last, policing the retail banking sector to the point where customers are beginning to feel that a properly authorised bank is trustworthy, whether UK or foreign, whether they've heard of it or not. People care less about who lends them money, but ING Direct and Egg seem to have proved that deposit taking is not strongly influenced by brand, but by marketing, and in particular word-of-mouth awareness. As for service, if that means branches across the nation, then supermarkets are seriously advantaged. This is not because they have more of them, they have far fewer. The supermarkets are better located, with parking, and the customer is going to visit them at least once a week anyway. A customer's most frequent contact with their bank is through an ATM or POS terminal, which are brand independent. Any bank can participate in a shared network, giving their customers immediate access to tens of thousands of ATMs and hundreds of thousands of retailers in the UK alone. So brand and service are vulnerable qualities for established banks.

Overall, that suggests that of the four competitive variables of brand, service, price and product, then success is most likely to come from a focus on products that are fit for the customer's purpose(s) at the lowest price and/or the best rates possible. Should this surprise us? Be honest. What can be wrong with the right product at the right price, in the right place at the right time, and with the least onerous and clearest terms and conditions?

This is not to downgrade the importance of customer service or brand. But it is to say that established banks prefer to fall back on these at every opportunity, since they have them in abundance. But service only needs to be appropriate to the task, and since the majority of bank costs are staff and staff-related, this deserves the closest scrutiny. As for brand, with the various regulators and the general oversight of the market, there is much less fear in using a lesser bank, and none at all when borrowing money. People trust their lives, more important than money surely, with budget airlines, and they comfortably live within the customer service provided, since they get a product that is fit for their purpose at a price they are happy with. The two largest budget airlines now each carry more passengers in the UK than British Airways does worldwide. ING Direct has few staff and no customer locations to visit, and the public know little of ING. In itself, Virgin is a most unlikely fit to provide comfort to the same level as Barclays or Lloyds TSB for a person's life finances. Marks & Spencer, Sainsbury's, Egg – is an established bank really that powerful a brand as opposed to other brands?

To our thinking, the most important of the variables is the product or service, and its fitness-for-purpose as perceived by the customer (Figure 6.12). In this regard there has been a tacit belief that all products from all banks are much of a muchness. They may be called different names in different banks but they're all much the same. This is changing. It is all linked together, in some way, to the events and lifestyle requirements

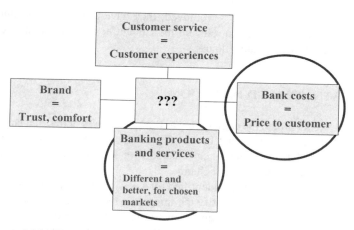

Figure 6.12 The two most important variables are products/services and price

of customers. Banks are increasingly choosing, or consciously not choosing, to develop niche products and services to address niche requirements. Unfortunately, given that they are all dependent on their legacy systems to support these niche products, the complexity of their product portfolios is increasing, with the inevitable consequence that customers will become confused with the choices and wary of the accumulated terms and conditions that they are undertaking. This problem is avoidable, but not if the solution has to fit into the existing systems, which define the way business is currently done. Anyway, why concentrate on niches when the mass market is waiting for something new, and when that something can accommodate the niches as well?

The second most important variable is price, in the form of rates, fees and penalties (Figure 6.12). Bank products are seen as commodities, and in that circumstance, price is everything. Bank advertising reflects this strongly in spirit, if not action. We have done this to death throughout the book so far, so let us just reiterate that the price is a direct consequence of costs. Competitively, all other important things being equal, a cost advantage opens up many opportunities for a bank to use as they see fit, just one of them being to price their products aggressively.

The way to minimise cost is to adopt manufacturing techniques and approaches wherever possible. Although equivalents between banking and manufacturing are sometimes tenuous, the concepts of inventory control, work-in-progress, wastage, lead times, requirements planning, capacity planning, unit costs, are all pervasive in banking. Many banks have called their operations their manufacturing divisions, and give some staff factory titles, such as factory manager. Unfortunately, they have not taken to the concepts as ruthlessly as manufacturers. And for ruthlessness, consider the way plant is closed and reinvented elsewhere. That is ruthless. Reimplementing a call centre in a cheaper country is not ruthless. Reinventing a plant with 30 % of the labour cost and with double the capacity of the old plant is.

The majority of costs cannot be removed; they have to be designed out. Manufacturers habitually redesign and reinvent their manufacturing to capitalise on new technologies. Established banks do not.

6.7   REINVENTION AND INVENTION

At the outset, we identified the engineering as the key to the systems, that is, the overall way in which things get achieved in banks. We said that the art will change, the science cannot change, and the engineering can change with some pain. We probably should have said that the engineering *must* change.

As things stand, when a niche is identified for a new product, or some other changes are needed, the first step is to identify the impact on the existing systems, from customer and staff interactions, IT systems, new forms and procedures, training and what have you. The critical path to the implementation of the new capability is invariably around the IT components of the systems, in duration, risk and cost. The upshot of this is to make the requirement fit the existing IT parts as closely as possible. This particularly applies to the applications software. In thousands upon thousands of instances, this has led to implementations which work, the tick goes in the box, and the next change is wheeled out. The systems have got that bit more complicated, there are now a further six options available to the bank staff, the call centre has been trained on the new questions that will be asked of them, another form has appeared (to join the 1300 already in use), and two more standard letters have been drafted (to join the 1700 already in use). Twelve more pages have been added in the procedural manuals, bringing that up to 1236 pages. There comes a time to say enough, and we are there, or thereabouts.

Yes, the system works in a functional sense, it does what it says on the tin. In fact, it works exactly as dictated by the systems engineering. Worse, knowing that this was to be the upshot, the requirements were probably originally written to conform to the limitations of the engineering in the first place.

Other businesses cannot operate in this way. In this example, it's only a new product that we introduced when all is said and done, and we probably do that less than once a month. Surely there is something to learn from supermarkets. They add or drop dozens of products each month. Neither should you think that that is a trivial process, but they do use IT to integrate contracts, supplies, distribution, delivery, placement, pricing, billing, MIS and much else before a single customer takes a 38p can of soup off the shelf and checks out at the cashier. Oh, and it could be delivered to the customer's home if they shop over the Internet.

We can imagine that BskyB has some interesting systems behind its schedules and pay-per-view capabilities. It's likely that the low-cost airlines, adding routes, aircraft and staff quickly, have some interesting systems. We know that their check-in systems are far more fit-for-purpose than those of the major airlines. We know that ING Direct or Direct Line have one-quarter or less staff to run a deposit bank or car insurance company than the established players. We suspect that the mobile networks also have interesting stories to tell in this regard. They offer x tariffs with y variations using z handsets, you can switch it all around instantly, and they can match competitive pricing tariffs.

Established banks have got to reinvent their engineering. New and small banks will invent their engineering.

The important thing to do is to look at life as we find it, and apply an artistic approach to providing the products and services that suit life today, taking into account all the societal influences that customers are living with. Within that, the key areas of reinvention, or invention, needed are shown in Figure 6.13.

▶**Simplification**
- Fewer forms
- Fewer signatures
- Fewer terms and conditions
- Fewer penalties
- Fewer options/bands/tiers, etc.

▶**Straight through processing**
- Real time processing
- Reduced workflows
- Less paperwork
- Minimal errors

▶ **Customer centricity**
- Stronger relationships
- Managing profitability
- 'They know who I am'
- Reduced paperwork and costs
- Intelligent pricing

▶ **Electronic manufacturing**
- Rapid product development
- Faster speed to market
- Product fitness-for-purpose

▶ **Risk management**
- Credit
- Interest rate
- Operational
- Regulatory
- Country, legal, equity, etc.

▶ **Capitalising on technology**
- Real, useful information
- Fewer system 'operatives'
- Greater flexibility
- Lower cost
- Greater choice
- New technology opportunities
- Integrated architecture

▶ **Delivery strategy**
- Proven strategies
- Certainty and predictability
- Scalability
- Early paybacks

▶ **Total cost of ownership**
- Efficiencies designed in
- Low support requirements
- High productivity
- Rapid start-up
- Quick knowledge transfer
- Reliability

▶ **Regulation and Compliance**
- Information
- Conformance
- Controls

▶ **Speed and responsiveness**
- Delivery
- Accuracy

Figure 6.13 The key areas of reinvention, or invention, needed

All we've tried to do here is boil down much of what has been written earlier and present it as a checklist of what needs to be achieved, given that we know what we will be providing to consumers. These are all interrelated and possibly better shown as a pyramid or some other structure. The key point is the first one, which is to simplify everything that can be simplified.

6.7.1   Simplification

There is a huge number of variables at both customer and product level in retail banking. The reasons behind these having been accumulated over many years are varied, and most often have no continuing justification. This leads to increased costs, service problems, complexities and much else. It is noticeable that new entrants are offering simple solutions with minimal small print.

6.7.2   Straight through processing

Having everything operational automated greatly reduces costs, speeds things up, reduces errors, improves controls and removes paperwork. The great majority of all transactions should require no staff involvement.

6.7.3   Customer centricity

Whatever this turns out to be, a bank wants it. Hopefully, it leads to a customer preference to consolidate their own, and perhaps some of their family's, accounts with the bank. Pricing and risk reduction are two large corollaries to this. If relationship management is to become something, then it has to start with a customer-centric view.

6.7.4   Electronic manufacturing

The new IT architecture should allow products to be rapidly engineered and developed. The benefits of electronic manufacturing are obvious to users of Microsoft Office. The speed of development and the quality of code are both greatly improved.

6.7.5   Risk management

Risk remains the bogeyman. Information is an antidote. Better access to better information is a first line of defence in lending.

6.7.6   Capitalising on technology

Banks have been unable to capitalise on information technologies as they would like. They should be looking to enlist its help in reducing costs, improving productivity and adding value for customers and the bank. The existing systems hold this back.

6.7.7   Delivery strategy

Channels will increase and become more powerful. To the logical extent, channels should be ubiquitous for customers.

6.7.8 Total cost of ownership

Banks are not interested in component costs but the total cost of ownership. This includes all associated staff costs.

6.7.9 Regulation and compliance

This is becoming a significant cost item, aggravated by an inability to be flexible to the requirements. Again, the resolution starts with the availability of information.

6.7.10 Speed and responsiveness

These are clearly desirable, but they are pivotal to providing efficiencies, controls and service.

6.8 HOW BIG IS THE OPPORTUNITY?

Evidence from the real world does suggest that retail banking is out of step with the experience of other industries. We believe that some 20 % or more of bank staff within the retail banking sector of banking do not add value because they are feeding and reacting to an outmoded 'system', they are slaves to the processes accumulated over many years. Further, banks have clearly been driven more by tactics than strategies. Retail banks have had few predators.

Most cost is directly staff cost, or strongly related to staff numbers. A 20 % decrease in cost translates into a huge benefit to be shared between customers and owners. The benefits to customers will equate to better rates and fees, and to a more simple relationship with quicker service, particularly at event points in their lives. Thus, taking the opportunity should both reduce cost and stimulate sales activity. We would expect to realise a 20–40 % improvement in bottom line performance, and a significant improvement in most measures of performance indicators. The new banks, like Egg and ING, do have customer/staff ratios in excess of 1000. This is primarily due to the design of their processes and the productivity and efficiencies that were designed into these processes at the beginning. They have simple, straightforward, flexible products. The customer/staff ratio in the retail operations of the large banks can be less than 400 customers per staff member.

How big is the opportunity? It's as big as the leadership strategy can make it. The point is that the strategies can be fully supported, quickly and at less expense than the current methods, which have to accommodate legacy problems.

7
The Propositions

7.1 CUSTOMERS

Customers are clearly the most important part of a bank, bar none. Customers provide the basic raw materials of deposits and the demand for loans, which are the revenue streams of net interest income, and they provide the fee income. The bank provides an intermediation service between customers with excess funds and those with a funds deficit. It borrows and lends wholesale funds to keep the two piles in some kind of balance. Try this on – customers are often borrowing and lending with the same bank at the same time. How sweet can that be?

Clearly then, the success of a retail bank depends on its ability to attract and retain its customers, and how much of the customers' business it attracts. There are many books on banking, but few spend time directly on customers and the customer value propositions that are being offered. The normal approaches are to figure out how to provide/improve on channels, or how to package up what engineering/operations can offer, and on setting interest rates and fees to optimise revenue. The differentiation between banks, as a result of this approach, is minimal. Most banks offer similar value propositions to customers, thus becoming commodity providers of commodity products and services.

In competing for customers, a common approach is to segment customers into a few large groups with distinct characteristics. Typically, it comes down to five or six market segments based on wealth, such as those shown in Figure 7.1.

Hidden behind these market segment descriptions lie many thoughts. Although there is a large number of mass-market customers, they have low balances, often only a current account with high transaction volumes, and are not profitable. The wealth banking customers are profitable, use several products, have substantial balances and generate good fee income – but there aren't many of them. At the other end of the spectrum is the non-prime market, a truly horrible description to impose on about eight million people in the UK. We prefer to think of it as the micro-banking market, where people need a few hundred pounds to help them balance their books. This is a

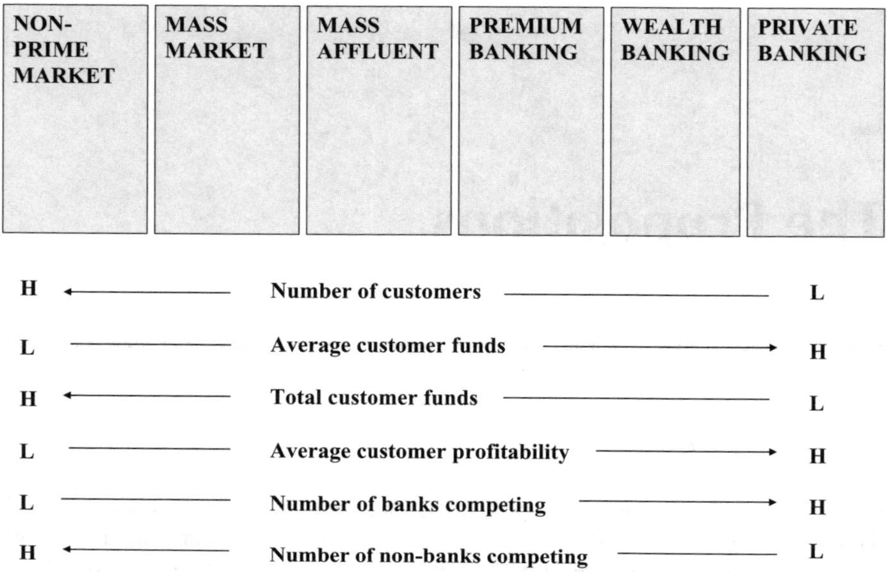

NON-PRIME MARKET	MASS MARKET	MASS AFFLUENT	PREMIUM BANKING	WEALTH BANKING	PRIVATE BANKING

H ←——————— Number of customers ——————— L

L ——————— Average customer funds ——————→ H

H ←——————— Total customer funds ——————— L

L ——————— Average customer profitability ——————→ H

L ——————— Number of banks competing ——————→ H

H ←——————— Number of non-banks competing ——————— L

Figure 7.1   Market segments based on wealth

perfectly noble market segment with needs, and you may be surprised to know, a good credit performance. The problem in the main is the small value of the transactions and balances, but our engineering capabilities can support these at low cost. Interestingly, South Africa will probably drive technology progress in this market segment. Banks have to service society as it is.

The skill is in providing product services to the level where customers can be attracted and retained, and where the profitability of each segment is optimised. An important corollary to this is the classification of customers, and understanding customer needs in their entirety so as to consider all their business with the bank. This can extend to other related customers such as family members. This engagement process rarely happens in retail banking. The customers have to sign up for this or that product and service, sometimes prompted by bank staff, but more likely by them having to prompt the bank staff themselves.

Perhaps the objective is simply to maximise income and minimise costs. However, this does have imperfections. A customer typically starts with a current account while at school or around the time when they leave school. Most employers pay wages/salary into a bank account, and in any event, a transaction account is almost a necessity for any level of independence. At this point the account will undoubtedly cost the bank more than it earns, but that's OK by the bank because the current account is a cornerstone to an ongoing and growing relationship. The problem is that these first interactions with their new bank establish their experience of banking and their attitude towards that particular bank. Service appropriate to the customer's needs is not much differentiated from bank to bank.

A second problem harks right back to the account-centric nature of banking systems. You're an account holder more than you are a customer, a number not a name. Over some twenty years, banks have sought to make their relationships customer-centred, but have not bitten the bullet. They have overlaid the accounts with a customer file, and more recently a customer relationship management system.

Some years ago, banks had superior customer relationship management that was fit for those times. Forget the myths, few people had banking relationships, but those that did really did. The bank manager knew every employer in town, knew who to introduce to whom, knew what made the town tick, knew the estate agents, vicars and doctors. They added value. It was only for the few, and it was not, as we say today, scaleable. It fell apart as society changed and more people wanted more from their bank. Banks focused on reducing costs via the implementation of technology from the 1970s onwards. Back office functions were centralised in the name of efficiency and reduced costs. The expensive utilisation of a cashier's time at the teller window was partly replaced by ATMs, on the promise that these would be cheaper for the bank. This was not always the case when customers made five £10 withdrawals over the week instead of withdrawing £50 on one visit to their bank. Still, a secondary consequence was better and more convenient transactions for more of the bank's customers. The branch manager's expensive position was reduced in importance, and therefore cost, into a supervisory administrative function. Personalised evaluations of a customer's creditworthiness were replaced by centralised credit scoring systems.

The net result of all this, in the name of efficiency and cost savings, was a loss of the relationships they did have, and a major change in the nature of consumer banking. For instance, customers with an unblemished thirty-year history with the bank might be refused a loan because of some combination of living in rented accommodation, not living at the same address for three years, earning less than some standard amount, being in their job for less than a year, being self-employed and whatever other selected credit scoring variables might show. The effect on small business banking was similar. The introduction of business banking centres manned by inexperienced 'business bankers' was not a successful substitute. There was nobody in the bank to hold a meaningful conversation with.

In recent years, the intent has been to re-engage the customer in a personal relationship with the bank. This has been targeted across all channels, at great expense and with mixed results. But without this re-engagement it is not possible to establish a relationship on which to develop and expand in a meaningful way. But quite how does a bank engage a customer?

A third problem is that, implicitly, a relationship has to be a two-way street. By definition, there can be no such thing as a one-way relationship. If customers feel that banks bring little to the relationship in terms of benefits, then the relationship proposition looks pretty thin.

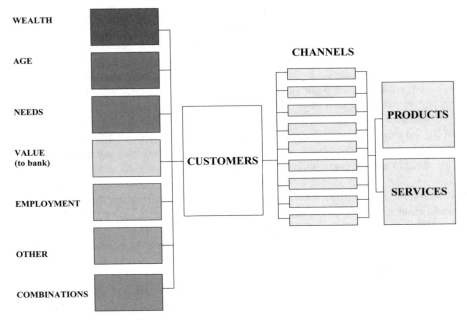

Figure 7.2   Different approaches to segmenting the market

Yes, the customer is at the heart of a bank's success, but it is unclear that many banks are addressing them with clearly better value propositions, which means fulfilling their part in having a relationship. Especially with people in the first half of their lives, when they are primarily transactors, a bank has to look at the future value of a customer, not only their current value.

The simple segmentation of the market in terms of customer numbers and wealth makes obvious sense. But there's a lot more to it than that. Consider Figure 7.2. Wealth, the standard basis of segmentation, is but one approach, and the most obvious and bank-centric of the lot. Certainly, it is one way of doing it. At the time it was introduced it was probably the only way. Banks didn't just segment the market, they segmented their service too. But are some of these others not more appropriate? There are some pretty lacklustre approaches to groups such as students, but they fail to break out of the historical tactical account acquisition approach. They do not functionally 'travel' with the student and their lives and careers. Banks take no note of the customers from whom they earn the most money – they will probably not be the wealthiest.

There are some observations to be made about this wealth approach to segmentation. It's a little clumsy. It is not necessarily true, for instance, that the non-prime market is unattractive and the private banking market is highly attractive to a bank. Why antagonise customers by imposing arbitrary 'class' distinctions? We doubt we'll see checkouts in supermarkets for people earning 'more than £50 000, more than £25 000, more than £15 000, poor people here'. Professionals, say a doctor, are unlikely to compromise their services based on wealth. You have to say that this approach is a bit of a social throwback. It is easy to understand first class and second class seating, and the difference between theatre seats in the stalls or upper circle, and private and NHS patients. It is not so easy to see inequality with no such clear justification. The intent is clear, but the method is not. Wealth segmentation is probably not one of the better ways to segment the retail market. It is hardly believable that we expect to have a relationship with a non-prime customer with this approach.

The obvious big group segmentation will be based on customer needs, but the segmentation that ultimately makes sense is a market segment of a single person or perhaps family group. It was not thinkable years ago, but IT can handle this with ease today. Current banking segmentation is, yes believe it, engineering driven. Because of this, that and the other, this is what we can support so this is what you'll get.

The old wealth segmentation itself was appropriate when that was all we could offer. Rich customers wouldn't stand in line for 30 minutes to be served, when their account needs couldn't be met with the standard products, when they needed to speak to a bank employee who actually understood their needs. None of this is, or needs to be, so today. Such brutal segmentation conflicts with a customer relationship approach.

Once true relationships have been established, then the capabilities of CRM can be deployed. CRM is a marketing project not an IT project. A vital aspect of this is that CRM must be used intelligently, not as a crass sales initiative, but aimed at further developing the relationship through adding value for the customer, based on the bank's awareness of the customer's situation and with the customer benefits shown in a transparent and unambiguous way. This requires a segmentation of one, which IT can supply easily. Perhaps the customer is wealthy, perhaps not.

For the moment, let us ignore profitability, regulations, legal requirements, accounting, gravity, night and day, and anything else that can be classified as 'science'. Also ignore how our systems work, the existing products and services, ignore the concept of accounts, where it's done, how it's done, ignore all those things that can be classified as 'engineering'.

Let's concentrate on the art of meeting customer needs at the right price. Their needs stem from society, economics, demographics, actuarial likelihoods, wealth, age, ambition, responsibilities, personal risk, personal security, handling life's events, and what have you. I need this, what can your bank do for me?

7.1.1   Does the customer want a mortgage?

Not necessarily. What the customer wants is a way to buy the property of their choice within their ability to afford it. They will want to know that their home is safe and secure, and that if misfortune were to happen then life can carry on. That sounds like insurance. Others may want to assume the payment and security risks themselves. Some will have saved a good portion of the purchase price, others not. Some may want to buy a house as an investment, to rent out. Some may want to buy a run-down house, renew it and sell it at a profit, that being a business proposition for them. Some want buy-to-rent, some want a second dwelling in town or in the country. Young adults wanting to get on the property ladder may choose to buy-to-share.

What they all want is a loan that can be paid off at a speed that they can afford, with or without some level of security attached. The repayment speed can vary up or down, and the level of security can be increased or decreased.

The customer recognises that the bank requires collateral for the loan, and a lien on the property is the obvious method. The customer would like that rate to be as low as possible, and they would like to see fewer fees, penalties and restrictions. They would prefer that a single institution address all aspects, as long as they are confident about the price and quality of the services. The bank holds the deeds on the house to secure the loan. The risk to the bank is as close to zero as you can get if the buyer has put, say, 20 % of the purchase price into the transaction.

This sounds a lot simpler than a mortgage. Buying a house in the UK is not easy. And a chain of events is associated, which includes other buyers and sellers, and that always takes months, it can fall flat, and does cost. Arranging bridging loans cannot be classified as fun, it is up there on the stressometer.

Received wisdom tells the buyer and seller that they are best advised to shop around for the best loan rate, life insurance rate, surveyor and solicitor fees and household insurance rate. Good advice, because the quality, service and price do vary. Experience shows that it takes months to effect this single large, but simple, transaction. For many, it is actually selling one property and buying another. Two transactions. Many now take out personal loans or business loans and then have the flexibility of paying at their own pace. But since tax relief was abolished for mortgages, the differences as compared with any other secured loan have gone. Some customers now take out commercial loans – banks want to lend. This is a secured loan, after all. Others take out multiple unsecured loans with the objective of repaying as fast as they can. With a mortgage account, a borrower cannot always just pay off a little extra from time to time, and have it credited immediately (the systems may not allow it). Many banks charge extra, or only apply these extra payments on an annual basis. You'll never be sure about anything until you try to do something that is normal for a person to want to do, and that often irritates the bank's rules.

It is mostly an arcane business. Home loans can be easier elsewhere, some of the complexity has to do with the law of the land, but more is simply the procedural and process choice of banks.

7.1.2   Does the customer want a savings account?

Not necessarily. The customer wants a way to save money safely, and earn a good rate of interest on their savings.

The customer recognises that the rates paid change with the amount and withdrawal notice period, and the committed length of the savings. Still, customers do not want to open up multiple accounts either. They just want their money to be safe, to save more money and earn the highest rates. The customer may well be happy with the 'jam jar' idea so they can segment their savings, but receive the highest rate on their total balance.

Bank savings accounts have been challenged in court under the Trade Descriptions Act, in that they are not savings accounts. Apparently, some customers think that they should earn more in interest than they lose in inflation, which may not make much sense to the government's so-called 'independent' enquiries of the world, but does seem a reasonable position to hold.

7.1.3 Does the customer want a current account?

Not necessarily. The customer wants a means to accommodate transactions. These transactions can be handling incoming payments, as from a payroll, outgoing payments for mortgages, purchases using a debit card, withdrawing cash from an ATM, and the myriad of other payment and receiving transactions. The current account is the key account for a bank on which to base its relationship with the customer. Even though the great majority of current accounts cost more to provide than the value of the funds they bring in, they are crucial to a retail banking relationship, and are competed for aggressively.

It is doubtful that it would take more than a day to sketch out a replacement for the current account that would satisfy 95 % of customers, and be far less expensive to operate.

7.1.4 Does the customer want an insurance policy?

Not necessarily, not as we know them. The customer wants insurance. For most men, insurance is a revelation that usually raises its head in that hurly-burly of marriage, children and property. What they really need is the certainty that if something rotten were to happen, then their family would be financially secure in the short/medium term. Well, it may be an insurance policy as we know them, but it takes little imagination to come up with alternatives and a more appropriate solution to that specific need.

And so on.

Banks see every need in the context of what they offer. Customers want to see it in the context of what they need. Because customers have become familiar with banking products, they will decide upon the account that appears to provide the nearest fit for them. We've all become conditioned to expect a standard set of products. However, there is a mismatch if the customer's true requirements are considered. But the bank has a series of these one-size-fits-all, predefined accounts that usually exceed the requirement and are more expensive to operate and support than needs be. Competition will close those gaps over time by introducing more and simpler products that focus on the real requirements.

7.1.5   The point is . . .

Such words as accounts, products, mortgages, savings, time deposits, personal loans, home improvement loans, home equity lines of credit, and so on, were contrived by banks, and endowment and term life policies by the insurers. Perhaps they are not what the customer wants, that is, needs, in today's world. They are pushed into assumed sets of capabilities, with several variations on each, and they have various options, dictated by what the systems can handle. The reasons are purely because of the inherited practices of banks, not necessarily because it makes sense today. This is confusing at the least, and threatening at the worst. The customers do ask themselves – what if this happens? What happens when this might happen? Does all this small print need a lawyer to read? And, above all, are there some surprises down the road? Where's the catch?

The customer wants the banking equivalent of a garden shed, this size at this price. Instead, we sell them all styles of lumber, nails and screws, stain, the choice of handles and window latches, paving slabs, bricks. Banks do not give them the instructions on how to put it all together. Necessarily, this requires explanation, and if it is not explained completely, then surprises might arise. Also, personal circumstances now change at a faster rate than in the past, and customer decisions and actions previously undertaken may be inappropriate for their changing circumstances. So, where's the flexibility?

Please, just show us the pictures and prices of garden sheds. This is pretty much the way most companies work, so why not banks?

A bank says, we'll give you 5.0 % on all your savings, there are no tiers of interest rates, there are no hidden traps, no minimum or maximum limits on the size of balances or transactions, you only get a printed statement once a year (the law), and you do not need to visit the bank (actually, there is nowhere to visit). There are no 'introductory' rates or benefits, and neither are there minimum periods after which the rate will revert to the standard. Whatever you want to see is on the Internet. Don't call us, and we won't call you. This is preferable because a customer can make of it whatever they will, without any constraints. With mortgages, some banks are now offering a mortgage agreement 'for life', which is transferable to any other mortgage offered by the bank at any time, with no penalties or fees at transfer other than a simple mathematical adjustment in some cases. These flexibilities are advantageous to customers and the precursor of things to come. We do lead flexible lives. Banks do need to keep up with society.

7.2   CUSTOMERS – LIFE EVENTS MANAGEMENT AND LIFESTYLE CHOICES

The laws of the marketplace stand above all else. So, what are the customers looking for? Events that happen to customers, and the choices that they make about their lifestyles, cause them to require products and services from banks. Successfully handling single or recurrent customer events is a path to market success.

It is difficult to cause a customer to change their accounts, especially their current account. There is little genuine churn. They have to want to change, the acquiring bank has to sell the idea that there is a better account, and it has to persuade the customer that their bank is a better choice. At an event point for the customer, when they will proactively want to open an account, the decision to purchase from some bank has already been made by the customer. This only leaves the choice of which particular bank, which is a lesser challenge than creating the demand in the first place. At event points, the demand is already established. Needing a mortgage is not at all the same as deciding whether to switch mortgages. Various studies and reports from within banks and from consultants place the cost of acquiring a new customer at some level, from about £50 upwards. Quite how the various reports calculate the numbers is unclear. Banks buy and sell other banks or their account portfolios, and that again points to a customer acquisition cost of £100 or more per account. Clearly, it is sensible that customers get help from the bank in making their decisions. That is really adding value – being productive. These are important decisions. They require trust.

Various initiatives have sought to capitalise on customer life stages and relationship management, but they become diluted into marketing or sales programmes, and have had limited success. They have most often become tactical sales efforts rather than strategies in action. As perceived here, serial event management is an overarching strategy to build true relationships with customers.

Customers will experience many events through their lives, and those of their families. There are many interdependencies, causes and effects and influences. There are many choices to be made and actions to be taken. Each event is an opportunity for a bank.

A bank can specialise in a single event, such as helping a customer to start saving seriously, or to buy their first property, or to plan for their children's education, start their pension fund (both the traditional preserve of IFAs and life insurance companies), and so on. By excelling in one or more events, a company can prosper and will establish significant barriers vis-à-vis the competition. It may even be able to establish something closer to a relationship than exists today.

The size of the company is not a major issue today, since a properly designed product and service can have low operational costs, and the entire operation can be based on variable costs rather than high fixed costs. This is primarily about leveraging IT against a clear objective.

Events come in all shapes and sizes and start right at birth, with, supposedly, a grant from the government and a little nest egg from relatives and friends. They may move through educational savings, with parents minimising taxes on these savings, and through college, finding a partner, getting the first job, renting, engagement, buying a flat, buying a car, moving, marrying, buying a house, changing job, having a first child, relocating, another child, bigger house, pension saving, insurances, and so on, way past retirement to preheritance and inheritance planning. For many there will be separation and divorce, remarriage, an inheritance, redundancy, starting a business,

CONSUMER   **SME**

Birth	Redundancy	Concept	Pension
Primary education	Self-employment	Business case	Tax planning
Secondary education	Inheritance	Birth	IPO
Savings account	Divorce	Seed capital	Personal insurance
Tertiary education	Marriage 2	Working capital	Factoring
Car purchase	Empty nest	Second tranche	Disability/Medical
Car insurance	Retirement	Account management	Business insurance
Credit card	Estate planning	HR management	Growth
Partner	Preheritance	Staff	Liquidation
Job 1	Trusts	Systems/processes	Bankruptcy
Flat 1	Buy-to-let	MBO	.
Job 2	Buy-to-share	Trade sale	.
Personal insurance	.	.	.
Mortgage	.	.	
House purchase 1	.	.	
Household insurance			
Marriage			
Family			
Pension			
Relocation			
.			
.			
.			

Figure 7.3   Events/lifestyles

and all kinds of pleasant and unpleasant, expected and unexpected events along the way (Figure 7.3).

Almost all such customer events have a financial aspect to them of varying value and duration to the bank. Staying with simple banking, we have three basic products – deposits, loans and payments – with many flavours. These three products are the raw materials of our banking acquaintanceships. Banks make some attempt to form the raw material into a subproduct that is more of a fit to a specific purpose, such as a mortgage or a current account. A bank will claim perhaps two hundred such subproducts, however they are most often just slight variations in terms and rates on perhaps ten themes. For instance, there are just two types of mortgage – interest only, and interest and capital repayment. Other mortgages are product variations only.

Whilst there is an acknowledgement to relationships, this is shallow, since it does not extend into its logical conclusions, such as risk-based pricing or customer bonuses based on the value of the relationship to the bank. Banks have ventured into the investment arena with unit trust, life and pension products with limited success. There are no loyalty cards and few frequent flyer points here. Generally, one size must fit. Selling commodity banking products and constructing life-serving financial strategies are different beasts.

The traditional approach has been to provide a range of products with a variety of subproducts – this to try to satisfy diverse consumer needs. It is like providing the Lego blocks for customers to build their own creations. Unfortunately, these particular Lego blocks don't always plug together. So we buy another block from somewhere else.

What we really want is for the bank to help us cocreate our creation, with us in the driving seat and the bank helping. But the bank is in the driving seat, and not much interested in our needs and creations. It needs to sell what it's got, with the staff that it has trained itself.

Financial events come in three basic flavours – credit products, investment products and protection products. There would appear to be plenty of room to innovate products and product packages. But more to the point, there is plenty of room to innovate solutions. Certainly, consumers and their requirements are varied and range from simple to complex, but there aren't that many profiles for which a solution couldn't be constructed to provide the creation that the customer seeks.

7.2.1 There are many opportunities to simplify

For historic reasons, habit, or legacy experiences, most banks appear to have an in-built requirement for overly complex processes, which generally remains unchallenged.

This appears to be in our blood. Consider the UK Government initiative for post office accounts, which are being introduced to make things easier for the public, and to cost less than the existing arrangements for government payments.

In order to open these post office accounts:

1. The Department of Work and Pensions issues a form.
2. It is filled in and sent back by the applicant.
3. The department sends a letter asking the applicant to phone them.
4. The applicant phones to say how and where they want the money to be paid.
5. The department sends a form.
6. The applicant completes and takes it to the post office.
7. The post office hands out another form.
8. Applicant fills out form and hands it back.
9. Post office sends applicant welcome letter.
10. The applicant takes the welcome letter to the post office.
11. The post office issues a card that cannot be used yet.
12. The applicant sends the post office welcome letter to the Department of Work and Pensions.
13. The department sends a letter asking applicant to confirm the account details.
14. The applicant returns letter of confirmation.
15. The department writes back with a start date.
16. The post office issues a letter giving the applicant their card PIN number.

You couldn't make this up. Meanwhile, you can open a checking account at a few banks, online, without visiting anywhere, signing anything, or sending anything through the mail. Oh, and it takes less than five minutes, as opposed to an elapsed month. That's a few thousand more call centre seats. Most of us could suggest alternative approaches and it is terrifying to think what the government might do if you wanted to borrow money from them. This is all simply so they can give it away to us. We await the first instances of people driving a bus through the process anyway.

The natural progress in banking has been that when something springs a leak, or a new demand occurs, we add a process to control it. Over many years, the old bank procedures have sprung several leaks, all of which have been rectified by first aid attention. We now have processes and procedures that are going around with so many band-aids, crutches, plaster casts and slings that you ask whether they should be allowed onto the ski slopes. There does come a time, and we are there, when you have to consider that a review of the whole purpose needs to be undertaken. Employees today cost a lot more proportionally than they did in the forties, fifties and sixties. A common sense view of the clerical and non value-adding burden leads to some common sense conclusions. It is not the law that imposes most of these burdens; it is the bankers' choice. There is a repair culture – sometimes you simply have to buy a new boiler.

On the one hand, banks embrace straight through processing, whilst implementing obstacles on the other.

Massive simplification is in order. The differences in the tiers, penalties, rates, fees, terms and conditions are so marginal that they upset customers. If you need to take £2000 from a term deposit account and you lose one month of interest, do you have to try to understand the bank's point of view that this makes such a difference to them when they have £30 000 000 000 of assets, and if everybody behaved like that it would be chaos? It is doubtful if the large banks with £700 000 000 000 could put a good case together. Is a relationship with a bank worth much? So few people do this, it's likely to be a distress situation after all, that the bank should consider whether it needs the £5 extra that it makes, rather than helping the customer through their distress and retaining the loyalty. After all, banks will tell us that it costs £100 or so to gain a customer – why risk losing one for £5? And does it make sense, logically, to be penalised for repaying a loan early?

Part of the argument for these terms/conditions/constraints stems from fundamental banking needs, such as liquidity management. In fact, no bank could survive a run on the bank on its own. It is calculated that liquidity would disappear after about five days in most banks if the market truly believed it was in trouble. The notice periods on bank withdrawals for retail sized amounts of money do little to protect against liquidity risk, in fact. In any event, customers can withdraw funds early and assume an interest penalty.

Simplification in most things is the key. Fewer products achieving the real customer goals, fewer valueless options, fewer tiers, fees, bands, minimum amounts, notice periods, frequencies, and other nonsense.

It is a paradox, but simplification will lead to important differentiation. This will lead to a massive reduction in the number of support staff, a reduction in the need for customer support (customers are not so confused, concerned or puzzled anymore, so have no need to call), an improvement in service (staff are not always practised in the myriad of accounts on offer themselves), and a massive simplification of systems, processes and procedures, and a reduction in their associated costs.

7.2.2 The pity of it all

From this focus on customer needs and a major simplification, a great deal follows.

In starting with open minds, and still having retained them, we have tried to look at the major ways in which better banking could come about – could it be relationship management, less expensive IT systems, better trained staff, more use of direct channels, hard-nosed cost reductions, something to do with marketing or sales, partnering with distributors, partnering with product suppliers, pricing changes, price transparency, risk pricing, funding, treasury management, specialisation, or something else?

There are some important caveats. There is little room to manoeuvre between the spreads dictated by the market and the costs dictated by the bank's processes, the bank's chosen ways of doing business, and its selected markets.

There is no doubt that vigilance in controlling and managing costs is essential; or that the displacement of staff with isolated process improvements and automation will save money and can sometimes improve service; or that a stronger relationship between the customer and their bank will lead to more business. However, it is difficult to see step function improvements to get us there.

Whilst banks will pursue M&A when it is strategically and economically viable, it can also be the default option, born of frustration with trying to improve business-as-usual, despite the fact that, generally, 80 % of acquisitions fail to fulfil their objectives.

The pity of it all is that the solution has been clear and known for many years – the processes need to be greatly simplified, most likely instigated from a major simplification of products, processes and procedures. This will greatly reduce costs, and from that point the bank has more freedoms.

7.3 THE VERY DIFFERENT STARTING POINTS OF BANKS

The spectrum of institutions that might seek better banking will range from the largest of banks, with perhaps a 20 % market share of their domestic retail banking business, to those considering entering the banking business from scratch. In between are mid-sized banks and small banks (Figure 7.4).

The most obvious differences between them are their size and their existing degree of complexity. Each existing bank or de novo bank will decide to what extent it wants to progress its business, and in which directions and how. This will be based on its perception of the size of the opportunities, the urgency to act, its risk appetite, and its perceptions of its own abilities and freedom of movement.

More than any other factor, the choices boil down to the husbandry of expensive capital to ensure that the bank earns an appropriate return. This focus materially impacts its decisions on change investments. The amount of these investments does not track bank

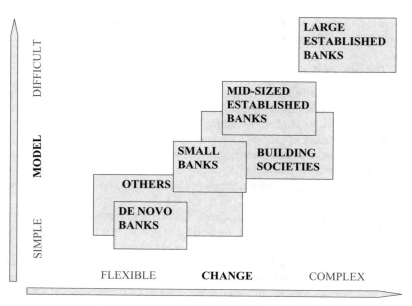

Figure 7.4   The size of the institution affects flexibility and the ease with which change can be implemented

size proportionally, but rather increases geometrically with the size and complexity of the institution. Non-banks find the decisions much clearer and easier to make than established banks, and they might also be attracted by the opportunity to diversify. Established banks will want to look twice or three times at this. They have been here before.

The greatest barrier for a non-bank to enter banking is its ability to attract a significant number of customers in what is, at first sight, a saturated market. There are holes in the market, underserved segments, and inappropriate banking solutions for particular customer circumstances – but do these constitute a worthwhile market? A new bank has to be confident that customers will beat some size of path to its door.

An established bank has choices, which are not mutually exclusive. It can be active on several fronts. Given a sensible target market, these banks are not as concerned about attracting customers as de novo or small banks. On the other hand, they have complexities that hinder their flexibilities in both market and operational matters. We will do well to look at the standard approaches taken.

7.3.1   For established banks

- *Acquisition and consolidation.* The most visible means of performance improvement for some years now has been the opportunity to acquire a similar business and then rationalise the two cost bases down, based on cutting out duplication and gaining scale. There are limits to how far this can go because of the number and price of the targets, and for the largest banks because of competition issues in their domestic market. Still, this is the safest route to growth, and growth into other countries is not constrained.

- *Improve the status quo.* Every year a bank chips away at its operation to improve its performance. This has been a tactic in retail and commercial banking forever. The cost/income ratio is reduced a little each year, credit controls are improved, risks are better managed, marketing is sharpened, and branches are closed/opened/resited/redesigned. Staffs are trained better and aligned towards selling. Systems are selectively enhanced, and sometimes re-placed. Clerical jobs are further automated. Staff and functions are outsourced. Poorly performing businesses are sold/closed. Complementary businesses are acquired. Vendors/suppliers are beaten down on price. Staff headcount is contained. It is hard work, but it works. The result is that the bank grows its revenues at a faster rate than its costs.

- *Diversify and/or specialise.* Since the primary measure of performance is the return on equity employed, the deployment of capital into businesses that have an inherently higher return on capital, or exiting from businesses with lower performance where such actions would not damage the bank capabilities for its customers, is a common strategy. Banks have their core competencies, which may revolve around product, geography, the markets served, cost advantages and/or some other competence acquired over the years. The addition of activities directly related to the core competencies serves to boost the levels of business, with lower levels of risk and costs than launching a totally new competency itself. This is closely allied to the acquisition approach.

- *Be a fast follower.* If somebody comes up with what looks like a good idea that appears to be enjoying market success, copy the idea, and quickly, or buy them out. This is a well-trodden path. From time to time, a new product or service gains market acceptance, and others follow. Usually, the new product is a variation on a theme, which is easy to replicate. Sometimes it cannot be easily replicated, so the originator has a market advantage for some period.

These and other strategies can have large costs associated with them, and can be intensely difficult to engineer into the existing infrastructure. But they are all proven in practice over many years. These strategies will undoubtedly continue. Together, they present an evolutionary approach to bank progress, although many of the individual decisions have been hugely brave and ambitious. Starting with something that works, and making it work better is safer than starting with an unproven idea and model.

7.3.2 For new banks and small banks

- *Why do it, do what?* It makes no sense to provide a comprehensive banking presence when some of the business can be loss making. Credit cards that are always paid off, current accounts with low balances and high numbers of transactions, and poor quality credit cards for instance, do cost more than they earn. The objective is to seek a reasonable margin, low transaction volume (low costs), and to compete on fitness-for-customer-purpose and price. The need for physical presence, as with branches, also varies. Most often, the target is towards the most attractive, and therefore most competitive, market opportunities, in particular gravitating to credit cards and personal loans, which do not need a physical presence. An association with a retailer that has physical presence is an option.

- *How to do it*:
  - establish the legal/regulatory capability, perhaps by partnering with a bank;
  - ensure that the business model has low costs;
  - design the end-to-end system to avoid all possible expense;
  - leverage customer convenience;
  - leverage customer trust.
- *Advantages*:
  - there is the opportunity to establish much improved business models;
  - the ability to capitalise on technologies;
  - incorporation of all best practices.

Perhaps it is how this has been written, but it does not sound compelling. Attracted by the high leverage of banking, and the high potential returns, a large number of companies around the world have launched new banks. And these include existing banks. Bluntly, few have enjoyed success.

Whereas established banks can successfully build using evolutionary approaches, the new and small banks have to be more revolutionary in their approach. For certain, their business models and their operations will have to be superior in their chosen markets to those of the established banks. And this has to be so, even though it has not been established that they are, or are not, proven in any way.

7.3.3   So, nothing is new then?

It seems that the established banks continue to plough their furrows in the same ways as always, and with success. It seems that to break into the banking business, whether in your own domestic market or in another country, is a lot harder to achieve than it appeared to many, many bright people and companies.

Nothing is new then? Well, yes and no. What is not new is that there has always been the opportunity to excel at banking by offering better banking. Because of the intense concentration of the mass of retail banking assets into a few institutions, there were few new, small, mid-sized or large banks prepared to compete aggressively on the streets. And what on earth was the basis on which they were to compete? Brand, scale, price, products, advertising budgets? The grounds for competition were mainly regional and specialisation. And indeed there have been great successes in doing just these – Bradford & Bingley, The Co-operative Bank, Northern Rock and Alliance & Leicester have each proven that a bank can profitably gain market share from the largest banks. With respect, that was primarily from their focus on the accurate selection of their served markets – and that is a key. They can be more attractive to their chosen markets than one-size-fits-all competitors.

Somewhere in all that we had the Internet hots, which for most seems to have turned out to be nothing much more than a competitively neutral delivery channel. Every bank has one. Some, such as Egg, *smile* and Alliance & Leicester are doing more with the channel, making it less just another channel, and more an integral piece of the customer and business value propositions.

What is new is that customers are questioning the value they get from their banks. They know that the One account effectively gives them about 6 % on their current account balances, thereby reducing their mortgage payment commitments by some years. They know that their regular bank is a bit behind in matching these rates. Indeed, in many large banks, multiple brands seem to be a growing tendency, much moderating the belief that a single, strong brand is the only way to go. Perhaps large size does convey strength and security, but it may also convey bureaucracy, expense, poor value, inflexibility and arrogance – even the impossibility of a relationship.

Because customers en masse are rational, it is inevitable that they will migrate towards a path of cheaper lending and higher savings rates. The established banks will either provide the rates, or they will lose the customers. In this regard, the high fixed cost model of banks means that any loss of incremental revenue could be dangerous. However, it is difficult to see how a bank used to an interest margin of 3 % could prosper on a margin of 2 %. That would cut their largest revenue stream, the net interest income, by one-third, and perhaps halve their profit.

Losing £10 billion of customer loans, on which a 2 % spread could have been anticipated, is losing £200 million in revenue, and more with associated fees. If the post-tax ROA was just 1 %, then on the £10 billion assets, profits would decline by £100 million. For sure, a thousand or more jobs would go. As we saw earlier with the FTSE 200 banks, losing 10 % of revenue would be the equivalent of losing between 20 % and 30 % of profit. That is serious. So look for customer retention programmes in banks, and new customer retention silver bullet software packages from the IT industry, although the latter will probably not help. If your bank doesn't give you the rates you can get from other banks, then inform them you will switch, and increasingly they will then match the rate, and even waive penalties. That approach will hurt about as much as a mosquito bite, and hurt less than losing customers, but it will hinder competitors.

So yes, something is new. There are improving business models coming from within the mid-sized and smaller banks, and there are new business models emerging as a result of experience gained from the Internet banking debacle. The large established banks are not vulnerable to relatively small rate differences from competitors; this has been proven over the years. But the newer models are able to support substantially larger rate differences, and all bets are off as to how the market will react, and at what speed.

One large mortgage bank showed 40 % of its mortgage business in 2003 to be remortgages, and the building societies had a similar figure. That's an indication of how the market will react, and at what speed. So is the growth of ING Direct. Not dissimilar, Direct Line insurance. The market can move, and it can move fast. Such market movements once underway, whatever the trigger, are largely irreversible. BT and British Gas are at last managing to reverse their customer defections, which were triggered by regulatory changes in their industries.

7.3.4   How ambitious do we have to be?

Clearly, any initiative has to have some idea of the light at the end of the tunnel, and this comes down to the need for a competent market performance. This is of primary importance to new banks that need to establish a critical mass of business as quickly as possible.

Let's imagine an initiative called the *Idea Q*. Using an example value of £1 billion as the initial target total value of all accounts, then we have to attract some number of accounts at some value. Depending on Idea Q, we must be able to realise an interest spread sufficient for the business to be worthwhile. Of course, there could be fees associated in addition, and we temporarily assume that the costs will be reasonable.

The charts in Figure 7.5 only multiply two numbers together, but they do hit the point. Whatever Idea Q is based upon, we have to attract sufficiently high account balances at an appropriate spread from deposits, loans, or both, to make the results financially worthwhile. That comes down, ultimately, to how many customers the initiative will attract, and how valuable the account balances will be.

The asset size of £1 billion is not large by any means, but the top chart shows that even at this level we have to attract £1000 of business from 1 million customers, irrespective of rates or anything else. Now £1000 outstanding on a credit card is quite aggressive, and many credit card customers clear their cards regularly. To attract £1000 savings from 1 million customers is also a challenge.

Obviously, the goal is to attract higher account values, and the higher the account value, the more the customer stands to benefit relative to the average rates available.

Achieving £10 billion in assets is more than ten times as difficult as achieving £1 billion.

Depending on the model, there will be a target spread, and it will be significantly less than the average. Probably less than 1 % on a savings business and 2–3 % on a lending business. If the average spread was 1.75 %, then on £1 billion that represents net interest income of £17.5 million. That is not a great deal of revenue to support marketing, sales and operations. Certainly, there will not be any profit.

Well, strictly in size terms, that's not enough to be bothered about for established banks, given the risk that customers may or may not embrace Idea Q, and that Idea Q may confuse their market position.

7.3.5   It's not enough for an established bank ...

Each of the banks can point to a year on year organic growth of, shall we say, 5–10 % in terms of their asset size. With a GDP growth of 3 %, a societal movement towards

Account balance in £ billions based on number of accounts and average balance of accounts

Number of accounts (thousands)

Average account balance £	50K	100K	200K	500K	1M	2M	3M
£100	0.01	0.01	0.02	0.05	0.10	0.20	0.30
£200	0.01	0.02	0.04	0.10	0.20	0.40	0.60
£300	0.02	0.03	0.06	0.15	0.30	0.60	0.90
£400	0.02	0.04	0.08	0.20	0.40	0.80	1.20
£500	0.03	0.05	0.10	0.25	0.50	1.00	
£1000	0.05	0.10	0.20	0.50	1.00		
£2000	0.10	0.20	0.40	1.00	2.00	4.00	6.00
£3000	0.15	0.30	0.60	1.50	3.00	6.00	9.00
£4000	0.20	0.40	0.80	2.00	4.00	8.00	12.00
£5000	0.25	0.50	1.00	2.50	5.00	10.00	15.00
£10 000	0.50	1.00	2.00	5.00	10.00	20.00	30.00
£20 000	1.00	2.00	4.00	10.00	20.00	40.00	60.00
£30 000	1.50	3.00	6.00	15.00	30.00	60.00	90.00
£40 000	2.00	4.00	8.00	20.00	40.00	80.00	120.00
£50 000	2.50	5.00	10.00	25.00	50.00	100.00	150.00
£100 000	5.00	10.00	20.00	50.00	100.00	200.00	300.00

Total value of accounts £ billions

Net interest income £ millions on account balances with varying interest spread

Total value of accounts £

Interest spread	100M	200M	500M	1B	2B	3B	4B	5B	10B
0.50%	0.50	1.00	2.50	5.00	10.00	15.00	20.00	25.00	50.00
0.75%	0.75	1.50	3.75	7.50	15.00	22.50	30.00	37.50	75.00
1.00%	1.00	2.00	5.00	10.00	20.00	30.00	40.00	50.00	100.00
1.25%	1.25	2.50	6.25	12.50	25.00	37.50	50.00	62.50	125.00
1.50%	1.50	3.00	7.50	15.00	30.00	45.00	60.00	75.00	150.00
1.75%	1.75	3.50	8.75	17.50	35.00	52.50	70.00	87.50	175.00
2.00%		4.00	10.00	20.00	40.00	60.00	80.00	100.00	200.00
2.25%	2.25	4.50	11.25	22.50	45.00	67.50	90.00	112.50	225.00
2.50%	2.50	5.00	12.50	25.00	50.00	75.00	100.00	125.00	250.00
2.75%	2.75	5.50	13.75	27.50	55.00	82.50	110.00	137.50	275.00
3.00%	3.00	6.00	15.00	30.00	60.00	90.00	120.00	150.00	300.00

Net interest income £ millions

Figure 7.5   What it takes to implement Idea Q

accepting responsibility for retirement income, and an increasing sophistication for more banking, and with customer wealth growing faster than the notional 3 %, and with standard competitive customer acquisition and retention efforts, that growth in asset size is not surprising. In terms of numbers of accounts, this is not a zero-sum game. If a bank gains a current account, it does not necessarily mean that some other bank has lost one. The increasing sophistication of the market is pushing customers into a greater number of relationships with financial suppliers. The first target must be to serve that growth.

Therefore, the annual asset growth of banks may well be 5 %. In the case of our banks, that asset growth could be £20 billion for RBSG and £9 billion for Abbey, as examples. What is the point in busting a gut to gain further extra assets of a billion or five when the outcome is unpredictable, as compared to our standard acquisition and organic growth options? For £5 billion assets we have to attract one million new accounts with balances of £5000 to us. It has taken Egg almost five years to amass three million credit card accounts with a total product balance of £3 billion. That is a good performance, giving them 6 % market share and 10 % of the net growth in UK card balances as at the end of 2003. But really, why would an established bank bother when it can tune its existing model, cross-sell to its customers and attract some new customers, and be successful?

On the other hand, as tried and tested and often proven as the bank strategies are, there is the ultimate risk of customer desertion over a period of time. If that period is ten years, that would be bad news. Any lesser period would be progressively more dangerous. Still, significant desertion will not happen quickly. If it can be seen coming, then something can be done about it. British Airways, BT, British Gas and Marks & Spencer may show the difficulties in how to respond, but they did have plenty of warnings.

M&A doesn't always work well either – not every merger or acquisition is a love story. Unless executed decisively, they can degenerate into guerrilla warfare. Neither are de novo initiatives all plain sailing. Prudential diversified into banking with Egg, with mixed success, Zurich with failure. Only inside information can truly show all the successes, supposed successes and failures, and the reasons. The point is that these strategies are not as predictable or certain to deliver on the objective as foreseen. Most of us will never know the facts behind many of these initiatives. How confident does a management have to be, and where do they find that confidence?

It is understandable that entrenched companies do not dabble. Call it R&D instead of dabbling. As soon as the dabbling becomes formalised, the essence of a new model inside an established bank inevitably becomes diluted and compromised. It is probably exactly the right response to avoid compromising or supplanting the existing business. This is the point of departure.

It seems reasonable that established banks will respond differently to the improvement opportunities in banking than will new or small banks (Figure 7.6). It may seem difficult and strategically illogical for an established bank to create a separate brand.

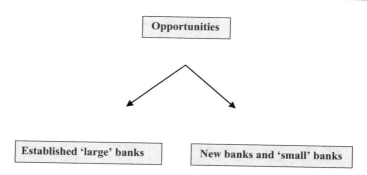

Figure 7.6   Established banks and new, or small, banks respond differently to opportunities

This flies in the face of events of the last five years, and no doubt hindsight plays a role. An analysis of new banks created from established banks will show the facts. It is noteworthy that of our twelve real banks, HSBC and RBSG were among the seven banks that didn't try to start a new, separate bank. Another two did but beat hasty retreats, two are 'hanging in there', to use a phrase, and the twelfth bank (Egg) is the only genuine new bank to be successful in its UK operations. *smile* is the successful direct banking unit of The Co-operative Bank, and it has a different model.

For well-managed banks, the indications are that organic growth, plus selective M&A opportunities, will continue to result in good performances, but it will be more difficult for the larger banks as acquisition opportunities in the UK reduce in size and number, and increase in price. Still, there are plenty of 'smaller' acquisitions occurring for strategic and tactical gain. For several reasons, not least leadership, we can point at likely peer winners going forwards. But competition is growing. The initial spread between the most aggressive savings and lending products in the market is about 1.5 %. With initial discounts and promotions, it can indeed be negative. Ignoring fees and whatever terms and conditions apply, a single bank could hardly match both of those rates, unless its operations costs and loan losses allowed it to operate profitably on a spread of 1.5 %.

As secure as customers' funds are in a bank, investment in bank equity is one of the least predictable figures. The high leverage of a bank gives a low level of equity requirement, but relatively high stock price volatility means that business misfortunes that may occur can make life uncomfortable. The high fixed/low variable cost model in place at banks means that a decline in market share will hurt financial performance disproportionately. The fear for the larger established banks has to be the double whammy of competition on rates and a loosening up of customers' attitudes towards changing banks.

The best strategy for an established bank, and one that can hardly be disputed, must be to work towards getting their cost structure into an optimal shape, and thus to have the financial flexibility, courtesy of the reduced costs, to retain market share. But it is difficult for entrenched bankers and their support units, having spent their careers building the bank, to construct a strategy, sell it to their leadership, and implement it. In addition, they will have to overcome internal objections and barriers that have little merit other than conservatism and fear, and the huge investments in the status quo have erected high mobility barriers for many banks.

While our emphasis has been on growth, it is salutary to consider the impact of a 10 % decline in revenues on the same cost base. On average, that would reduce profits by a whopping 30 % and seriously impact the market capitalisation. Because of the diversification of banks, and a dozen other good reasons, it is unlikely that such a scenario will emerge. However, the retail banking sector of these banks could experience a serious walloping if, if, if and if.

In other industries, and we have superficially mentioned retailers, airlines, telephone companies, food producers, clothing businesses, supermarkets and what have you, it is generally true that innovation has not originated amongst the established players, but has rather come from maverick initiatives from smaller or new competitors. Once proven, many get acquired, all get copied. If the success is spectacular, then the horse is out of the stable before the door can be shut, as in the cases of Ryanair, Vodafone and Arcadia.

Retail banking innovation will take a different form, no doubt. But the once impregnable BT, Deutsche Telecom and France Telecom now stand as a warning. BT has a market value only four times that of Alliance & Leicester, and half of HBOS. There was a time when . . .

Established banks, uninterested in the opportunity to make a small amount of money at the risk level required, may still choose to act in order to protect their market position and image, and to contain the threat and gain experience. Generally though, even that's not enough to act upon.

7.3.6   . . . But it is enough for a new or small bank

The scorecard for any bank, as we have discussed, is the return it makes on the investor equity it employs, and the likelihood that the returns can be sustained over the short/medium-term future. This presupposes attracting and keeping customers with its value proposition. There was a time when giving capital to a bank was seen as similar to giving beer to a drunk – the only unknown being which wall he'd use. Times have changed. It is now necessary to know exactly what the capital is for, and how success will be monitored and measured. Here we look at a start-up model.

Now, let's be brave about this, and act like grown-ups. We don't show the business plan for this model, but it is brilliant. It is just what consumers need, their prayers are answered.

Figure 7.7 discusses the growth of a new banking initiative. So as not to have too many things moving all at once, we are going to make some basic assumptions over a ten-year period.

Equity market value appreciation

Tier I capital ratio — 4 %
Tier I and Tier II capital ratio — 8 %

TOTAL INVESTMENT £500M

Illustrative only

No dividends
Expenses kept flat at £40m each year
Provisions included within revenue figures

	1	2	3	4	5	6	7	8	9	10
	Investment added £m	Cumulative investment £m	Expenses £m	Total assets £b	Revenue net of provision as a % of tot assets	Pre-tax profit £m	Post-tax profit £m	ROI %	Input P/E X	Market capitalisation £m
STAGE 1 – getting established										
Year 1	100	£100	40	0.8	0.0 %	-40	-40	-40 %	n/a	n/a
Year 2	100	£200	40	1.5	0.0 %	-40	-40	-20 %	n/a	n/a
Year 3	100	£300	40	2.4	0.5 %	-28	-28	-9 %	n/a	n/a
Year 4	100	£400	40	3.5	0.8 %	-14	-14	-3 %	n/a	n/a
Year 5	100	£500	40	4.8	1.0 %	8	8	2 %	n/a	n/a
STAGE 2 – tax loss carry forward £114m, breakeven profit achieved, self-funding from profit and Tier II capital raised	tier I + II cap									
Year 6	0	£750	40	9.4	1.0 %	54	54	11 %	10	£540
Year 7	0	£860	40	10.7	1.0 %	67	65	13 %	12	£804
Year 8	0	£990	40	12.4	1.0 %	84	59	12 %	12	£1008
Year 9	0	£1100	40	13.8	1.0 %	98	68	14 %	12	£1170
Year	0	£1230	40	15.4	1.0 %	114	80	16 %	12	£1368

Callouts:
- Can we attract this investment?
- Can we attract this volume of right quality assets?
- Can we make this revenue, net of provisions, as a % of total assets?
- Are we worth this P/E multiple?

Figure 7.7 The growth of a new banking initiative

1.   Investors give £100 million each year for the first five years, to cover operating expenses and provide the capital.
2.   That £100M is split, £40M for operating expenses (staff, advertising and so on), and £60M to provide the capital required by the regulators to support the bank.
3.   Halfway through, after five years, and this is a bit technical, the Tier II capital is provided through normal channels, not by the investors, as it was for the first five years. This has the effect of doubling the ROE on the Tier I capital. We only mention this so as not to cause grief for readers who enjoy looking at spreadsheets! Don't worry about it.

This model gives us an opportunity to introduce several other aspects of our thinking, as well. In Figure 7.7, column 1, we see the £100M being added from the investors, and in column 2, we have their cumulative investment. In column 3, we have the operating cost of £40 million. It is unrealistic that the costs will remain flat over the ten years, but it doesn't matter for the purposes of this illustration, because we are not working out the performance from the income/expense method, but rather by making assumptions on performance based on the ROA input in column 6. The point is that £60m of the investment goes to providing the bank capital. The maximum size of our assets is calculated in column 5. The regulators require that our risk weighted assets are supported by 8 % of Tiers I and II capital, which, in the first five years of this model, will both come from the investor funds. So, in the first year, with £60M capital, we can have £750M of assets (60M/8 %).

The ROA measure in column 5 is a pretty clumsy measure, and is net of provisions for loan losses, but aspiring for a 1 % ROA is a credible goal and helps us deduce the profit amount in column 6.

Our bank will start off making losses, but as it gets moving, it will generate profit. We guess at the ROA that the bank will make in column 6, and that enables us to calculate the profit in column 7 (col7 = col5 * col6). For the first five years, we can now work out the return on investment on Tier I and Tier II equity in column 8, and for years six to ten, for just the Tier I equity, because the Tier II equity will be funded more cheaply from the capital markets from year six onwards.

We make another assumption in column 9 as to the market price/earnings P/E ratio, leading to an estimate of market capitalisation in column 10.

You will notice that after the fifth year there is a leap in asset size and the ROE. This is because we were funding the Tier II capital requirements from the investors for the first five years, whereas after that time, having been able to establish market credibility, we provided Tier II funding by more normal means, effectively doubling the investor returns. This would be done more gently in practice, over several years.

That then is the spreadsheet. It is unrealistic in some ways, but not badly so. It should convey a realistic length of time, ten years, to achieve a meaningful size of £15 billion assets, which will make our bank the tenth largest retail bank in the UK. Such a story as this illustration would be a major achievement. The costs in years five to ten are clearly too low, because the bank will have perhaps 1000 staff by this time. But hey, who knows what business model this bank has? Perhaps it is a breakthrough model! The nature of the costs changes greatly over the ten years, from being primarily marketing and sales costs with few staff, to a staff-dominated cost base. In any event, the cost/income ratio does move towards 25 %, which, while aggressive, may not be far away from the reality of a highly automated and effective retail bank in the future.

The investors did well – having established a market capitalisation of £1.3 billion on their £500 million investment.

At the end of the ten years we have a profitable bank with £15 billion in assets. How profitable it is helps to determine its market value. But in addition, there is value attached over and above its pure financial value. This additional value can be large, depending on prospective purchasers. For instance, while Egg has not become profitable yet, it has a strategic value in excess of £800 million. Our bank is slightly larger and profitable, so it has a higher value.

7.4   THE STRATEGIES

The required strategy comes from thinking and behaving like the enemy, be it a supermarket, predatory bank, retailer, network operator or well-financed investor. This applies both to established banks and new entrants.

The most common strategy for new entrants has been, has had to be, to develop a 'new' bank, with a de novo approach, thus to be unencumbered or prejudiced by the status quo. The successful new entrants had no more than a few people each at their inception. Prior to operational launch, there were less than ten people influentially involved in IF, Virgin One, PayPal, Sainsbury's or Tesco. The approach and plans took only a few months. The subsequent implementations, marketing and live operations clearly required more staff. It seems fair to say that the less successful initiatives were unduly influenced by entrenched approaches, and had significantly more staff involved.

Existing banks, in the main, quite reasonably in theory, leveraged from their existing engineering and customer base. There is not a great deal left to see of these initiatives since they now seem to have become subsumed into the main bank as just another channel with marginally differentiated pricing. Two notable exceptions are ING Direct, which was always kept entirely separate, and the Co-operative Bank's *smile* Internet bank, which was positioned uniquely.

But all that flurry of activity was linked to the hype and expectations emanating from the Internet. For certain, many of these initiatives were defensive in nature, and lacked the true conviction from the top. Many more were no more than allowing their engineers to have some fun, and far more declined to become involved for positive or negative reasons. This was probably the sensible approach. It kept some good company anyway; Warren Buffet advised sticking to bricks, paint and carpets at the time.

The objective should not be to launch a revolution, thus to destabilise a perfectly good business model. It is not to try and replace the bank and its systems. The complexity of replacing banking systems is intense; systems being a word to encompass the totality of the ways things are done overall, due to their functions, evolution, scale, or the interactive dependencies of the many staff units. There are many moving parts. The resultant engineering solutions, both beautiful and contrived, make replacement doubly difficult. Replacement over a short period without risk is impossible.

Knowing what is known now, and having today's information technology available, there is simply no way that a bank business model, defined from scratch, would or should look much like the business models that we currently use. From scratch, we could not possibly 'invent' a cheque, or have a postman on a bicycle deliver a tiny piece of processed tree several days after we have adorned it with hieroglyphics at a cost of £1. That is a bank statement. We could not possibly invent many, perhaps most, of the things banks do internally. We could certainly not have invented the merry-go-round we subject customers to when anything requires any deviation from our rigid capabilities. We could not invent manned call centres. We could not invent the need for two FTE staff to support the actions of every one who is actually facing customers. That some banks did, is truly amazing. Banking expertise is not only about knowing how banks do what they do.

Many of the first wave of initiatives were dominated by traditionally thinking bankers and IT, rather than by the business case. This is not the case for any of the successful initiatives mentioned above. Although PayPal was singularly dependent on the Internet, the focus was all on consumer payments as a business. The channel did not come close to dominating the thinking, even though it was the sine qua non. The IT form followed the business function in all successful cases. This was not so in the unsuccessful initiatives. Mostly, they sought to reduce risk and uncertainty by falling back on established systems and practices – basically, this came down to doing the same thing better. That was not a good enough approach. The risks and uncertainties need to be embraced and managed, not avoided.

7.5   FOR ESTABLISHED BANKS

Figure 7.8 shows the positive impact on operating profit by improving revenues and costs for an existing banking operation. The base case sets a starting point for the revenues and costs; scenarios 1 to 12 reflect a variety of changes to revenues or costs. This is a brief reprise on a key point made in the first part of the book.

In practice, banks tend to grow their assets/liabilities through the increased values of loans and deposits, caused by net customer acquisitions, growth in wealth and inflation. They aspire to reduce their cost/income ratio but it usually remains fairly constant. Once a good level of efficiency has been achieved, it is difficult to improve much further unless there are significant operational changes, so whilst the gains from cost reduction are attractive, the first priority then becomes to increase revenues

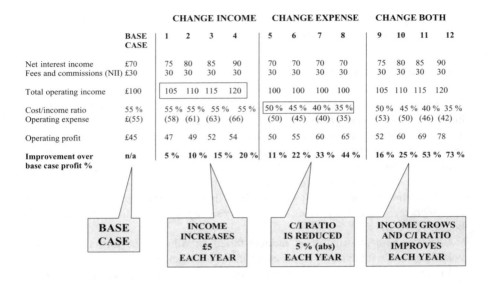

	BASE CASE	CHANGE INCOME				CHANGE EXPENSE				CHANGE BOTH			
		1	2	3	4	5	6	7	8	9	10	11	12
Net interest income	£70	75	80	85	90	70	70	70	70	75	80	85	90
Fees and commissions (NII)	£30	30	30	30	30	30	30	30	30	30	30	30	30
Total operating income	£100	105	110	115	120	100	100	100	100	105	110	115	120
Cost/income ratio	55 %	55 %	55 %	55 %	55 %	50 %	45 %	40 %	35 %	50 %	45 %	40 %	35 %
Operating expense	£(55)	(58)	(61)	(63)	(66)	(50)	(45)	(40)	(35)	(53)	(50)	(46)	(42)
Operating profit	£45	47	49	52	54	50	55	60	65	52	60	69	78
Improvement over base case profit %	n/a	5 %	10 %	15 %	20 %	11 %	22 %	33 %	44 %	16 %	25 %	53 %	73 %

BASE CASE	INCOME INCREASES £5 EACH YEAR	C/I RATIO IS REDUCED 5 % (abs) EACH YEAR	INCOME GROWS AND C/I RATIO IMPROVES EACH YEAR

Growth and reductions of £5 and 5 % are simple absolute figures, not compounded
Variables such as loan loss are, unrealistically, ignored
C/I ratio is the cost/income ratio

Figure 7.8   The impact on operating profit of improving revenues and costs

by gaining customers or increasing the number of products customers already have through cross-selling initiatives.

The combined impact of both revenue and cost improvements can be dramatic. The problem is that both are difficult to achieve – the one because of competition and the difficulty in differentiating one offer from another to interest consumers, and the other from the in-built processes and procedures that shield the cost base from major surgery.

A bank cannot blatantly compromise or supplant its existing business. That would merely create an independent market position, which would be confusing for customers, and would in any event not directly meet competition. Actions that are unrelated to customer demands are often disastrous. Better banking does address the real market forces of customers and owners.

The proposition is that existing banks should quietly develop and pilot better banking, starting by defining banking and sketching out the systems that will be needed. This is primarily the art and science of banking. Engineering has little part to play, although there is plenty of talent within engineering that could contribute – engineering is not mutually exclusive from art and science. But, the art is to be dominant.

One important outcome of this, and our focus has been towards customers and owners, is to address the problem that banks will increasingly have – keeping their staff interested in going nowhere. What can they aspire to? The vibrancy, contribution and earnings of staff will be materially impacted by the changes, particularly as their numbers will reduce greatly over time.

7.6   FOR NEW BANKS

New banks have the choice of battleground. They can select the products that afford the highest combination of growth and efficiency consistent with customer needs. This is especially so if they already have a physical presence, as with retailers, supermarkets or the Post Office. These can provide a low-cost front office. They can use presence, mail, the Internet and newspapers to great effect. A stretch target cost/income ratio of 20–25 % is not unrealistic for this kind of retail bank.

This optimising of the cost base enables them to share the benefits with their customers through lower lending rates, higher savings rates and lower fees across the board.

Because the cost structure is variable based on volumes, performance is not as volatile as it is with existing banks as business grows and changes.

Figure 7.9 contrasts an existing bank with a 'new' bank. The key points are that the new bank has a spread of 1 % less than, and charges fees one half of, the existing bank, yet makes the same ROE. The customer will enjoy significantly better rates, and be aware that these rates are not promotional but are in-built to their ongoing advantage. We have used a Tier I (equity) capital ratio of 6 % in this example.

Missing from this is the loan loss. This is always important and can be pivotal to success. Credit management – how much we will lend to whom – is of critical importance.

	Existing bank		New bank	
Assets/Liabilities	£100		£100	1 % customer interest rate benefit
Equity @ 6 %	6		6	
% Spread	3.00	* * *	2.00	
Net interest income	3.00		2.00	
Fees	1.00	* * *	0.50	
(non-interest income)				Fees reduced by half
Total income	4.00		2.50	
Cost/income ratio	50 %		20 %	
Operating costs	2.00	* * *	0.50	Far lower costs
Operating income	2.00		2.00	
Tax @ 30 %	0.60		0.60	
Profit	1.40		1.40	Same ROE
ROE	23.3 %	* * *	23.3 %	

Figure 7.9   Comparing a new bank with an existing bank

7.7 SWOT SUMMARY

Figure 7.10 summarises the strengths, weaknesses, opportunities and threats for established and new banks.

ESTABLISHED BANKS		NEW AND SMALL BANKS	
STRENGTHS	**WEAKNESSES**	**STRENGTHS**	**WEAKNESSES**
Franchise	Mobility	Fitness-for-purpose	Investment
Strong on science	Politics	Price	Market awareness
Good BAU growth	Staff reward schemes	Simple terms and conditions	Marketing costs
Major room for improvement to status quo	Organisational glue	Selective	
	Need of proof	Design	
Buy out serious competitors	Lack of flair	IT	
Customer inertia	Don't understand customers	Staff reward schemes	
Product range	Fixations/Past successes	Flexibility	
Ancillary services	Too small to bother with de novo bank	Huge prize for success	
etc.	Old dog/New tricks	New dog/New tricks	
	Legacy IT	Simple organisation structure	
	High degree of vertical integration		
	Complex organisation structure		
OPPORTUNITIES	**THREATS**	**OPPORTUNITIES**	**THREATS**
Positive service	Competitor rates	Build fitness-for-purpose	Copying existing bank methods
Recognition	Competitor fees	Can compete on price	Time to profitability
Ahead of politicians	Short time to improve	Service	Failure of model
Value awareness	Staff issues	Pricing transparency	Regulations
True relationships	Customer disloyalty	Small size, cherry pick market	
Flexibility	Regulations	Word-of-mouth sales	
Whole relationships	Disruptions	Early proof of model	
Lower costs		Buy-out	
Word-of-mouth sales			

Figure 7.10 SWOT summaries for new and established banks

7.7.1 If the costs are 'right', the rest can follow

Established banks have to take the view that their costs must be greatly reduced, pro rata to the size of business, over a short period of, say, five to ten years maximum. In terms relative to their size, that might mean a reduction in costs of 10 % per annum. Benchmarks for performance at this level in both deposit acquisition and lending have already been established in the market, so competition is certain to increase as that goal is pursued and achieved.

Recent years have seen a relentless assault on costs, and there can be little left to take out as long as the business does much the same things in much the same way. A continuation of these cost reductions based on the strategy of working harder, faster and smarter could now easily trigger other problems, that is, it could backfire somewhat. There seems to be a misunderstanding between efficiency and effectiveness, stemming from the intent to 'increase productivity'. Productivity is the value that is added to the raw materials in order to attract a higher price for the products or services. The existing processes do not allow value to be added, they were designed simply for efficiency in a different era. Those efficiencies have worked their way through into slightly better rates for customers, and many of these engineering investments have in fact been damaging to performance, and the useful ones are competitively neutral as they become adopted by other banks. Instead of cajoling the organisation to work harder, faster and smarter, the focus now has to be on working differently, such that the resulting model gives a flexibility that allows staff, at all levels, truly to add value.

The development of the new business model is the critical step, irrespective of whether the bank is established or aspirational. Focus on cost gives a negative connotation. Perhaps it shouldn't be that way, but that is the way it is, and all banks know that. As a cop out, we talk of increasing volumes without increasing the cost base, we talk of using IT to increase productivity. We talk and talk and talk. It's rather like diets, except we're looking for organisational weight loss. There is this thing called 'The Second Law of Thermodynamics', which basically says that we cannot destroy energy. Food is energy. This gives the great majority of us only two strategies for losing weight – eat less and exercise more. Still, we embrace all sorts of diets in order to try to disprove a fundamental law of nature. The truth is that if people do lose weight from their diet then they either did eat less and/or they did exercise more. Our diet is our business plan, so it must both help us eat less and exercise more. Costs are the result of the business plan, not an input into it.

The consequences of lower costs are all good. It opens up vistas to products and services, pricing, distribution and the entire gamut of better banking. But then comes the point of departure between established banks and wannabe banks (Figure 7.11).

An established bank will find it extremely difficult to get from where it is to where it needs, and hopefully wants, to be. One thing seems certain, however. Starting a separate entity bank brand is not the ideal way to proceed. These banks will need to work out a displacement approach with a long-term view of obsolescing many of their existing operational practices, procedures and systems.

New banks and small banks wanting to enter the retail banking market will follow different approaches to the same end. They will first have to implement their banking systems without replicating existing systems. So they should be cautious of hiring banking experts who only know the way it is being done, not the way it could, or perhaps should, be done. Some of the less successful new airlines implemented check-in systems just like the established airlines, with the consequent check-in times and queues. Some Internet banks simply emulated today's banks, and of course failed to get anywhere.

Once over that hurdle, the biggest problem remains, which is attracting and retaining customers. Ultimately, the most powerful force is word-of-mouth and media interest. Do Ryanair or easyJet run much TV advertising? Come to that, does Tesco Personal Finance?

7.8   THE STARTING POINT

It would be a surprise indeed if anybody were to 'discover' an overlooked factor with massive potential that banks were not already aware of. Nobody will, and nothing written in this book is new to bank managements. However, we did set out to look

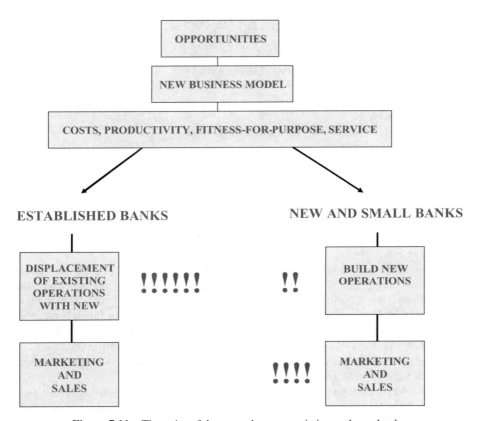

Figure 7.11   The point of departure between existing and new banks

for step function improvements that would be pervasive, and benefit the bank and its customers.

Pervasive is the operative word, since this involves all aspects of the bank and its customer relationships. We have looked at:

- the basic value proposition for customers;
- the basic value proposition for investors;
- sharing the benefits with customers in a positive way;
- the high level of working capital involved;
- the significant amount of effort that is not adding value;
- the importance of process;
- the burden of process;
- the unnecessary and unwanted numbers of variations and variables;
- difficulties in competing in the marketplace against new business models;
- understanding what it is the customer is really looking for;
- the IT approach, which is still based on data processing and automation;

- the value-adding opportunities growing from IT;
- the inability to leverage IT;
- empowering staff to add value;
- stand-alone operations, shared operations;
- aggregation;
- low cost and low overhead;
- adding value;
- getting carried away with a shared cost base;
- vertical integration.

We have now got to a point where the indicators and directions might support a formal rethink of the retail banking business in its entirety. In itself this is quite a challenge, because a bank has become compartmentalised over many years. The organisational structures and responsibilities have become strongly independent of each other in one sense, whilst being highly interdependent in day-to-day operations in other senses.

The starting point is to look at the organisation. The number of units in a retail bank is counted in the hundreds. In purely arithmetic terms, the interactions could be unlimited. An established retail bank with a selective market will have at least 50 discrete products and services that it is selling and supporting, the larger banks will have more than one hundred products and services. Actions at any one unit, or group of units, within the organisation can affect multiple other units of the organisation, be they credit, treasury, operations, customer service, branches, payments and so on. And vice versa. These interactions can be fiendishly complicated.

With a large customer base and active sales, the number of customer-initiated events is high. Even in level flight the average current account customer will actively or passively initiate some thirty transactions each month in the form of employment pay, direct debits, standing orders, ATM withdrawals, cheques, funds transfers, and so on. Some customers will initiate far more, especially small businesses. Bank staff cost no less than 20p per minute, so unless their function is enhancing value, a bank needs to avoid the need for staff involvement. To minimise unit costs, these normal service interactions avoid the need for staff involvement. But cheques with insufficient funds in their accounts, incorrectly filled out forms, wrong passwords, cheques having to be physically transported and handled, ATMs needing replenishment and errors having to be rectified cause work. Many other expected events arise, and many unexpected demands occur too.

The processes and procedures have been finely tuned over many years to achieve this goal. Technologies of various types have been used. For instance, if an ATM holds £100 000 cash and the average withdrawal is £30, then interaction is required once for every 3000 interactions or so, which means that for 99.7 % of the time it is all OK. Banks have optimised this by outsourcing ATM servicing, and otherwise trying to reduce the relatively small cost that this represents. The particular unit, or several units, that are responsible for ATMs have managed to perfect their little piece of the business.

Much of retail banking is in the detail, and if every unit can increase its efficiency by 5 %, then that is surely a good thing. But it's nowhere near enough of a good thing.

Normal customer servicing, where staff cannot and do not add value, must require few staff. By that we mean *few* staff. By how much can the efficiency of a unit be improved, recognising that it has been repeatedly crawled over? The answer is – not much.

Table 7.1 is about as pure as it gets. Doing the same things harder, faster and smarter has limits. Perhaps in banking it is only a 1 % per year improvement that we can get from cracking the whip. Many banks at the moment are achieving a one or two percent improvement in their cost/income ratios year on year. The growth in the market size even flatters that performance gain. Each unit of the bank can only improve its efficiency a little if it is to do the same things in the same way, even with some additional technology or other. If the unit is doing much the same thing in much the same way, then much the same results will follow. If indeed there are opportunities to improve, then something or some things must be done differently. Yes, some units are bigger than others, but you get the point.

Table 7.1   World Records – men

Event	1950	2003	Change 1950/2003	Change per year
100 m	10.34 s	9.78 s	5.4 %	0.11 %
400 m	45.9 s	43.18 s	5.9 %	0.12 %
1500 m	3 mins 43 s	3 mins 26 s	5.0 %	0.10 %
10 000 m	29 mins 03 s	26 mins 23 s	9.0 %	0.18 %
Marathon	2 h 20 mins 42 s	2 h 04 mins 55 s	11.0 %	0.22 %
High jump	2.11 m	2.45 m	16 %	0.32 %
Pole vault	4.77 m	6.14 m	29 %	0.58 %
Long jump	8.13 m	8.95 m	10 %	0.20 %
Shot put	17.82 m	23.12 m	30 %	0.60 %
Javelin	78.70 m	98.48 m	25 %	0.50 %

All the cards are face-up. Now it gets tricky because banking is indeed hugely complex, and the art involved in going forwards successfully has never been more important. Arriving at decisions and implementing the consequent strategies will take years, and funds. Decisions and strategies have never been more difficult to make and settle upon. Banks will change their fundamentals only with extreme caution.

Well, just stating all this is the easy part. So what? There are several so-what scenarios. This is fundamental root and branch change. We are not talking about departmental tweaks, or sticking in a bit of imaging so as to relieve document handling, or redesigning branches.

The staff in banks are highly competent in their areas of expertise. We do not imply that there are general weaknesses or obvious opportunities going begging. In 80 % of it all there is little or nothing a bank can do anyway. But if that is all there is to it, then extraordinary performance improvement is not achievable. It is fair to say that the banks themselves know this to be true, and most are experiencing difficulties of some sort as to how best to proceed down the road they know they are going to have to take. But doing much the same thing in much the same way will not suffice. Working harder, faster and smarter on the existing model has limited potential.

As well as setting the strategy, which we believe to be the single most important function of management, management has the challenge of making the entire organisation respond in an orchestrated and singular way to the successful achievement of the strategy.

Perhaps the orchestra is an appropriate analogy. The strings, woodwind, brass, basses, percussion are quite different, and in isolation each is of limited interest. But when playing to a musical score, with a conductor balancing the sections, regulating the pace, the volume and so on, the result becomes far more interesting. So it is with the bank organisation. Each section should be playing to the orchestration of the leadership.

It is accepted that the quality, size and the sustainability of the return on equity is an ultimate management goal. We have also offered the fitness-for-purpose and rates charged/paid to customers as the attributes for retail banking market success. The simple chart in Figure 7.12 gives an idea of the many units in the bank that

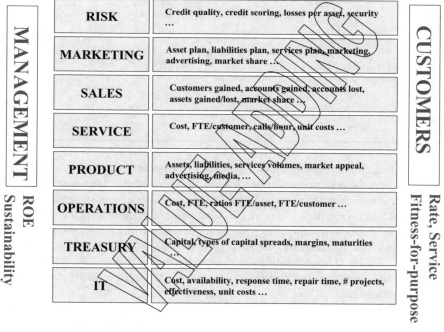

Figure 7.12   The contribution of each banking unit and their key performance indicators

need to contribute actively, and their respective 'key performance indicators' (KPIs). Converting the customer KPIs into the bank management KPIs is like converting lead into gold. They are two quite separate sets of indicators. As we have said before, the bank itself is between a rock and a hard place.

The eight organisational units shown in Figure 7.12 are each further subdivided in practice, and there are dozens more involved that are not shown. Just how can they all work most effectively in cooperation to win the team event, rather than concentrating on winning their individual gold medals? Are the individual performance indicators and incentives encouraging team success? Should incentives be split between team and individual achievement? Should all rewards be linked only to team achievement?

The difficulty is well known. For instance, in order to offer an attractive product, we need marketing, sales, IT, operations and product management to work tightly together. But any of these units, say IT, has performance indicators from which it cannot move, such as budget. So it can or cannot contribute as it might like to, or be able to, unless its requirements and constraints are balanced – which they rarely are. What is worse is that with shared costs and shared this and that, a business unit of the bank gets some almighty cost allocation from marketing, operations or elsewhere that does not give them the value or benefit that they would expect for that expense.

Information technology is, to our minds, a crucial case, because the IT intensity in a bank will be extremely important in the new models that will emerge. IT intensity is not about how much money is ploughed into IT, but rather to what extent value can be realised from the IT investment. Suffice to say that to put a spending cap on IT for the next year is to say that any possible contribution from IT will be limited. Of course, every other unit argues similarly about their situation.

The outstanding opportunity to achieve a step function improvement, and ahead of all others by a mile, is to address the processes within a bank – both those that involve customers, and those that are internal to the bank. The role of IT is simply to offer capabilities, and then to implement the processes that the business chooses – it is not to lead or dictate.

As simple as it sounds, the starting point is to develop a new business plan. Established banks will have the problem of migrating towards it, but that is a different problem. The existing business plan is inadequate for the future, and has been adjusted too many times and for too long. Enough, let's get on with it.

8
Preparing for the Future

8.1 EVOLUTION, TACTICS, LIMITS – THE OBVIOUS STUFF

Let's clear the decks a little. Retail banks will avoid disruptions, internal differences of opinion, significant change, more work and more expense whenever possible. This is a biological certainty. The bank organisation itself is actually a real organism, and cannot help but resist threats, perceived or real. The resistance of its immune system is strong. This is a natural reaction anyway, and it is additionally what the organisation has evolved to do. The actual response to competition is to fiddle with the rates and terms and conditions, T&Cs. We think of punchy slogans, and shout louder to consumers. When that ceases to work, the natural response to competition is to leave it to evolution. Banks do evolve, but they don't of themselves change much or often. In evolutionary terms the competition is slow, and the competitors may have just developed keener eyesight or sharper teeth. So a competitor launches that product, and if it seems to be doing well, other banks match it somehow. A competitor refurbishes branches, so do the others. All stimulating stuff, no doubt. But it is hardly worthy of the word evolution, or the process of rational selection. It is simply a reaction.

Even in the face of successful competition, the organisation will instinctively fight, even if it cannot match the new threat. True evolution is pretty hit and miss stuff and takes much time, and it can go wrong. Chickens, turkeys, emus and ostriches still haven't got wings that work. Don't blame them, they have no serious natural predators. Then again, *Homo sapiens*, that's us, is the result of a dozen or more turns at evolutionary Y junctions, inspired by survival.

Still, at whatever speed competition emerges, and however effective it turns out to be, there are too few decades around for banks to rely on evolutionary speed. Proactive speed is needed.

The only influence that can adjust this behaviour is the bank leadership. It will causally introduce disruptions, internal differences of opinion, significant change, more work and more expense. This is the critical stuff, and quite opposite to the organisation's 'natural' response. Let's face it, the leadership has had to change quite dramatically over these last ten years. But it's still the same old tanker underneath their bridge.

But first, as a bank, let's look at some semi-evolutionary progress that can be made to strengthen defences and sharpen attacks. We can modernise the branches. We can have meeting rooms to talk with customers, space to mingle, uniforms, brochures, video kiosks, more staff education and free coffee. We can cross-sell our products, perhaps. We can introduce more products on the web, better presented. We can have imaging of documents. We can have all kinds of telephonic services. We can let customers use their mobiles to find their balances, and they can top up mobiles at ATMs. We can have a CRM system, chip and PIN cards, customer segmentation, cute pricing/fee/penalty deals and grabby promotions. We can develop our branding and sales. We can enter partnerships with non-traditional suppliers. We can put in more terminals, offer access, resite branches, even provide parking – there is nothing we cannot do. But it's not enough only to be able to pat your head and rub your tummy at the same time.

All this is reflected in articles, books, internal communications, consultants' mouths, and so on. One consultant even uses the word 'terra-space' to talk about branches. Clever or what – cyber-space, terra-space? The consultant didn't smile or look embarrassed. Oh dear!

Previously, we had 'concluded' that focusing on customer needs and a major simplification of products and services were two of the goals to drive for. Does all this last lot relate to these goals, given that we have the same products, services and staff knowledge? OK, so the other banks are doing it all too. We like the giving of staff education, and the partnering bit, but hold little hope for the rest in general, although some might be nice to have. There seem few foundations in all this towards a step change improvement.

But unfortunately, we have to, almost must, stay within the limits of the existing 'system'. Pretty much all the articles, papers, internal suggestions and the rest stick within the limits of what can be done today. You do not start out an article on marketing, customer service, profitability or whatever with the words 'Once you've got rid of what you've got . . .'. Neither can a bank memo start by saying that the entire infrastructure has to change, that the staff are incapable of doing what's needed, that we need a massive advertising budget . . . and once that's all in place, then this is what we can do.

And spare a thought for the staffer in the branch selling a new XYZ capability. They have to achieve that within the existing infrastructure. Staffers can only sell what is in the back of their trucks, and that is the products, services and skills that they have, albeit 'new and improved'.

So, look for new paint, bonding, and team signals like uniforms and all of the above. They require no changes to the 'system'. Look for ethnic marketing and disguised products. Admire the TV advertisements. This is all business-as-usual, and is going to happen anyway. It is improvement with the least disruption, in many ways the easy way.

Alas, in fact, branch designs, mobiles, CRM, imaging, better Internet sites, subsegmenting, smart words, advertising, nice brochures, sharp staff, call centres, technology toys, and so on will make absolutely no competitive difference that matters. All banks will do them. Predators will do two or three, and try to meet customer needs.

Unless retail banking is looked at in its entirety, all these things, offered as the future of retail banking, will disappoint customers and investors. Offered as improvements, that they are. Consider the other kind of competition. In the unlikely extreme that they were to offer more appropriate products/solutions, and could work on a 1.5 % margin, then it has to be goodnight to those that cannot do so. In that event, most of the above issues will not matter quite so much.

And then again, banks can provide Indian customers a way of sending money to India, they can provide Islamic banking, and gain consumer trust in Liverpool or London. Neither is it a brainwave to finance large ticket household goods like fully installed plasma TVs, or serve the many other particular market segments and subsegments. This would meet customer needs, and simplify things for them.

A new bank, an old bank, a big, mid-sized or small bank, a non-bank, or a wannabe bank has first to decide upon its strategy and its own abilities. What do they want to put in the back of their trucks?

The established banks in particular will have to seriously ponder on the future, and of course they do. That pondering needs to be uninhibited. It is constrained today by the 'system'. Cross-divisional interference, or whatever other term you fancy for organisational reality, is not welcome. So such discussions are also inhibited. Buying another company that already does what you want to do may be easier than getting your own bank to do it – even if you're the top person in the bank.

8.2   THE CRITICAL STUFF

Whatever the future may hold, there are four major areas that banks and any other businesses will continue addressing aggressively, and differently. This is irrespective of the business they are in, their business strategies, whether the main intent is to perform better at what they do, to introduce new lines of business, merge or acquire, and/or what have you. It seems that most things we can and should do come down to customers, marketing, costs and the alignment of staff to the mission.

The first concerns our understanding of what a customer is, and how we intend to relate to the customer. Who are the customers, and what are their needs? The specific case of banking is different in that the customers provide much of the raw material in the form of funds through their various deposit/savings/current accounts, and they buy the manufactured products in the form of loans/mortgages. It's a little like the Victorian colonial model, where the UK imported raw materials from countries and sold back finished goods. Independence messed up that model. A retail bank would find it difficult to run a business if it only had the money markets as its primary source of funds, so the two-way nature of customers is important.

The second issue is marketing. Marketing may not be what most people think it is; it is definitely not just placing advertisements in newspapers. It should be matching consumer needs with bank competences, and greatly influencing those competences. Only a small part of marketing is fluff and puff, important though that can be. The important pieces of marketing are critical to a bank's success. The consumer momentum inherent in retail banking has been on the side of banks for a long time, and has kept them moving in a straight line. The need for manoeuvrability introduces zigzags, responsiveness, uncertainties and other phenomena. Marketing will be in the driving seat negotiating the bends; it will no longer be 'full ahead all engines'. More skill will be required, and there are no nautical charts of these waters. A wonderful opportunity.

The third point revolves around cost. Cost cannot itself be directly addressed because it falls out from the myriad of situations and activities, primarily revolving around the chosen practices, processes and procedures. In this regard, information technology, or more precisely the appropriate usage of it, is a bank's great ally. For banks, costs resolve down to processes, procedures and the division of the work done by staff, customers and technologies in cooperation. Surely we have shaved individual staff costs as much as we can over the years, so just how are we meant to halve them from here? Scale economies are real, but there are limitations depending on a number of factors.

The final area is the bank staff, from top to bottom. The functions, the availability, the skills, the numbers, the management and much more are going to change enormously. The performance of the bank is going to be raised to a higher level, and its staff in total will become far more professional in the sense of their knowledge and empowerment, and usage of technologies. Quite what this ends up meaning in terms of staff impacts is unclear, but it certainly means major change.

8.3 CUSTOMERS

Mention the word customer, and the world fast-forwards into customer relationship management (CRM). Certainly, the IT part of the world does. CRM is a dream application for IT, in theory, and particularly in its engineering opportunities. Plenty of banks and vendors have become heavily involved in CRM over the last five years. In practice, the experiences of CRM have been variable, and most frequently below the low end of the original expectations and above the high end of cost projections. There is no surprise that CRM has been a bust in banks so far, but there is a surprise that it has not been more successful in many other businesses. The churn of customers in gas, electricity, communications, retailing, broadcasting, newspapers, airlines, washing powder and so on, where one could reasonably expect a properly thought out and implemented CRM to work, simply proves that the gap between the impeccable theory and the practice is not as small as we assumed it to be. Perhaps pricing is more important than the incumbents acknowledge. Banks in particular should play around with the word customer before they fast-forward into CRM. Customers are not simply product users or account holders.

A starting point is to look at the three words in CRM – customer, relationship and management. They are not customer, cost and management; not customer, product and sales; not marketing, product and customers. They are customer, relationship and management. It is evident that for CRM to work, the bank needs customers, relationships and an ability to manage the relationships.

For certain, the first thing is to agree quite what we mean by the word 'customer'. There is no intention to become involved in semantics, but is a customer different from an account holder? Customers are people who buy goods or services from a shop or business; people you have to deal with. On such a basis, there is no suggestion of anything special or valued about a customer; account holders qualify as customers. A customer is a 'thing' that buys stuff, or that you have to deal with. In one infamous memo leaked from a large airline, customers were referred to as 'walking cargo'. Again, customers are things. Customers in general do not appear to be special in the scheme of things, and in many ways they are not. Twelve million of them hoof around Tesco every week, 2.5 million people visit McDonald's in the UK each day, 14 million shop at Marks & Spencer – how special can one person really be? It is hugely impressive how such businesses have developed even a modest relationship with so many of their customers.

The word 'client' is different, a client is a person using the services of a lawyer, architect, doctor or other professional person. It seems that a customer is a 'thing', and nothing special, and clients are on some higher plane because they seek professional help. Private banking has clients, and retail banks have customers. It seems also that clients pay fees, customers do not. Is that really the way retail bank customers want to see it? Is that really the view of banks? Are customers seeking non-professional help? This is most certainly not the view of the FSA when disciplining banks for mis-selling – they assert that banks must exercise a professional duty of care to their customers when selling them complex products.

A bank customer is a good deal more than just a person who buys goods or services from the bank. If the customer entrusts the bank with their money, and relies on them for loans and transactions, then surely the customer is closer to a client. This is not comparable to buying a tin of soup, which makes you a customer of Heinz. We need to know that bank staff qualify in customers' minds as professionally competent to help them manage their finances. If bank staff can't do that, what hope is there for a relationship? How could we know that the bank is doing the right thing by us?

The pity is that whilst the bank accepts professional responsibilities for customer funds and manages them, it does not qualify as a professional service in the mind of the customer. This is self-inflicted by banks. They have told customers that they sell a commodity, and have reduced their costs. In so doing they have damaged relationships and access. It is clear that their branch staff have little or no authority to override 'what the computer says'.

To move a customer onto a higher plane, where the bank is regarded as a cosolver of financial concerns and a cocreator of the appropriate financial services, requires dialogue. It requires that the bank knows enough of the customer's circumstances and desires to be able to help materially and advise. It requires that the customer trusts and respects the bank staff with whom they have the dialogue. You certainly will have a dialogue with your painters, and the likelihood is that you will take their advice on a few points. They most likely do have your best interests at heart. With the dialogue in place, the customer moves upward from being just a customer, into becoming something more than that. This is the beginning of a relationship.

Having this bank/customer dialogue can be seen as an onerous burden. Imagine that each customer spends just one hour in total each year talking to the bank about his or her needs and circumstances. If a bank had one million customers, that million hours would roughly equate to about 500 man-years of bank staff time. Simplistically, if we divert time from non value-adding busy-work into dialogues, then we can convert customers from product purchasers into relationships of varying degrees of strength. The push of a telephone call from a bank is not the most welcome channel for customers; it puts many of them into a flap. Again, banks should spend less time on what they think is good for them, and more of it on what is good for their customers.

We have to establish the relationship first. Therefore, we have to know something more about the customer to be able to help, and we have to expose the customer to our staff to establish their confidence in our ability and willingness to help them.

We have banged on about costs. In this regard, CRM has been somewhat useful. It has been used to reduce costs through streamlining some processes, reducing duplication, 'bringing things together', reducing delays and improving efficiency. We were of course able to do all that with the CIF precursor. CRM has been hijacked by engineering, but these efficiency benefits are not CRM's real goal. CRM has far greater potential and power than has been practiced in banks. CRM should be concentrated on the business, the revenue generating side. If it can help on the cost reduction side, as a consequence, but that's a bonus.

In exactly the same way as the Internet, bill payment and a number of other seemingly sensible opportunities fell under the control of engineering and missed the entire point, the first wave of CRM has precisely missed the point. It, like the others, has become some sort of engineering adjunct, touted as full of promise, and as IT people like to say, 'just leave it to us'. Before undertaking projects that are logical, tidy and clean, the more important question to ask is 'why are we doing this?'

What a missed window of opportunity this has been. The hope is that having learned from the mistakes, we'll get it right next time around, and banks surely will. The first time around on most things, banks always over-intellectualise, over-analyse, over-theorise and under-realise. Then the practical issues get a chance, often after the engineers have been put back in their box.

Customers will decide whether a bank practises effective CRM. The customers will decide whether they feel that they have a relationship – it is not for the bank to tell them that they do indeed have a relationship. They would like to see that the bank is looking after them without having to be prodded. They would like to see the bank give valued advice voluntarily, to point out how they could make more out of the relationship. The implication is that a customer explicitly pays to be a client, the payment being some form of 'professional' fee. If that fee is implicitly bundled in the relationship, then that is somehow different?

Banking is an occasional purchase as it is, and a distress purchase at that. Consumers take more care with occasional purchases, and they value quality. Quality breeds customer confidence in the bank. Customer usage of the bank's products and services responds to growing confidence in their relationship with their bank.

We acknowledge that managing customer relationships will be a key source of competitive advantage in the coming years. We also recognise that the subindustry of CRM has tremendous skills and capabilities for banks to use. However, the prerequisite for any success is that the bank has the basis for a relationship in the first place. At this moment, banks would be far better off putting 80 % of their effort into establishing the basis for stronger relationships and 20 % into CRM, than putting 80 % into CRM and 20 % into cross-selling efforts which are not relationship building, quite the contrary because they are seen for exactly what they are.

These dialogues have to be encouraged. Branches and trained staff are the resource, available at the customers' convenience. We cannot see any shortcuts to establishing these relationships. Generally speaking, the customers have decided what they want from the bank independently, from media articles and the opinions of their peers. To be able to help them we need to be able to help them make these decisions cocreatively, where the bank is invited to, and can, make a useful contribution.

It may be that the development of a relationship is not possible because of the inability to attract enough business from a customer to develop the base knowledge about that customer. If competition and customer decisions point that way, then monolines, or companies with multiple monolines, may be in the ascendant. If the relationship in fact belongs to another entity, such as a supermarket, then financial products themselves can be secondary in the relationship.

8.4 MARKETING AND BRAND POWER

Marketing itself grew out of the need to differentiate mass-produced goods and to create trust. The success of bank marketing as practised today can be judged on the basis of the achievement of such differentiation and trust. Bluntly, it's not been that successful. Banks bemoan the commodity nature of their business, but the reams of small print, forms and processes undermine trust, and distance a relationship.

As one full-page bank advertisement says:

> 'We're fast, practical and down-to-earth. If there's a way to do business, we'll find it. If there's not, we'll do our best to invent one. You can't do that if you look at things the same way as everyone else does.'

There can be no argument with the sentiment, and although it was for corporate banking, the sentiment is close to being appropriate for retail customers too.

It is ultimately the consumers, by their decisions and actions, who will determine the direction and pace of the market. Marketing has never played as key a role in banking as it does in most other consumer businesses. Memorable bank marketing is infrequent, and no examples come to mind. It was never clear why an American actor wandering around the middle of Kansas was relevant to a UK consumer.

The objective of marketing is to gain customer market share and share of the customer wallet. Bank marketing departments vary widely in their roles, reporting and size. Some are still traditional with leaflets and newspaper ads; some are tactical and include advertising and direct (postal/phone) marketing; and some are strategic, where product, pricing and overall communications are major roles. As a result, marketing may report into different parts and levels of the organisation. In a few cases, marketing now encompasses sales, profit and channel responsibility. In some banks, the marketing function is also seen to be the custodian of the brand and the customer, which has led to the proliferation of customer relationship management initiatives.

The evolution in most cases is historical but what is becoming increasingly evident is that marketing must be a bank-wide philosophy embracing all employees. Further, specific functions like product development, marketing communications, pricing, market research/intelligence/evaluation are best located across operating, sales, or central resource functions, rather than in some isolated and remote unit.

Whatever the organisation or structure, the key is that the fundamentals of marketing are delivered. Find out what the customers want, then design, price, communicate and deliver this through the most appropriate channels, and ensure that this is evaluated and done in a profitable manner. How this is coordinated, structured and delivered will differ from bank to bank, but it is clearly a pervasive activity.

Since marketing (primarily advertising) budgets are usually large, they attract scrutiny, if not criticism. Increasingly, such spends are being evaluated and approved by procurement personnel, alongside them buying stationery, furniture, computers and all else. Bank marketing is not delivering. Could this spell the extinction, rather than the evolution, of bank marketing as we know it? Hopefully, yes, and the new marketing will have a far larger remit.

It seems that the word marketing means just what the person saying it wants it to mean, and just what the person hearing it wants it to mean, and that the two aren't necessarily in agreement.

If marketing is to be a bank-wide philosophy, and if it is to find out what customers want in order to design, price, deliver and communicate to the market, then that is a major departure from their current roles. But that is precisely what we see happening. Marketing has largely been about shouting louder about what the bank offers, not actually changing what it offers. It has been about burnishing the brand to a high gloss, not about causing facts to change. Nobody in banks really listens to their marketing people. Marketing and consulting have become two abused roles, so let's think of alternatives.

The true marketers in other industries actually do design the products and services that their companies sell. It has never been like that in banking, and marketing has usually operated as a tied advertising agency, rather than an original and creative spirit. Their job has been to sell what's on the truck, not to decide what to put on the truck. Like retailers, if a bank cannot sell what is in the stores, then it may have to change what it is putting in the stores. The role of bank marketing is going to grow rapidly, and it may not be the existing type of marketer that is needed. High profile situations, such as Laura Ashley, Boots, Burberry's, Tesco, Sainsbury's, Marks & Spencer, and even Coca-Cola and McDonald's, show this right up there in the business headlines. The focus of a business renaissance is on marketing, which is the identification and fulfilment of consumer needs and desires. We frequently see that marketing is key to pulling a business out of the ditch, so it must also be key to keeping a business on the road.

Marketing as custodian of the brand is on equally thin ice. Brands are meant to convey values to the served markets. Well, one size does not fit all. The brand that appeals to City financiers is not the brand that appeals to the non-prime market, and vice versa. The brand for a credit card or car insurance might not gel with a wealth client, and vice versa. We are seeing a proliferation of brands. A brand doesn't have as much elasticity as was assumed by marketers just a few years ago. Virgin demonstrated that best. Most clearly, there are corporate brands, product brands, demographic brands and pricing brands. You cannot simply mix them together, but they can be complementary. The Sony Walkman is two sets of brand values – Sony may mean innovation, technology and quality, and Walkman may mean music on the move in an attractive and usable package. The kids may only want the Walkman, but the parents are glad it's from Sony.

The net outcome of all this is that we are seeing the early stages of the dissolution/disbandment of the marketing function as we've known it. Marketing will split into two distinctly different roles. One is to capture market share through a customer, product and service focus, much along the lines that have been written about – need, design, development, implementation and product advertising. This will require a different breed of cat. The other is corporate in nature, to include brand management, public relations, investor relations, sponsorship and community involvement and corporate advertising. These will go their different ways.

The first will be new, and dispersed throughout the bank in some fashion. It will become the driving force behind the bank and may be the primary source of added value. The skills needed will not come from media studies, but from solid cross-disciplines. There is much substance in this job. For starters, they'll have to really know banking.

The second is closer to the marketing departments that we know today, and is largely mechanistic and tactical in nature with little value added.

To those who have sensed that marketing in banks has been little more than a straightforward job, wrapped up in the justifications of a pseudo-science, your suspicions are about to be rewarded. Marketing is extremely important, but not as banks know and practise it today. We expect it to become more proactive, assertive and value adding. Welcome to retailing.

The new marketing will also drive R&D. Few banks have any such function, since historically it has been about copying a competitor rather than researching or developing products and services. Innovation and differentiation are important forces, especially for market leaders. Erecting barriers to competitors is a powerful and fair way to compete. Whether the R&D is product or service focused, or aimed at understanding customers and their relationships with banks, there seems to be a huge amount of scope for R&D based simply on the fact that so little is done. Where it is done it tends to be engineering dominated again – yes, they've hijacked this too.

8.5 COSTS

The first reaction to cost discussions in banks is pretty hostile. It's seen as a negative subject, and most middle management see little opportunity to improve on their costs. They would far rather concentrate on growing revenues, training staff and undertaking other positive activities. And quite right they are too, on all counts. In the big scheme of things there is little they can do to improve costs within their remits. They have no remit.

There's nothing fancy in all this – costs in banks average half as much or more of the total revenue. The somewhat unique thing about banks is that about 80 % of all costs are systemic. That is, it is not a question of playing off suppliers against each other – the bank and its own staff are its own main supplier. Costs are self-imposed, and improvements have to be self-directed. As we have banged on about earlier, the costs are the outcome of the chosen processes, procedures, practices and a bank's choices on how to address them. The worst aspects are how large they are and how they get allocated. You can be certain that if a business's revenues go up, then as night follows day, its cost allocations will rise too.

Costs are a pervasive problem, and they are generally far higher than needs be. They cannot be much influenced at local/departmental levels.

Again, starting with a focus on the customers' true needs, and ignoring our own received wisdom on how these can best be supported within the existing operation, we can open up entirely new approaches.

So, and not without some problems, we can define a target business model and the ideal operations. This leaves us with the largest problem of effecting the change – how do we get from here to where we want to be? How do we define and effect a pervasive change?

The size of the bank is important. Whatever the maths is, the complexities and difficulties rocket up with size. The small and mid-sized banks are more able to make, and indeed in many cases have made, pervasive changes. They typically have more focused business models, a finer aim towards their selected, served markets, and a more flexible organisation. They share less. OK, they are simpler.

Especially after having arrived at a new business model, with highly efficient processes and procedures designed in, it would be the same size of task for an established bank as a new bank to introduce the system. The far greater challenge for an established bank is how to migrate to the new model (Figure 8.1). This has to be achieved within a short period in which the costs of the old business model need to be supported, as well as the costs of the new business model. It must not lead to customer or staff confusion. It must improve revenues and profits within a short space of time.

**EXISTING BUSINESS MODEL
AND OPERATIONS**

**NEW BUSINESS MODEL
AND OPERATIONS**

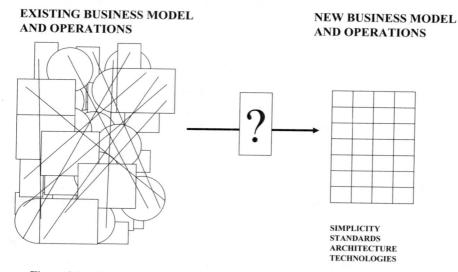

SIMPLICITY
STANDARDS
ARCHITECTURE
TECHNOLOGIES

Figure 8.1   The challenge for established banks – how to migrate to the new model

The reality is that we would really like to base it all on the existing system. There is no acceptable way to remove the legacy systems quickly, and particularly not the core accounting and controls.

Nevertheless, what a bank should develop is a clear model of where it would like to get to, and it should not compromise that model with the difficult realities of the transition. The transition is a separate problem, and can be immensely difficult. But there will be a way – relax about that until you get there.

It is no wonder that much management time is spent addressing costs. And costs are removed, especially with consolidations. However, it's pretty slow and painful to watch cost/income ratios being ever so slightly improved year on year. When costs are so embedded, it is impossible to impact them, and because costs are the consequence and not the cause, it is largely futile to address anything other than the cause of the costs.

8.6   STAFF

Staffing is the ultimately complex topic. Staff are 70 % or more of all costs. Staff are what the customers see of the bank, and they can strongly influence the opinion of the bank's customers. Staff are the primary opportunity to add value to a relationship. Staff need to be managed. Staff need to be trained and retrained. There are a great many staff to work with.

Staff used to be the face of the bank; they are now becoming the voice of the bank. In either guise they can strongly influence the bank's customers. Staff need to know and understand the strategy of the bank and the role they have and where it fits in helping to deliver on their strategy. The strategy is not the mission statement. The mission statement is most often a valueless, vacuous string of words. Replace it with the *action statement* that shows what has been done. It has to be believed by the staff. They have to hold some level of belief, even a little passion, that a consumer will be well served by their bank. Bank staff are consumers too. They can spot a banking trick from a thousand yards, and have integrity. They deserve to understand fully the whole business model, and to be told honestly about their role in all this. Should they just smile harder, talk louder, dress sharper . . . is that it?

Whatever anybody wants to believe, banks have got the staff they asked for as a consequence of a long and cumulative series of decisions, primarily relating to cost and management style. The quantity, skills, talents, preferences are as they are. This reservoir of staff will not be wholly appropriate for a changed business model. So the characteristics and skills of the staff will need to change at a faster pace to meet customer needs – all in the face of competition and the changing business, process and regulatory demands. This has to be easier if they want to contribute.

A look to retailing, service and manufacturing industries as sources for future staff at all levels will, in our opinion, become the norm. For example, much of the back office is a factory, and the optimal skills to handle this environment are unlikely to have been picked up in a wholly banking environment. This of course is the basis of the IT outsourcing market, and indeed office cleaners.

But quite innocently and passively, staff will be a source of major difficulties. So the premium on all aspects of superior staff management will only continue more intensely. We believe that education is the key to staff – the development of character and mental powers. Training is something else – learning a skill or discipline. We train dogs and monkeys. We educate staff. We train children to cross the road safely, but we educate them to be able to achieve.

8.7   DECIDING ON THE CHANGE ITSELF

There need to be targets to be achieved over a period of time. They have to be aggressive, such as these for instance:

- develop 50 % of customers into proper relationships;
- attract a large number of new customers/relationships;
- develop customer solutions so as to increase customer balances by 25 %;
- reduce the cost/income ratio to 30 %;
- increase staff productivity (value added) by 75 %;
- introduce two additional value-added fee services to 20 % of customers.

Such goals will not be achieved, or approached, by pussyfooting around. The bank has to work out its 'go to' state. Nothing should be considered safe. Product variations will be cut, forms will go, procedures will be removed; complexities go, and simplicity is in. Every customer form to fill in is a hurdle. All through the book, many of the areas have been pointed at.

As difficult as it may be to approach this challenge ruthlessly and confidently, that's as nothing as compared to effecting the change itself. How on earth can the same people doing the same things achieve such targets? Will working smarter, faster, harder do it? Clearly not. So we have to do things differently, and the same people may or may not be up to it.

8.7.1   Differently

Our view is that it makes little sense for an established bank to 'invent' a new bank, unless it is itself a tactical step towards the reinvention of the main bank. First Direct, now part of HSBC, was the granddaddy of direct banks and is successful, but most banks-within-banks have not had the same experience. As it happens, First Direct was not invented as a stand-alone bank, but a tactical step along a wider strategic path that was thwarted, for whatever reasons.

You would think that new and small banks would have no alternative but to invent or introduce a difference. Sad to say, that has not been the case. In taking old software and practices for their base of operations, by unleashing dyed-in-the-wool bank staff into the sand pit, they tended to neither invent nor differentiate, but to emulate existing banks, costs and all. This is the worst of all worlds. With large initial investments, largely the same operational cost structure, and no scale, the outcomes were inevitable. They should have spent quality time up front on their models, rather than jumping into the hype and hurry of starting a new bank, Internet-based or not. Don't blame the Internet for that.

New and small banks do have the opportunity to invent, but few of them have taken it. We are not talking about anything more than starting with the question 'what do the customers need, what do they value?' Most started off with the premise that, irrespective of customer needs, what the customers actually wanted were unsecured loans, credit cards, mortgages, savings accounts and what have you. Or to put it another way 'what have we got that they'll buy?' These are not the same.

Large banks have many difficulties in inventing, but no restrictions on imagining the end state. Their problems are how to implement their imagination speedil, and how to handle the disruptions and costs that they will incur.

The end result of invention or reinvention is somewhat the same – more appropriate products and services at competitive prices. The main difference between invention and reinvention is that with invention there are no inhibitions, but large banks do not have, or want, that totality, and there will be enforced or chosen restraints. For them, reinvention is far preferable (Figure 8.2).

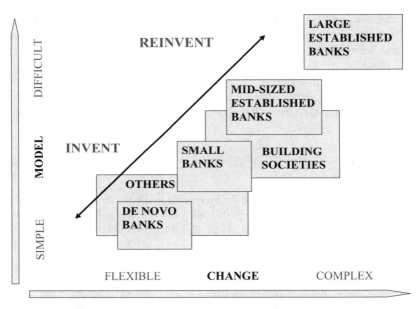

Figure 8.2   Invention is easier for smaller and newer banks, while larger established banks prefer reinvention

8.7.2   New and small banks

The main risk for new and small banks is in building their business models. Their main challenge is in marketing and attracting customers. The business model can only be realistic if there are significant differentiators in the product or pricing – which means offering something different for, and valued by, customers, and/or at a markedly better price.

What is or are these differences, and at what pace will customers change? For customers to open and use an account with another bank, new or established, there simply has to be a major justification. It is not clear that promotional pricing does much more than attract uncommitted customers who will desert that account when the next promotional offer arrives from another bank. Creating customer awareness, through marketing in some form, is a significant challenge. However, the standard methods of TV advertisements are not as effective as far cheaper newspaper advertising supported by being near the top of the best-buy or best-rates tables in the financial press, and supported by an excellent Internet website that is clear and easy to use. Telephone usage is to be dissuaded. Postal communication is more acceptable than many assume. Word-of-mouth awareness is best by far, but has to be primed and can only be totally truthful, by definition.

There is not much to add as regards new and small banks. The reasons for the lack of success in this area have been the fundamental flaws in their initial business models, or the unwillingness within the bank for staff to be honest with themselves and each other. Plenty of those involved in new banks questioned strategies privately, but were unwilling to argue against all the consultancies and vendors. Those that did, did not help their careers. Some of the initiatives were so insane or naïve, depending on which consultancy was used, that there should have been serious embarrassments. There have certainly been more successes from consultant-free strategic initiatives, and they are less expensive, cleaner and quicker. Either a bank knows its business or it doesn't. The role of consultants to our minds is in education in its various forms. Ultimately, the bank has to do things for itself, on its own. People will be fired for doing the wrong things, wherever their advice came from.

Once the business model has been decided upon, the task is to build the new operation. This is another bear-trap. The obvious pressures were the need for speed, the inevitable and quite correct response being to seek a solution from a third party or third parties that were deemed to be pretty close to meeting the bank's requirements. Here they usually went wrong again. The brave new world of Internet banking meant that, despite the bravado, the bank staff did not actually know much of what they were talking about or looking at. That is to say, the bank and its staff, or the bankers it hired, had never implemented a complete banking system from scratch before, there was little experience in the new technologies, and little savvy in the area of consumer marketing and sales. The result was domination by consultants, vendors and marketing companies, who themselves knew little about what really mattered, but knew everything about maximising their own revenues. A series of travesties ensued. It is important for better banking that these bad experiences are seen for what they are, which is incompetence by mismatching skills to the task. The successful exceptions should be seen as the realisation of the possible.

8.7.3 Established banks

This is a more complicated matter. Still, irrespective of the difficulties, it is necessary to develop business models as to how life could be. The natural tendency has been to discount approaches early, simply because they are quickly judged to be difficult or impossible to support within the existing organisation and operational environment. That necessarily curtails discussions right at the beginning, and we revert to slight improvements to the existing business model. As an illustration, the large banks' Internet models have become little more than a delivery channel onto the pre-existing accounts, which does have its uses, without doubt, but it's not first prize.

It is tempting to reconsider zero-based budgeting, whereby each group of staff functions is questioned with a view to designing them out of a new model. But these approaches have been tried many times, and fall flat when the staff functions are shown to have been totally designed into the existing model or have become an integral necessity. As a result, the addition of an extra channel has not reduced costs, but rather increased them. This was not the plan. Please argue that it has improved service and so on, but the performance numbers show that it has not contributed – customers do not pay for it. Customers are making twenty enquiries a day, and it is not costing them anything. Banks talk of millions of 'hits' to their Internet banking services with little to show for it. A good portion of these bank actions were transformed into defensive plays in the end.

8.8   ESTABLISHING THE BASIC INPUTS

There will have to be a formalised, disciplined process to provide the framework for change, leading to the target business model. There is nothing new or different in the process outlined here from similar processes that banks undertake regularly. There is a difference in spirit though.

We wish that we had identified some things that are radical or dramatic. Our recommendations, however, all come down to good, solid work. Fulfilling customer needs at the lowest cost is hardly a useful or new recommendation – but how to identify customer needs, and how to deliver them at the lowest cost most definitely is. Improving, or cementing, investor ambitions is as important. Both must win.

Looking for boulders in a haystack is a lot easier than looking for needles. We are not looking for slight improvements, only step function improvements. The consequence is that the analysis and research work is a minor part of the mission with major consequences. We are looking in the main for what comes before the decimal point, not what comes after the decimal point.

Importantly, open minds will find interesting thoughts, only some of which will be opportunities, and only some of those opportunities might be worth pursuing a little further, and only a few might justify action.

You will assume that this goes on all the time in a large bank. Perhaps it should, but it doesn't. You would be amazed at how compartmentalised, and therefore parochial, the majority of the many bright minds in a bank are. Experience has taught them that they have to be that way. The multiple disciplines required, and the finely tuned competencies in each actually discourage, or at the least inhibit, team progress.

Most, yes most, and we do mean 90 % or so of bank staff, could not give a one-hour talk to first-year business studies students on the subject of the business of retail banking. They can tell you 101 % about what they do, and rest assured, they can tell you how to improve performance within their expertise, but are not asked genuinely. If banks are to be professional cocreators of solutions, then they will need to know about the subject. True or false?

The imperative is that the activities are not dominated by engineering and science, but continuously relate to the art of defining and meeting customer needs, solution development, marketing and aligning staff towards solving customer needs. Question everything with a view to greatly improving productivity throughout the bank. The result will please customers and investors.

The ball has to start rolling somewhere, and so we need to establish cross-disciplinary discussions focusing on the strategic goal of providing better banking. Something such as the following, perhaps.

8.9   DISCOVERY PROCESS

There do have to be thought provoking opportunities, and displays of thought leadership. One approach is simply to examine the facts and the opportunities, and to establish a basis of common knowledge around the subject of banking and the challenge.

A proportion of participants will have an intimate understanding of bank customers. This may seem an unnecessary statement, but one half of many banks' staff have never met a customer in their business. Less have had a long and wide involvement with them, and even less have expertise in the subject of banking. Promotion has often meant getting out of the line of customer fire. Still, the objective is to develop a profitable business, and for that purpose it does require much greater insight into the business than these same people might have. Therefore, one purpose is to transfer rapidly key knowledge and information on the retail banking market, the constraints and freedoms it needs, the behaviour of customers, and so on. But experience of working with customers is no less important.

The second objective is to address the topics and steps outlined earlier in this chapter to arrive at the robust outline(s) of an approach.

To a large extent, one can say that this is little different from the processes already undertaken by banks. In fact, there are three basic differences. First, the main focus begins and ends with customers. The normal approach is to focus on market activities that are usually generated from within the banking industry itself, which is why we simply tend to end up with product variations rather than any new approaches.

The second difference is that today's concerns are dominated by what the bank can support most quickly and easily, which should be a secondary consideration.

The third, and most important, difference is that we are not trying to *improve* performance, those mechanisms are in place. We are trying to *change* performance positively for the customers and the bank.

In order to frame these discussions, we suggest a standard analysis. It is not necessary that the analysis be laborious and detailed, but it should concentrate on high-level measures of performance as we have done throughout the book. The challenge is to identify how we can be profitable with a spread of 2 % or less when we currently depend on a 3 % spread, or whatever the appropriate figures are for the individual bank and its served markets.

The objectives are to:

- discuss the opportunities;
- outline the essential business cases;
- identify what is needed to support the business cases;
- research;
- produce findings;
- make propositions;
- select the business model;
- outline plans, resources, costs, and timeframes;
- refine the business plan;
- analyse key staff requirements;
- set the project management framework and governance;
- set sales and marketing strategies;
- set partner strategies.

8.10   ESTABLISHING THE BUSINESS MODEL

The business plan, particularly the customer value proposition and the cost model, are absolutely key. The quality of the implementation is important – news of a bank's call centre problems or operational snafu travels fast. There will be pressures to take shortcuts; to utilise something that exists but is not really what is needed, to put things to one side because they're too awkward, and so on.

The degree to which the plan and implementation are compromised will greatly impact the benefits to the bank.

Depending upon your freedoms, getting to market will require you to follow one of three broad courses.

8.10.1   New model

A new bank, or a new self-standing initiative in a bank, will require investment and the building of substantial infrastructure well before any benefits accrue (Figure 8.3). This is high risk insofar as a sequence of decisions is needed, and needs to be made optimally, before the customer solution can be launched. Even then, customers have to be gained from a zero base against mounting competition. The business model has got to be right, the customer proposition has got to be strong, and the execution has got to be near perfect. Success in the short term will be measured in gaining assets of, say, £1 billion. An ROA of 1 % would only give a profit of £10 million,

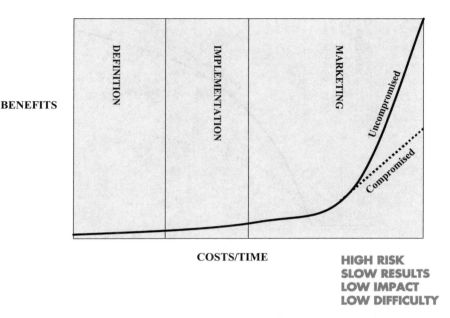

Figure 8.3   A new model

which allows little leeway for any drift. If the plan is over a period of five years, then there will have to be some barriers to competitors copying in order to sustain a growth to a comfortable critical mass. The best competitive barrier is to capture the market. This has been the standard model for the new wave of banks of the 1990s. There are non-mysterious, quite obvious reasons why most failed to make the hurdle rate required. But some did, and no doubt most of the others would do better next time, but are unlikely to get another chance.

This approach seems best suited to monoline approaches, and where physical presence is not needed, indeed, designed out. Direct Line, First Direct and ING Direct are good examples. Pretty much, you get the business model and the implementation right, and then you succeed. If not, you don't. To the extent possible, the implementation itself is best based on standard, off-the-shelf systems, and can be rapid.

8.10.2   Enhancement model

The second approach is where there is sufficient room for manoeuvre for an existing bank to capitalise on its infrastructure to a useful extent. This is nondisruptive to the bank, in that it is not resource intensive, and utilises proven and familiar components to mitigate many of the risks and to accelerate growth. The supposition is that this is attractive to a flexible organisation. We are adding value to achieve the goals set out in the business plan, but relying on selected, solid foundations (Figure 8.4).

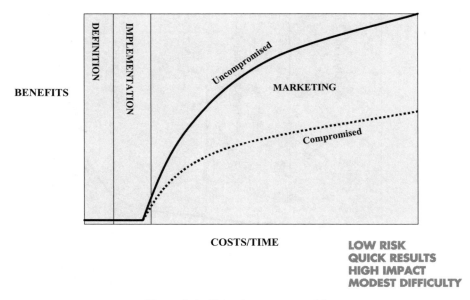

Figure 8.4   The enhancement model

Depending on the technical and organisational flexibility, this approach can make sense for small, mid-sized and large banks. This approach too has been embraced by many initiatives in recent years, and again with mixed success, but few failures. To our knowledge, The Co-operative Bank's *smile*, Northern Rock and Alliance & Leicester are three positive examples. The large banks seem to have followed this approach with their Internet banks, however the weight of their organisations and many complexities seem to have led to so many compromises that what is left is little more than channel improvements linking customers to the self-same value propositions as before. That is, their models did not lead to better banking, but rather to another ho-hum 'improvement'. The three banks we mentioned have indeed introduced better customer value propositions.

With this model we are 'simply' bolting on new capabilities and plumbing, and wiring them into the existing infrastructure. This is not easy for large and complex banks, where the existing systems are brittle and there are many interfaces to be developed to other parts of the systems.

This approach is also well suited for multiline initiatives. It would seem that utilising the in-place capabilities of a bank, that is the accounting engines, controls and customer contact mechanisms, has much merit. The value added, which comes from a change in the customer value proposition, is in the selection of which parts of the infrastructure to use (and to pay for), and which not to use (and not to pay for). Sainsbury's Bank and Tesco, who utilise the account processing, accounting and control mechanisms of large banks to minimise their risk and gain high impact and quick results, use a variation on this approach. The only caveat is that they must be able to use these existing components at the right price, and it isn't clear that they do.

Irrespective of the difficulties that Tesco and Sainsbury's caused in the systems areas of RBS and HBOS, this was moderated by the similarity of their products to pre-existing bank accounts. It is not at all clear that their dependency on inflexible capabilities enables them to strut their stuff as strongly as they would like. Their major business appears to be insurance. It will be interesting to see if they can make the impact in banking that they made in petrol, newspapers and magazines and pharmaceuticals and toiletries, given their reliance on bank legacy systems.

8.10.3 Change model

If the needs driven by the business plan are substantially different to the existing infrastructure capabilities, then the time may come when a step change is needed. This is a big time problem, big time that potentially leaves the large, complex banks out on a limb, and indeed any others that have inflexibilities for whatever reasons – technical, organisational, political or creative. This third and final approach addresses such situations. The reality is that to overcome the inflexibilities and rigidities does imply disruptions of some sort, to some degree. The accommodation is that change is slow, incremental and safe. The business model does not carry a step function improvement or two, but rather a series of changes that combine in time to form a step function improvement.

Although the definition and implementation challenges are more difficult, the marketing is significantly easier (Figure 8.5). Anything that a large bank does is subject

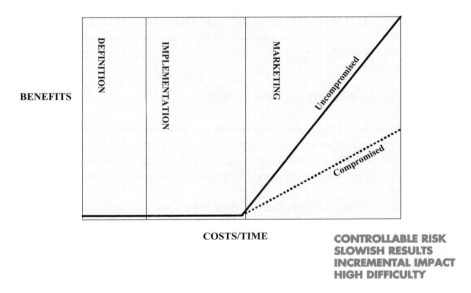

Figure 8.5 The change model

to serious dilution, whether intended or unintended. Each organisational unit, be it department, region, division or business has its own survival mechanisms. But, more powerful for (or against) success is the single-mindedness which the bank leadership brings to the mission, itself balancing the efforts from the impacted organisational units, not allowing them to act in isolation. This calls for flying in tight formation, not just all heading in the same general direction. The benefits will be achieved only to the extent that comfortable compromises are avoided. If most units 'get what they want' then the customers will certainly not get what they want, so neither will the bank or its investors.

Irrespective of whether the goal is to provide better banking or just another year's worth of 'normal' improvements, there is plenty of evidence that this approach has difficulties. The risk is controllable, which is good news, but the results are slow and the impact incremental, which is not so good, but acceptable if the end result is indeed a step function improvement.

To illustrate how difficult this third approach is, for whatever reason, we can simply say that no large bank appears to have achieved a step function improvement in its performance except by M&A or some other peculiar change. So we cannot bring any successful examples to mind. This is the more surprising when we look at the concentration of spending in the large banks.

This change model is the general approach of the major banks. Frankly, they have to change from their legacy constraints if they are to protect their business a few years out.

A last warning is that pressures to compromise are intense, if for no other reason than to minimise disruption. There is a long history of this, which is why this legacy problem exists today. It seems unthinkable that mainframe applications systems originating from the 1960s and 1970s will still be supporting banks in 2010. However, unless this problem is addressed, it seems that they will. That being so, the large banks with their inherited systems will be at a serious disadvantage with an unsustainable cost model and an inability to compete effectively.

8.11   ESTABLISHING THE BUSINESS PLAN

The business plan will inevitably come down to a sheaf of spreadsheets, and it will be complicated, but not necessarily complex. We imagine that it will be the outcome of an iterative process considering customers, products, services, tasks, resources, finance, organisation, risk, legal issues, regulations, and just about everything there is to consider.

The mission of defining the business model is not a part-time effort, and cannot be compromised with pressures that would seek the easy way out. Giving the mission to staff as a sideline activity while they keep their day job, the job for which they get paid and rewarded, dilutes originality, creativity and boldness.

The working prototype of a business model can be constructed in months by a handful of staff using off-the-shelf components. They may say it can't, but it can. It costs little. They may say it costs a lot, but it doesn't need to. If the model is deemed to be a strong enough candidate when shown and explained to the good and the great, it can be geared up for a pilot trial. This pilot could use existing staff and families, thus to encourage thoughtful and creative feedback. Once, and if, the model has been proven to be effective, then the live rollout can be considered, and that will lead to some additional expense to ensure integrity against all-comers, robustness, good response times, low unit costs, scalability and so on. The third parties used will be familiar and competent in these issues.

This should be achieved at a high level first before diving into the minutiae, which is the tendency. A high-level business plan will stand on its own merit quite easily if it makes sense. The business plan must reflect the known realities of the business and the choices that are even now waiting to be made.

8.12 BIG BANKS IN PARTICULAR

In making bank valuations using the various methods, the sum-of-the-parts valuations show that retail banking is highly valuable, disproportionately from its simple asset size measures. There is a high value attached to the implicit customer equity, a surrogate for which is the cost to acquire a new customer. On this basis, the retail bank itself as an autonomous unit provides higher shareholder value than it does when incorporated into the many other activities of large banks. Investors may want both to maximise their shareholder value, and to invest in opportunities that are pure plays in the retail banking sector, rather than general plays in the banking sector overall. As the large investors increasingly practise global strategies, their comparisons become more difficult with large complex businesses having dozens of discrete and individually large activities, many of which can be counter cyclical to retail banking in performance terms.

The large banks, by our thinking, are going to find it the most difficult to raise their games to the levels that will be needed in retail banking to retain and attract new customers. Much of this comes from the complexities of shared resources and systems. We do not see that this sharing brings scale economies past a fairly low size of bank. Undoubtedly, the de-duplication of activities in an M&A situation is a strong improver of performance, but normal growth provides more inefficiencies of scope and organisation than efficiencies of scale. An autonomous retail bank does have a far higher efficiency than a retail bank embedded in a hugely complex organisation.

The bank leadership itself can have a staff count of 100 000 or more to manage. In fact, it is more accurate to look at the challenge as managing ten very different companies, each in a different business, with 10 000 staff in each. It is not the numbers of staff that is the concern, after all Tesco has 220 000 staff – but they only have the one basic business. It's not the volume of staff or customers that give concerns, it's the number of disparate businesses. The phenomenon of companies diversifying to get into counter-cyclical businesses and enjoy synergies and the rest, was soon followed by retrenchment back into their core businesses in preference.

Running the bank operations is no small business in itself. If split out as separate companies, the operations divisions of the larger banks would each be FTSE 100 companies in their own right. But that's not the way to do it. These operating divisions are to banks what Railtrack, or whatever it's now called, is to the independent train operators. The case for the train operators to take responsibility for their track is strong. Only then can they be held responsible for the service that the customers receive.

So, there will be a lot of thought given to increasing autonomy for the retail component of the bank, and its possible float as an independent company, still owned by the bank holding company, but separately traded.

8.13   IS THERE REALLY A CHOICE?

Bankers, consumers and investors either think that retail banking will continue to sail along happily, with only occasional storms to weather, or they don't. We don't.

We think that consumers should reasonably expect more of their banks, and that competition in retail banking will increase as new business models are introduced and gain traction in the market. These business models will appeal to consumers based on their fitness-for-purpose, price and the low effort required from the consumer because of their simplicity, flexibility and accessibility. We look to word-of-mouth marketing as a major growth catalyst, the Internet and the phone as the primary channels, and the quality of staff across the bank, all these combined will be the key market differentiators.

The leadership team of the bank – whether it be a large, mid-sized, small or new bank – will be the critical factor, because of its decisions and its ability to execute them.

Just because things are 'going alright' in banking at the moment does not invite a relaxation in effort. Quite the contrary is the case. There are business cycles and economic cycles. Nobody knows what tomorrow holds, even if the odds are that it will be much like today. There is no better time to think it all through than when things are on the up. Trees don't grow to the sky.

Figure 8.6 returns to the diagram we used in the Preface. Left to their own devices, and recognising who the owners of the bank are, banks are going to pursue profits growth and operational efficiency as their two primary objectives. They say so with every results announcement. This will lead to the continuation of a well-known trajectory – more of the same with higher investment performance as the goal. But it will lengthen the customers' perceived distance between them and their banks, and undermine attempts to develop relationships.

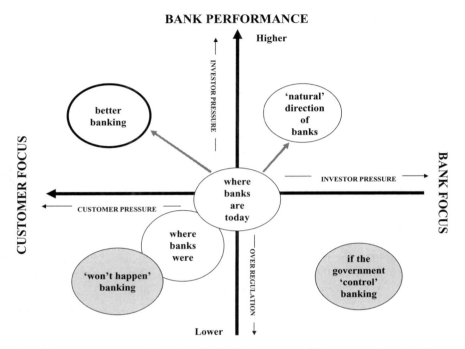

Figure 8.6 The two possible trajectories for banks – more of the same, or better banking

The investors will be happy though. And indeed, this trajectory might serve its purpose for more years to come. This would leave the top left quadrant of the diagram empty.

We don't think that this is the only way forward. We think that the trajectory towards better banking is the better trajectory to be on, because better banking will lead to greater and deeper usage of banks, and thus to improved investment performance.

The top left quadrant is where both customers and investors get more of what they want. There is a lot of emptiness to fill, and much room to play in here. There are major opportunities to serve consumers, and money to be made. It's enticing. How will it be filled?

It is not difficult to envisage better banking to fill this – customer-focused solutions and appealing products, good rates, new services for consumers, low fees, low costs, super easy and simple, speed and flexibility. Each one of these individual qualities is good for both customers and investors.

But the directions of the 'normal' and 'better' trajectories are quite different, and that's not a trick of the diagram – the diagram came before the thought. It is rather the result of approaching the future with open minds.

8.14 MUCH OF THE WRITING IS ON THE WALL

There are no surprises in all this. Certainly not from the customers' perspective.

- The need for banks, and the opportunities to fill the need, are both growing.
- Brand, service, quality – the mantra of market leaders – carry less weight now. Brand is trust, and public trust is with the regulators and media as much as it is with the banks themselves. Service is shrinking along with the cuts. Quality is indistinguishable – my loan is of better quality than your loan? Come to XYZ Bank for high quality mortgages? All three are pretty neutral.
- Customer relationships will matter. How can a bank help if it knows nothing about the customer? Will customers seek help from a bank that they do not have a relationship with?
- Customers want solutions, not products.
- Customers are happy to pay 'fair' rates and fees, but don't like getting hood-winked or paying over the odds.
- Customers are most likely to open, or close, accounts at life event points than in normal flight. Consequently, there is a lag between introduction and take-up. Conversely, there is a delayed run off of business.

Banks do have problems, be they organisational, technical, mobility, cost, regulation, administration, or whatever. They will need to address them soon.

Banks have to decide just what parts of retail banking they wish to own, partner or outsource. They have a complex business, and as it stands they are doing almost everything themselves and trying to be most things, if not all things, to most people. Figure 8.7 is a simple illustration of this, taken from our previous discussion on IT. After all, form should follow function.

Just how many aspects of providing retail banking does a bank have to be good at doing itself? At one extreme, it can do it all itself, which has been the normal approach. On the other, it will only handle the customer relationship aspect, and find ways to have all the rest done.

- Banks will be responsible for all customer relationships – from sales onwards.
- Banks will want to retain control over policies, financials, pricing and other aspects in the administrative space.
- All the rest can be bought rather than made, but it can be made rather than bought.

The decision on the business model and the business plan must include such decisions. There have been (reluctant) movements towards 'buying' components. But these have been in the face of an inability to provide the necessary capabilities at the right price/risk internally within the bank. Pieces of software here and there, outsourcing of various functions, and what have you.

Long term, we have little doubt that banks will retain all aspects of their customer relationship, and that they will buy, rather than make, wherever that is possible. They will buy processing, they will commission much development work, they will use

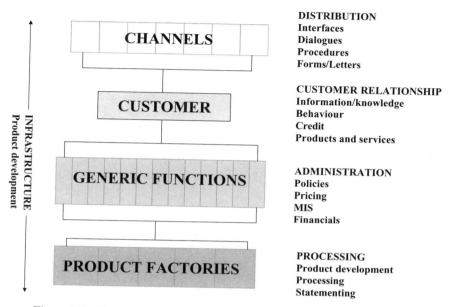

Figure 8.7 The components of retail banking – to own, partner or outsource?

shared counters with others for transactions, and they will have others look after infrastructure and the rest. The bank will become good at *retailing* banking products and services, not in making them.

In the short term, the appropriate preparation for the future is therefore to align the internal functions along such lines by defining and implementing such a model, using internal staff and components. At some point, the bank will then be able to buy superior, proven components from a variety of third party sources who will have the specialisations and scale appropriate to their component.

In the medium term, components can be wheeled in and out as the market evolves and superior components become available.

One suggestion has been to become simply distributors (have channels, will sell), and buy in manufactured products or the manufacturers of products. Or they could be simply marketeers and channel managers. In other words, they could become very single minded. The drawback of this approach is not having significant equity in the financial products themselves, thus having a greatly reduced opportunity to earn revenues and profits because they occupy smaller and less profitable parts of the value chain. The scale of revenues and profits, and the attractive returns on equity come primarily from the lending, deposit and insurance products themselves. To not be doing those functions cuts you out of the big time, and you simply become a processor, by any other name. You do however stand to make commissions and carry less risk; so it's all about getting the sums right, as usual.

9
Predictions for Retail Banking

Surprisingly, based on all the preceding material and pulling the strands together, we find most of the forward projection to be easier than we had imagined.

Let's not kid ourselves – banking today is recognisable from banking in 1960. Banking in 2030 will be less recognisable to today's twenty-year-olds when they get to their forties. That is to say that the pace of change is going to accelerate rapidly from here. In the same way as markers were put down in the 1960s, the markers that are put down now will determine the future. Banks have to play a long game as well as the short ones.

The health warning is not to get too caught up in what banks could do, might do or should do. We have to predict what they will do in practice, and that is subject to 101 influences, pressures, forces and circumstances. It is also of more use to predict that which is likely to be generally right, than that which might be precisely wrong.

Our predictions are in two parts – the simple ones, and the braver ones over the horizon.

In the last ten years or more there have been many predictions of the could/should/might variety, emanating primarily from consultants and market researchers. It is by no means certain that these 'experts' are capable of feeling embarrassment, but we can try for a little discomfort. The stock-in-trade seems to be shock, doom and gloom. Some big predictions relating to retail banking have included:

- Global banks – a handful of the largest banks were going to gobble everything up and rule the world.
- Internet banking – the costs were going to be so low and the service so convenient that traditional banking would go the way of the dodo.
- Disintermediation – banks were going to suffer death by a thousand cuts from the securities and insurance industries, as well as non-financial companies crashing in on the party.
- The end of branches – bank branches were to become obsolete.

- The glory of branches – they were to sell holidays, coffee, property, insurance, securities, medical plans, pensions, funeral services and so on. The financial services superstore-plus.
- Pan-European banking – large banks were going to acquire banks in other countries and construct dominant networks, according to some, with bancas-surance the new model.
- Relationship banking – hey, we're related!

There is an element of accuracy in all these predictions, but the timescales were certainly wrong. The pace of change in banking is stately, and we continue to assert that the sky will not fall in, and that the future holds a continuing process of improvement, opportunity and growth for retail banks of any shape and size.

M&A does continue with in-country and cross-border activities; the Internet does provide an exciting, inexpensive and convenient channel; non-banks will continue to compete for business; branch networks will continue to be both rationalised, and made more effective; banks will provide more than just bank accounts – specifically solutions and services; large UK banks will go where the opportunities present themselves, which is not necessarily in the UK; foreign banks will go where their opportunities present themselves, some of which will be in the UK; there is logic in relationships, but how will it be used?

But for all that angst, concern and consulting there have been no real shocks, and it is to be hoped that banks didn't pay too much for these predictions. Our predictions as to the future of retail banking are not so surprising, and are free.

A seismic shock is our least likely prediction, and doom and gloom nowhere to be seen. But there will be major, uncomfortable change, with relative winners and losers. And in that wonderful political phrase, there will be 'events, dear boy, events' which will be deeply uncomfortable for those banks that fail to make the cut.

9.1 A FRAMEWORK FOR THE 'SIMPLE' PREDICTIONS

All of the many parts of retail banking are important, and all have to work in harmony. Figure 9.1 has some twenty-eight areas or characteristics that we consider to be the most important. Just under half of these have been highlighted ($\sqrt{}$) as being the areas presenting the most difficulties and dangers. The chart is intended to be logical, not hierarchical, and our predictions range widely, often incorporating several areas at the same time.

We are not going to get worked up over those things that we can do nothing about, other than to absorb them into the pot. The large wave structural changes brought on by political pressures are for each bank to deal with themselves. Our aim is to focus on the emergence of better retail banking from the competitive mêlée, and to help some banks win competitively by helping them to help their customers better. These large wave influences, such as European enlargement, the European Central Bank and the like, are interesting and important forces, but they do not mean that Bank X

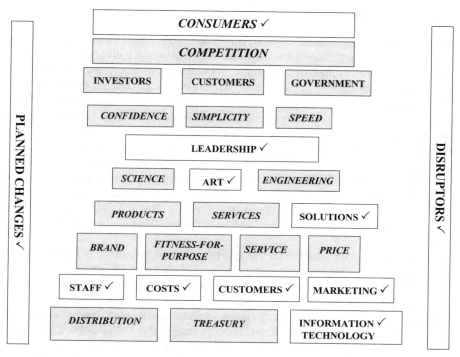

Figure 9.1 Some twenty-eight important areas, with the most difficult marked

is going to outperform Bank Y, and are happily irrelevant to consumers. These are for the banks to work out.

More importantly, we are concentrating on those areas where staff in a bank can make a meaningful contribution and difference. We leave all the large wave stuff to consultants, who will hawk around homogeneous solutions to Basel II, IAS39, FSA regulations, Brussels and Washington. 'Twas ever thus. Every year, a new sales target.

9.2   SIMPLE 'WE KNOW THAT ALREADY' PREDICTIONS

We start off with the obvious predictions. Way above all else is that the consumer proposition be appealing, effective and efficient. If this is not the goal, then don't bother. The basic premise is that retail financial markets will continue to grow world-wide. The growth will be strong and steady in developed markets, in line with the growth in prosperity and increased savings and pension provision. It will be rapid in emerging markets, particularly in Central Europe, the Far East and Latin America. Retail banking will continue to be an attractive business, simply because we need it and it is critical to success for each nation and its people.

9.2.1   Competition

Competition is going to intensify on all fronts. Established banks will compete harder with each other; non-banks such as major retailers will fan out their offerings and grow their account and customer volumes. The big non-banks, such as the supermarkets, may vertically integrate once they have gained sufficient volume, experience and skills, in order to reduce the processing costs charged by their partner banks. If this group sticks to basic commodity products, as we suspect that they will, then vertical integration will be the normal course to get to the optimal cost structure. We suspect that the current reliance on bank legacy systems will prevent meeting the needs of the supermarkets' vision of what banking is about. However, the banks provide much of the capital, so watch this space. Operating infrastructure and capital are two separate decisions. Partnering has been the favoured approach because supermarkets know what they know, and they know what they don't know. They're smart. But now, they know a great deal more about what they didn't know. This could be an interesting period for them.

Serious new entities will enter the market. We say serious because this is not a business to undertake without deep pockets. A realistic minimum critical mass of business is an asset size of perhaps £5 billion, which will require an investment of some £200 million in equity capital plus the cost to establish the bank and meet the staff, development and marketing costs. That size of £5 billion in assets, by the way, is half the size of The Co-operative Bank, and broadly comparable to Yorkshire, Clydesdale and Northern Bank. It is not trivial by any means, and would place it at about 500 in the world ranking of banks by size. Yes, the retail banking business itself is potentially hugely attractive, but new operators or small operators with big ambitions are entering into a crowded market. They will have to accept that their business models and value propositions need to be materially different or much better than those that already exist, and they have to be able to convey that to consumers who are already being blanketed with offers from others. To rise above all that noise, we see an imperative that word-of-mouth recommendations amongst consumers and the media are generated. To carry that off, the consumer value proposition must be immensely strong.

We therefore expect few new entrants, and those will probably be financial services companies from Europe and the USA. GE, MBNA and ING Direct are successful examples. Bank of Ireland has adopted a model with The Post Office, which has strong potential. Note that none of these four are attacking the indigenous banks at their own game – each has a new and focused model. But it is not the number of new entrants that matters, it's their quality. Just a few entrants with gripping propositions and effective marketing could have a large impact on market share in their chosen markets, as these have done or will do. It will not all be foreign. Within the UK there have been some important successes, Northern Rock as an example, but rather more muted in approach because they have been of an enhancement nature rather than a new nature, and that makes sense. Alliance & Leicester, The Co-operative Bank and the three NAG banks (Clydesdale, Yorkshire and Northern) look on track too. In fact, these six banks are the only mid-sized banks that the UK has. We suspect that these six have got the measure of their defined markets against the large banks and have made their strategic decisions, which includes divestment in the case of NAG, and the growth of their Clydesdale brand in the UK.

We will see finer definitions of served markets leading to more effective selling. We will see customer behaviour change and a willingness, or even a desire, to change allegiances if it makes financial and/or service sense, and is easy. The width of products and services will diminish in importance as the solution value increases and the purchase or change decisions are made easier by simplifications.

There are a number of smaller companies serving niche markets such as sub-prime, which we see as a growing business opportunity and consumer need.

9.2.2 Customers

Customers are changing. This is not due to anything mysterious; they are changing because they have to change. Our society is going through some monumental adjustments under our noses. Property ownership and pensions are two of the largest and most important needs of our society, and both are addressed differently by consumers than they were only ten or twenty years ago. Affordable housing is becoming an oxymoron; couples have to save hard to get onto the property ladder, often delaying marriage and family so as to have two incomes for longer, if not forever. Pensions are no longer always the entitlement of long and loyal service – they are increasingly the responsibility of the individuals themselves. Inheritance is now becoming an issue for people as the value of their homes exceeds the inheritance tax threshold. In these circumstances customers will become more concerned with value, most obviously savings and mortgage rates and fees, the investment policies of their pension provider and the cost of insurance, particularly protection. With the power of compound interest (which Einstein described as the most powerful force on Earth) and the long duration of mortgage and pension commitments, it will be no surprise to see consumers chasing the best rates and lowest fees to knock years off their mortgages and to accumulate savings, seeking the best investment advice to boost their pensions, and using taxation and estate planning services. As a consequence, fee revenues will jump.

The media will tell you that we are a nation of borrowers, but that must mean we are also a nation of lenders. The demographics of wealth are, however, quite frightening. Excluding property ownership, the least wealthy 50 % of those known to the Inland Revenue have just 5 % of the wealth. Savings as a proportion of income have been in steady decline over the last decade. Quite what the consequences of these and other figures show is unclear, except that societal change is going to continue, and more people will be needing more help from banks and the government in the future to guide them in key financial decisions which previously were taken by a person's employer or the state. Choice means that decisions are increasingly being pushed back on to the individual, and that is uncomfortable for many. A fear is that this will attract companies that sail too close to the wind, essentially 'ripping off' customers.

9.2.3   Government and regulation

Quite rightly, the government takes a close interest in retail banking matters. Since the collapse of BCCI, the government has put in place deposit protection schemes and regulations to stop banks doing stupid things and causing customers to lose money. Latterly, they have concentrated on the quality of products and financial advice given to consumers to try to prevent repeats of pensions and other financial products mis-selling. These two examples show that they come in after the horse has bolted. It is difficult, we're told, to know if a horse is about to bolt, so that is not a criticism. How long before another agency has to authorise new banking initiatives? This intrusiveness will only increase with the spectre of a generation of consumers arriving at the gates of retirement with insufficient funds to live on and of an inability of citizens to be able to afford housing. A reliance on heavy debt and other scenarios will have a significant impact. The government needs to mitigate such scenarios, as remedial measures on any scale are unpopular, difficult, lengthy and costly. Since most consumers have their wealth tied up in their property, any dislocation in the property market has severe implications.

Of course, there are ways to manage such requirements, but all of them are relatively unknown territory to government. The consequence is likely to be unsatisfactory legislation and regulations, leading to complexity, confusion, adjustment and a change of mind at a later date.

This is likely to be highly disruptive and the unsurprising prediction is that this is all going to get worse with government placing increasing reliance on regulators and, as a consequence, slowing down progress towards better banking.

Now, enthusiastic banking is one thing. Misbehaviour, chancing and deceit are quite another. Banks will increasingly try to police and enforce their own code of practice. The collective reputation must be preserved and if they do not do it themselves, government will do it for them. The banks invented the regulators, it wasn't the other way around. The banks keep the regulators employed.

For every positive action from banks there does seem to be an equal and opposite reaction from government, in some shape or form. We'd rather see wholly unequal and opposite reactions to consumer rip-offs. We all want and, indeed, need and must believe in a good regulatory regime. A real problem is knee-jerk and populist reactions from government and their regulators based on emotion rather than thought. There's not much can be done about that, we suppose. Still, banks and the many authentic non-bank lenders could help their reputations by better explaining some of their decisions.

9.2.4   Investors, and mergers and acquisitions

Investors are looking for high returns and to maximise shareholder value, but they do understand and listen. M&A opportunities to merge two independent and costly sets of operations and remove duplicated costs provide quick and significant performance improvements. Investors in the buying banks, and especially the selling banks, can benefit greatly. Investors will continue to encourage M&A activity, but typically overestimate the capabilities of management to execute the acquisition properly. Most management teams could not execute a major acquisition (there is no such thing as a merger of equals) and experience in the US with such banks as Bank of America and Wachovia shows that buying, stripping down and integrating banks rapidly is a core competence, and difficult to acquire except through practice over a long period of time. Only RBSG in the UK, with its acquisition of NatWest, and to a lesser extent HSBC, have demonstrated this on a large scale this side of the Atlantic. It simply has to be a ruthless process. The outlook is for a number of botched acquisitions at the second level, with the major players prevented from major domestic plays by competition laws. You don't get too many opportunities to practice mergers.

Internal UK M&A has already reached its finale, insofar as the market is already concentrated and we are running out of banks. More generally, there will be an increasing number of cross-border acquisitions, either by global or major regional players. Typically, these are not operational mergers, just a change of ownership. Except for the most experienced banking consolidators, an operational merger will tend to fail because of cultural differences and the difficulty in achieving the cost savings necessary to make the transaction fly financially. The more likely bank plays are US ⇨ UK (Bank of America or Citicorp/Barclays), UK ⇨ EU (Barclays/Allied Irish Banks), EU ⇨ UK (ABN Amro/Lloyds TSB) and UK ⇨ EU/International (Barclays to ABN Amro/Standard Chartered). There will be visionary pan-European acquisitions, which may well be driven by a core insurance company shareholder holding the purse strings and with deep pockets (e.g. Allianz, ING, and Generali). These, in particular, may end in tears through the combination of an inability to create an integrated management team or good business proposition, or to realise the required cost savings. Pure insurance companies seem not to understand banking; their track record here is dismal.

The danger in all this for the big players is that whilst they are wrestling with cultural differences and improving their own organisations, the field will be left to fleet of foot medium-sized players, and direct banks, and monolines and multilines having a ball at their expense. Such a development will not be lost on investors who could become disenchanted with the upwards potential of the large UK-oriented banks, and either walk or take remedial action. HSBC for certain, RBSG with its US acquisitions, and Barclays with its penchant for international expansion seem to be focusing outside the UK. A European bank coming into the UK will need to have more interesting things to say than 'me too' if it is to succeed in value creation, and that is a concern behind the BSCH/Abbey National purchase. The fact is that all but the largest banks could be either predator or prey, or both.

An associated thought is that estimates of bank values based on 'the sum of the parts' valuation shows retail banking to be a star attraction within a grouping of the related but disparate banking businesses. Not unusually, the performance of each business fluctuates depending on external factors. We therefore see a scenario of 'breaking up the bank' with investor pressure to break banks down into independently visible and valued companies, thereby making available the opportunity for pure plays in specific businesses such as retail and corporate/investment banking, and major monolines such as cards and mortgages. It is a fact that banks are conglomerate businesses, being in a number of lines that are often complementary – the performance of one line goes up as another one goes down. That portfolio effect is good, for those who want it. But when fund managers build their portfolios, some may well prefer pure investment plays on, say, retail, international, capital markets and certain monolines.

Typically, operating service businesses and investment management with high levels of loyal and repeat income carry the highest ratings, closely followed by retail banking. Investment/corporate banking, with a higher reliance on less reliable one-off trading income and transaction fees, typically carry a lower valuation.

Our prediction is that retail banking will be perceived to be the growth opportunity, whilst corporate will be viewed as a more annuity type legacy business. There will be growing divergence between the needs of retail and corporate banking for the basic accounting systems and operational infrastructure. Retail equals high volume/low value, flexible, single currency, mass customisation, supporting simple products. Corporate equals higher value/lower volume, bespoke, multicurrency, in support of complex products. Until now, banks have tended to paper over these cracks and have tried to force-fit a single solution out of their retail accounting systems, but in the large universal banks, the strains are showing.

The need for different operational support infrastructures will accentuate the trend towards distinct banking businesses, and therefore perhaps the need to break up the bank into individual financial entities. The growing opportunities to outsource will also reinforce this trend. Many of the more obvious, non-core activities have already gone; premises management, payroll, stationery, security, catering, travel and transport and the like. But going beyond this, there are more challenging questions as to whether retail banks need to run their own cheque clearing, urgent and non-urgent payments, data centres, call centres, card processing, bullion, cheque books, statements and much more. These are all commodity activities with no competitive advantage beyond cost, and they can be outsourced to best-of-breed providers. A big issue going forward will be what should be the residual core of the business beyond the sine qua non ultras of brand, capital management, treasury, investor relations, market management, products, risk management, the customer experience and customer contact. Is that not enough? A decision to diverge, encouraged by specialisation, business focus, and simplicity, contrasts with a decision to converge, enabled by technology and 'open' systems, shared services and perceived efficiency. These decisions will be debated passionately over the next year or so. It's not a question of right or wrong. There will be a different answer for every bank, each of which will need to draw numerous lines in the sand on such issues.

As part of this general slimming down, banks will need to get smarter at capital management in particular. This will include putting in more sophisticated risk management systems so that they can benefit from dispensations arising from the new capital adequacy rules effective in 2006 (Basel II), securitisation and other related capital market techniques. This will probably be quite straightforward for retail banks and for the market leaders, who are heavily technology based.

Generally, as part of their market and investor management, banks will need to be much cannier at market management. Short-term maximisation of ROE might no longer be the absolute aim. As the need to invest in a new operational business model gains momentum, we foresee a trend where retail banks will need to target investor returns to satisfy investor expectations, but where premium returns are ploughed back into building the new operational model, rather than being returned automatically to investors. This is easy to say, and will depend heavily on the ability of banks to make a clear case for their investment programmes and for a greater maturity from the investor and bank analyst community in constructively analysing and understanding those cases.

All of which takes us neatly into...

9.2.5 Leadership

The key differentiator between banks in terms of market performance is the quality of the leadership, individuals and teams, over a period of years. Leadership teams have to be joined up emotionally as well as in their mission. That is, they need an ability to pick the right things to be doing, rather than just doing things right, which in such a highly structured and disciplined industry as banking is the reverse of the past, where doing it right was more important than what you were doing – which was simply to do what every other bank was doing. The PIMS evidence earlier shows that doing the right thing explains 80 % of the performance difference between companies. Leadership is difficult to define, but if we look at the successes, we see characteristics of confidence, simplicity and speed in all cases. There is no arrogance, no resting on past successes or the brand in itself. Surprisingly, there is no strong cult of the personality. Leadership is expressed in a set of professional values set by example. Banks are so complicated and have so many interaction points that leadership is more about deciding what to play and where and when, and conducting the orchestra, rather than teaching the players how to play their instruments. Casey Stengal, a legendary US baseball manager, said that the key to being a good manager was keeping the people who hated him from meeting those who were still undecided.

Our prediction is that attracting or retaining a winning leadership team will become the single most important concern of investors and, by extension, banks' boards. Rewards attached to proven leadership will rocket in the UK. Big banks pay the biggest money; the proven leaders get to go to the races. It is no surprise that these leaders often served time in smaller banks. That's how you can get wide and deep experience fast.

The typical banking career path to the top, based on corporate credit and business development, will change. Hard-nosed accountants are in today. Marketing toughs will be in tomorrow, and then at some point in time, when the banking business cycle changes again, the accountants will be back on top again.

Banks will less and less provide, or expect, lifetime careers from their high flying staff. Staff will move between organisations in financial services and there will be recruitment from other industries, particularly retailing and IT – retail banking in large measure sells products and provides mass data processing and information services for retail customers. It just happens to be in the financial services sector of the economy. Inevitably, banks will move away from their roots, whether commercial banking or mutual, and a challenge will be to retain the best of the old culture – trust, integrity, discipline, reliability – whilst embracing the core business disciplines of modern retailing and information technology.

But can structures and organisations remain much as they are? What if banks become so large and so complex that management of the bank becomes too much for monolith traditional structures and organisations, as it will? This will lead to an increasing degree of separation of the businesses and less reliance on vertical integration and shared cost models, except for big bore factory-style data and transaction processing such as current accounts, cheque clearing, payments and mortgage processing. This trend is exacerbated by the reducing economies of scale available with new generation technology and a willingness by banks to cooperate with each other, supported by technology and venture capital partners on reducing the costs of non-competitive overheads. Such changes would suit some investor preferences, as touched on above. Banks increasingly will be able to have their cake and eat it – they will be able to develop their structures and operational infrastructure to achieve increasingly decentralised business autonomy, whilst retaining industry standard efficiency, tight corporate governance and financial and risk controls. Are staff following their leaders out of a shared belief and commitment, or simply out of curiosity, or because it's their job?

9.2.6   The balance of art, science and engineering

We see the balance between art and the historically dominant, but increasingly old hat and mechanistic, engineering being inverted. The art of meeting customer needs profitably will become dominant again, now that underlying business processes are being made hugely more efficient through engineering improvements. Most importantly, the staff will be needed, and able, to provide customer solutions, and this will be fee earning. There will be a noticeable growth in the art-associated activities of marketing and human resources. If there were two departments with little influence just a few years ago, marketing and HR must have been them. As for the science, the economics department or its equivalent won't suffer either, given its importance in predicting increasingly changeable economic and demographic trends. The science of finance will progress into new areas. By contrast, operations and IT will suffer. A bank can buy much of what its operations and IT departments does from various sources, but it cannot buy what its marketing and HR do. These, together with the Chairman, CEO and the leadership team, will explicitly become much more the guardians of a bank's soul.

9.2.7   Products, services, solutions

We see no need for banks to run the risk of dramatic change that would worry customers, so we see everything continuing in the way that products are packaged, sold and supported. But in parallel, we see the emergence of solutions, which may be no more than a prepackaging of a number of products along lifestyle or life stage needs, and along segment, subsegment and sub-subsegments of customers. In effect, the customer buys multiple products with a single application, and the high level of integration dramatically reduces forms and overheads with certain new product features providing the glue. Most importantly, the solution is just that, a total solution to their banking needs, priced competitively and supported by skilled staff.

Savings products will be enhanced through automated sweeping to highest yielding savings products, regardless of provider. There will be a major move towards stakeholder products (higher yields, lower commission, few conditions/less small print), driven by the low-cost innovators.

The imaginative use of derivatives and capital markets will drive the creation of more sophisticated credit products, and here we see increasingly expert product developers forging partnerships with investment banking providers of structured capital market-based products. For example, housing products that enable people to acquire better housing through equity sharing, or acquire access to a car with all the costs and risks, such as insurance and maintenance, bundled into a monthly payment, thus taking the various motor finance options to a higher level.

We see one big casualty – the current account, as we know it. For most banks, the current account is a disaster. In a moment of weakness and leading a collective industry death wish, the old Midland Bank introduced free banking for the man in the street. This gave a momentary competitive advantage and kind of worked when interest rates were high. But it is now a millstone around banks' necks. There is no free-if-in-credit banking for small businesses or medium-sized companies. Tacitly, the banks drew a line in the sand and resolved never to make the same mistake again. They are probably itching to charge for consumer transactions – but by stealth, as a full frontal attack would put them in the dog house.

So what will the consequences be? For consumers, expect to see a new breed of transactional account. There will be no high set-up and maintenance cost standing orders, cheques do not figure (except where issued centrally and for a charge). You can (already) credit any UK current account from any other using the Internet via BACS, but expect this to become same day, rather than three day, at some time in the future as the technology is upgraded and under the weight of government and consumer pressure. Also, to the extent that cheque clearing remains, expect this to become image based with a clearing cycle as low as one day. Cards, credit transfers and direct debits will be the only payment mechanisms. There will be a simplified interest rate payable on credit balances, all transactions and statements will be via the Internet and processed automatically – straight through processing, untouched by human hands. Branches as we know them will no longer undertake basic transactions and answer basic queries; there will be no need, as transactions will be straight through and error free and the basic products delivered simply, obviating the need for requests for information. Branches will now be there to advise people on the real things that matter, such as how to get that house or car that they want but they don't see how they can afford, rather than why the cheque they have just issued against uncleared effects has bounced.

For small businesses, expect to see the revenge of the nerds. For far too long, small and medium-sized business has been subject to extensive transaction charging and rates on deposit balances significantly inferior to those paid to private individuals. Why have they put up with it? There are a number of reasons, including the previously weaker competition than in the consumer market. That line in the sand mentioned above has been part of this, but an important factor for many has been access to credit. The unwritten compact has been 'give me your transactional business and pay our charges, and when you need credit we'll see you all right.' But in an increasingly more open, competitive and transparent world, there is the opportunity for some mould breaking. This is only for the brave and careful – small business credit is not the easiest part of a bank's business. But it is a substantial business in its own right.

Corporate banking capabilities and wealth banking services will continue to infiltrate the consumer market. Many of the solutions that consumers need are already available elsewhere in banks. So netting and offsetting of funds and a complete portfolio of services, such as taxation and pension management, will become available and find their way.

9.2.8 Staff, costs, customers, marketing

We'll take these in reverse order. Marketing is identifying customer needs and aligning resources to meet those needs profitably. This means that, increasingly, product development and customer relationship management activities, as well as the tactical marketing communications (advertising to us) to which many marketing departments have been reduced, will be centred on the marketing function. This is a key function, and our prediction is the emergence of a powerful and pivotal marketing function that will look strangely like those in retailers and FMCG (fast moving consumer goods), from which banks will no doubt recruit. Marketing will not be so much a department as a virtual business function across the bank – the brain and nerve centre of the organisation, typically reporting to the CEO and responsible for customer propositions and product design, procurement, pricing and profitability.

Led by marketing, we see a clearout of the causes of many of the costs. We look to a stretch target of reducing costs by 50 %, which gives a cost/income ratio in the region of 20–30 % from the current average of 40 %. Some are there already, primarily because of their intense focus on their served markets. The culprit for the others is their own processes and procedures, which are disliked by staff and customers alike.

Under these predictions, the skills alignment of staff to customers is significantly changed. Over a period of five or more years this should not be too traumatic, as increasing numbers of operational staff are provided by agencies or treat a job at a bank as a short-term placement, not a long-term career. But whether staff work in branches, operations, IT, marketing or elsewhere, this realignment of skills will still be a major challenge.

With this we will see a major commitment to staff learning, sponsored by the banks in a number of ways. This learning will be at a far higher level than the training that bank employees receive today. Bank employees themselves are going to be helped to move upmarket in their knowledge. Staff will be challenged in a positive, creative, structured and rewarding way.

9.2.9 Information technology and the real dot.com revolution in banking

There have been many predictions that the days of branch banking are numbered, with Internet access curing all the ills of banking and acting as the nemesis of bank branches. So why are branches still flourishing and why do most of the population use cash, go to branches and not use the Internet? The answer is that most Internet banking products are pretty dire – there is mostly no incentive to buy an Internet product and a combination of clunky bank access features and uncertainty makes the whole experience pretty frustrating.

We know that the Internet is the thing, but there were 'only' 200 million Internet purchases of all goods, most of them books and CDs, in 2003 (APACS figures), so it's not quite here yet – it will storm in though, quite soon.

So what's changing to support our prediction that the real dot.com revolution is just starting and will transform retail banking? First, the technology for Internet delivery of financial services is now well established and security issues are, by and large, sorted. Confidence levels generally are firming.

Secondly, the take up of domestic PCs and broadband is now growing fast, and consumers are quickly becoming used to being able to get information and transact over the Internet – who ever goes to a travel agent to buy an air ticket now when they can go to increasingly user friendly and informative websites? The same will happen to banking, when banks smarten up, which is not intrinsically difficult. So, why should anyone ever go near their branch when they have Internet banking plus an ATM network if they need cash or information on the move?

Thirdly, banks will increasingly put solutions and services onto the Internet that people want to buy – not just the same old boring current and deposit account balance and transaction reporting.

Our prediction is that as Internet banking take-up increases, branches will more and more be there to service a diminishing number of late adopters and an increasing number of customers seeking valuable financial (not just transactional) advice to enable them to run their lives better. The staff giving this advice will be a new breed of banker: mature, experienced in life changing events and with good advisory skills. A paradox at the moment is that a bank cashier in the West End of London is probably one of the least paid, least valued, least permanent employees of a bank. Many are from staff agencies. Yet that same person is serving well over a hundred of the bank's most affluent customers each day. Expect this to change as the nature of the branch purpose changes, with much more professionally trained (and higher paid) people in front of customers.

For the banks, migration to a different branch footprint will be critical, time consuming and costly. This is not the paint job that they have in process at the moment.

Most financial services providers (banks, building societies, insurance companies and major IFAs) will want a portal through which to do more business. Only a few will succeed and there will be major portal wars to gain customers. Casualties will be high and only a few mainstream portals will survive – up to a dozen or so banks and perhaps a few of the largest insurance companies, but even these numbers will diminish. IFAs in particular, will feel the squeeze.

As part of the deal to attract customers to their particular portal, portal providers will have to aggregate financial information from other providers (current and deposit accounts, cards, mortgages, personal loans, ISAs, investments, pensions) with real time valuations and the ability to switch at will between different types of savings or investment products. This departure will generate much heat.

As we look back in ten years' time, we will be amazed at the primitive nature of the Internet as it was in 2004. The basic protocols of question/answer and instruct/execute, which is the way we pick and poke at it today, will have been complemented, if not replaced, by volunteered, sensible and appropriate information, and there will be far more automation and resolution of needs. The primordial soup of technologies and gadgets that constitute version 1.0 of the Internet will become version 2.0, where customer needs can be anticipated to a large degree and delivered through bespoke e-mail prompts available at home, work or through mobile devices.

9.2.10   IT application software architectures

The banks' IT strategies will be migrated to more logical and simple structures. This will see the separation of function – channels, customer, accounts and internal functions for instance. This will be followed by the introduction of discrete modules such as pricing, fees, credit management and many other functions placed logically into the architecture. The use of standard reusable business objects will become the norm across the board. The result will be an IT capability that supports a 'plug-and-play' approach to systems development and maintenance. Most importantly, the huge burden of maintaining the complex legacy systems will be greatly reduced, thus freeing up IT resources to work on more business-directed initiatives.

A growing competitive issue will be that new generation technology is increasingly negating the laws of economies of scale, except for big bore processing such as payments and account data processing. Small is beautiful and can be as inexpensive as big, particularly when combined with outsourcing of the 'big' factory processes. Smaller scale players who manage to this model will have the ability to match the big banks in terms of both products and costs, if they wish.

Far from heralding the demise of IT in banks, we think that this will be the making of it. The number of direct IT staff will be reduced over time and not without pain – perhaps by 50%. But the remaining 50% will nearly all be working on go-forwards projects in direct support of business requirements. The contribution from IT will soar as a result. We regret moves to outsource IT development. While it may make sense to outsource boring, low value-added functions such as testing and maintenance, particularly of legacy systems, to a lower cost, like-for-like service, this cannot be the case for go-forwards development.

In the short term, we see the need for additional staff to support this transition. Whilst IT banking application vendors of all hues gnash their teeth at the size of the bank IT groups, until the IT vendors themselves get their acts straight and provide the channel, customer, account and function components, then their actions will only delay the architectural transition that is a core need.

IT vendors providing staff to work on these components and their integration will be in high demand.

IT vendors with the full suite of components that can be selectively used by banks will have a good time. Legacy vendors who are slow to respond will have a torrid time, especially with the larger banks. IT equipment itself will continue into a commodity business, banks will be more demanding, competition will be even more brutal and margins will be ridiculously small. Nothing that might happen here would surprise us. Ultimately, the desire is to fully support full and flexible interoperability across the full range of chosen and required activities – consumer, corporate, risk and capital markets – indeed, to have systems that really are 'open'.

9.2.11 Treasury and securitisation

Treasury is the glue binding together liquidity management, asset/liability management, capital requirements and risk management. It has an increasingly important job to do. At one end of the spectrum it manages balance sheets and liquidity, and does good things to enhance the yield on assets and minimise the cost of liabilities, mostly through the clever and intelligent use of derivatives. At the other end of the spectrum, treasury can help restructure the balance sheet and provide new products.

In retail, the greater punching power of good products and their acceptance by the market could create a demand for more capital than the bank has at its disposal, which is the US experience, where securitisation of assets has helped significantly. The idea behind securitisation is that if a bank has, say, £1 billion of mortgages, it requires some £40 million in capital to support those mortgages, as a regulatory requirement. Now, £1 billion in mortgages may sound a lot, but it's only 10 000 houses at £100 000 each as an example, and only one eight hundredth by value of all outstanding mortgages. Ten thousand homes is about 0.4 % of all UK housing purchases in a year. There are investors out there, such as pension funds and fund managers, who would like to buy the revenue stream from £1 billion of mortgages – these can be attractive fixed income assets yielding dependable low-risk returns superior to, say, most investment grade corporate bonds. So, they buy the rights to the mortgages for £1 billion minus a bit, the bank frees up its capital and can now go and sell another £1 billion of mortgages. Meanwhile, it made fees on the mortgage origination and it continues to collect fees for processing the mortgages. Mortgages are not the only products that can be securitised – personal loans, car loans and credit card receivables are equally eligible, as are certain classes of loans to companies. In theory, virtually any revenue stream can be securitised.

The whole point is that the bank can do what it does, and generate more revenue from its fixed cost distribution base. This enables it to develop a larger footprint than its capital would permit. Retailers hate to have capital tied up in stock, but that is the equivalent of what banks have always done – tie up all their capital in loans inventories. Securitisation is an important feature of US banks' balance sheet management, but so far this has not caught on in a big way this side of the Atlantic. It will – as the medium players with smaller capital bases successfully take on the larger players at their own game – gain efficiencies in most things that matter, including capital management. Banks will increasingly look to securitisation to accommodate new business rather than incurring the high cost of new capital. Northern Rock is a good example of securitisation in action. This is a totally safe piece of financial engineering, and has no impact whatsoever on the customer – their contract is with the bank, and stays with it.

Equally, as we have mentioned, treasury can help create new products through the creative use of derivatives, where the sky is the limit in terms of innovation, but equally the risks are not insignificant. That is, the greater the creativity, the greater the risks and the potential, which is a basic law of finance.

We have two predictions here. First, that we shall see creative products emerge, particularly in savings and home and motor finance. Secondly, that there will be a significant derivatives meltdown somewhere (perhaps credit derivatives, a somewhat arcane but nevertheless growing part of this sector). Not the Armageddon of some observers, but nevertheless one or more substantial financial institutions will bear some major and embarrassing losses. For bank management the aim should be to avoid major derivative plays which they do not understand – if they do not understand what is proposed, they should either not proceed, or they should get technically up to speed so that they do understand. Under no circumstances should they rely on the pointy head treasury maths masters and PhDs telling them that it works and that the black box computer model proves this – 'trust me'. Most banking disasters have been caused by generalist bankers deferring to specialists without understanding the implications of what they were going along with.

9.2.12   Payments solutions

With BACS and card systems, ATMs and their services to businesses, the banks control the core retail payments systems in the UK. That is not going to change – ever, they hope. The fees collected for the usage of payments systems directly or indirectly account for the majority of the banks' fee income, which itself is some 40 % of their total revenue. Indeed, the ability to make payments is all that separates banks from non-bank competitors, who have access to the systems for a fee.

Although technology is knocking at the door and theoretically permits non-bank providers to disintermediate virtually all of the banks' clunky settlement systems, banks are not about to cede their control over making payments, nor would the regulators permit a payments free for all.

Nevertheless, as with the Internet, technology will put pressure on the banks. In our view, there is looming competition from technology and telecommunications companies for segments of the payments market, particularly based on new payment switching or mobile phone technology. Mobile phones present particular opportunities and there has been a long running saga with many banks, network operators and others seeking the right business models to get mobile payments into the mainstream. To this point there has been a series of failures with a few modest successes. Worldwide, banks and networks in a variety of competitive and complementary models have tried a hundred or more initiatives. Cost and customer ownership are two non-trivial problems.

In the same way as expectations for the Internet exceeded the reality, mobile payments have disappointed. Still, the Internet impact, whilst lower than expectations, has been hugely important. We are certain that a workable business plan or two for mobile payments lurks out there somewhere, waiting to be found and implemented. The obvious initial gaps for such a mechanism to fill are for unbanked consumers and for all consumers buying low-priced goods or making low-value payments that are unprofitable using existing card systems. Reverse billing, where such payments are added to customers' phone bills, is expensive and a better way will emerge.

9.2.13   Disruptors

If planned changes give the problems that they do, the disruptors buffeting banks are far worse to accommodate. These stem particularly from governments and a number of regulatory agencies, particularly the FSA and the central banking agencies such as the BIS. They come from taxation and accountancy sources, as well as lawyers. The growth in the effort required to handle these disruptors is frightening. These disruptors often arrive with a deadline and an inadequate and often poorly thought out definition of the requirements. Especially with government inspired disruptors, the knock-on effect for customers and staff is high. And a few years later they change it all. Many of these disruptors are not competitively neutral either.

The risk is that the burden of handling these disruptors goes through the roof. The large banks are hardest hit. The Y2K experience, which was an unavoidable disruptor, is a good example. A seemingly simple requirement led to enormous amounts of effort with absolutely nothing to show for it. We could blame it on the Romans for the calendar, but in fact it was all an IT problem, and there are a lot more problems stored up where that problem came from. At what point will the burdens of disruptors become threatening? Soon. The 'simple' change is becoming a memory, and the systems are going to need to be able to handle increased numbers and severity of disruptions. To those banks that have old and brittle systems, forward progress is going to be hard to achieve, thus giving a clear operational advantage to superior, flexible systems.

9.3   MEETING CUSTOMER NEEDS AT THE LOWEST COST

The great majority of requirements in the retail market, satisfying more than 95 % of the market, can be accomplished far more simply and efficiently than at present. Figure 9.2 gives a picture of what is needed, as one suggestion. The reason we have

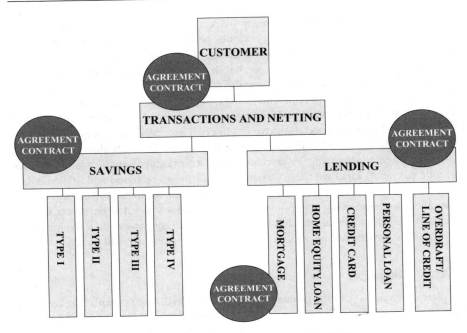

Figure 9.2 One suggestion of what is needed

shown it this way is because every component and practice shown is actually in use today in established banks. This is therefore just a mechanism to demonstrate what could be done if the customer proposition is joined up from the outset. Let us assume that a new customer wishes to start a relationship with a bank.

The customer signs a 'lifetime' agreement with the bank, giving their required personal details. The bank establishes the transaction account (much like a current account), with a debit card, direct debits and whatever else the bank chooses to support. It probably would not choose to support standing orders, at least not as we know them today. Neither do we need cheques when we can use the Internet to transfer funds to any UK bank account already.

At the same time, the customer can enter a 'lifetime' savings contract, which will enable them to open, manage and close any number of savings accounts. Because of legal requirements there will be explicit references to different types of account – for instance, tax treatments and government enforced practices, pensions, reporting, the investment and risk appetite of the customer, etc.

They can enter a 'lifetime' lending agreement to cover various loan types. Mortgages will require a separate, independent agreement, although this could also be a 'lifetime' agreement.

After that, the customer can open whatever bank accounts they need with no paperwork at all. The administrative burden is reduced for the bank, and there has been no inconvenience for the customer. One bank has reduced the number of customer application forms from over one hundred down to eight on this basis.

The transaction account does not support cheques. Under 30s write few cheques today. A customer needing a cheque can request a banker's draft made payable to the beneficiary at a branch or over the Internet, which can be fulfilled centrally and sent directly to the customer or beneficiary. Bill payment mechanisms are far preferable, particularly if they are of the new Internet bill presentment and payment type, where service providers such as utilities present bills over the Internet and all the customer has to do is click on a 'Pay' icon for their bank to pay the bill.

The netting capability allows funds to be shuffled to minimise the cost and maximise the return to the customer. Risk can be, but does not have to be, handled by netting off loans and deposits. That is, depending on the credit card balance being secured by savings, the interest rate on credit cards would be as for a secured loan, not an unsecured loan.

It's all a simple concept and all parts of this model are already in use in some banks.

The model is totally automated – in today's jargon this is straight through processing (STP). Terms and conditions are simple, and there are few options. Because of the low operating costs, the rates can be highly competitive. Because of this, when a new account is needed, it is easier for the customer to pick up a phone or open it through the Internet rather than shop around, because the rates will be amongst the best, and it requires little effort on their part to open an account. The only paperwork required is governed by the requirements of the regulators. Such forms are available over the Internet or by mail.

The point is, it can be done. Every single component exists, as do the IT systems.

In this scenario, the cross-sell problem is replaced with cross-buy opportunities, the customer relationship is established up front, and is reciprocal, in that the customer directly benefits from the relationship, most likely because of pricing and T&C flexibility.

The offsetting of surplus funds with deficit funds is automatic, not just a way of selling mortgages. A mortgage is not even necessary to benefit from offsetting.

So, we can meet customer needs with a low operating expense base. Procedures such as credit control, loan authorisations, and so on all remain in place, but with high levels of automation, where the question will be not 'can we authorise this loan?' but rather 'is there a reason why this loan cannot be granted?' Except for a minority who require protection from themselves, or are fraudsters, the vast majority of bank customers are responsible people who manage their finances well and invariably repay, except for some kind of unforeseen circumstance.

With some ingenuity, there are no reasons not to include insurance investment management products in the same model.

Importantly, bank staff are relieved of the process and procedure burdens, and can concentrate on helping customers achieve solutions to their needs. Basically, everything that the bank has to offer has already been sold to the customer; the issue is how they can use the capabilities to form the solutions that they require. The staff are therefore clearly adding value. Their focus is not on selling products, but rather on helping customers cocreate financial solutions for their lives, lifestyles and events. At its extreme, we can imagine the bank having literature not about this or that product, but rather aimed at customer needs profiles. That is, a brochure for students, young adults, the upwardly mobile, the sideways mobile, those near retirement, the retired, the single parent, the this, the that and the other types of profile, where their personal financial solution can be cocreated from the available components. This would be a radical change in many ways, but pivots around the ability of staff to add value for the customer. Banks do have juvenile questionnaires to 'help' customers 'work out what they can afford', but at best they are naïve.

9.4 RESEARCH AND DEVELOPMENT

R&D in banks will become a recognised function, but not in the sense of an isolated departmental role. Bank products and services are the result of complex interactions between customers and many parts of the bank, particularly treasury and credit, but also include staff, operations, IT and everything else. We see R&D fitting into a new, pervasive marketing function.

The cross-disciplines needed cover science, engineering and art, and these will need to be coupled with the business itself.

9.5 WINNERS AND LOSERS

The biggest winner in all this will be the consumers, who increasingly will be able to access their banks from home or work or on the move, choose simple best-of-breed stakeholder products, have access to a comprehensive real time statement of their aggregate financial position, and be able to consult their very own bank manager, in the flesh. If his traditional supplier is moving too slowly in providing this, there will be providers that will – and the regulators will hopefully ensure that there are no barriers to switching. Consumers will be able to get solutions to their needs. And the rates and the terms and conditions will be uniformly good. There will be fees attached to some of the services, but the customers will value them and pay the appropriate price. Relationship management will take root, leading to pricing improvements for customers and risk improvements for banks.

Investors in retail banking are aware that relatively small changes in a number of variables can have a major impact on bank performance, and hence the value of their investment and its performance in both dividend and market value terms. Banks that offer what customers will see as better banking will have a more sustainable level of performance, and given the certainty of demand for banking products and services, these banks will outperform their competitors. Therefore, investors in 'better' banks will enjoy both higher and more sustainable returns.

The challenge for the monolines will be that the relationship with their customers is purely transactional, unless they broaden out their product line, when they become one of a crowd. If they wish to break outside of their boxes they will want to avoid becoming comprehensive banks, but continue to select business lines for which they can develop a strong business case that is largely self-standing. We would expect ING Direct and others to move into second or third products. This still gives them the monoline advantages because they become, in effect, three monolines. The business model doesn't change. ING Direct doesn't do face-to-face or encourage ear-to-ear customer service and this is integral to its business plan and therefore to its customer proposition.

Direct banks could have a ball, but their problem will be broadening out their product range sufficiently and developing a softer (even if only cyber) side to what is mostly a transactional relationship. The strength of the direct model is the Internet channel, which is low cost. But this is now ubiquitous and an inadequate competitive differentiator. Most banks support direct Internet access, for it brings the ability to increase the bank's footprint beyond the geographic limitations of its own branch network. Alliance & Leicester is a good example of a bank that is using the Internet as a normal access channel but with differentiated benefits to customers.

Supermarkets are credible providers. Their strategies position them as retailers of financial products from third party providers of banking and insurance products. So far, the retailers have produced largely me-too products sourced from traditional banks and insurers. However, their selection of what products to offer has been successful. As well as savings and loan accounts, they have particularly attracted insurance business in cars, homes, pets and simple life insurance. Potentially, they are big winners, as are their partner banks.

Those medium-sized banks and building societies that are fleet of foot, in touch with their customers and able to reconfigure rapidly, should be big winners too. But the pressures on management will be immense.

Monolines are set to win. The supermarkets are set to win. Building societies are set to win. Responsive banks are set to win.

Retail banking is not a zero-sum game. Over and above the growth that comes from increased affluence and economic growth in general, the important growth will be from customers who make more use of the banks. All banks will grow, so winning and losing is more about the rates of growth, one bank to another, not about customer defections themselves. We do not anticipate major defections, but we do see that different consumer decisions will be made as life events occur, because that's when people shop seriously for banking products and services. The net effect of this is that as these life events occur, and our guess is that it is about five million times each year in the UK, then a large proportion of those five million accounts will be opened in 'better' banks.

Large banks may become too large for their investors to realise shareholder value fully, for customers to benefit from improved value and products/solutions, and for the bank leadership to manage effectively. They may well be the losers, but only in the sense that their retail banking business will not grow in size or performance as fast as it otherwise might, or as fast as the market grows.

Overall, our prediction is that the biggest losers, in only a relative sense though, will be the larger, more complex banks, weighed down by the complexity of their organisation and products, a major fixed branch network, a high fixed cost base and the need to square the circle of meeting market expectations with the cost of reconfiguring their overhead structure. Any succumbing to the temptation of regional consolidation will take their eyes off the ball. Only RBSG and HSBC have proven that they can do big acquisitions, and they are probably too canny to go into Europe in a big way. The retail banking businesses within the other large banks will struggle and will go through a torrid time, making them vulnerable to acquisition or a break-up of some kind.

The so-called global banks like Bank of America, Citicorp and HSBC may well struggle in individual markets, but they have the power and armour to ride through the difficulties. They, together with the medium-sized banks, are the most likely to pick up the action, and reconfigure themselves to the new model. The truth is that, except in their home markets, the UK representations of these global banks (except HSBC) are mid-sized banks themselves. The fact that they have a certain parentage is a bonus, especially in corporate banking terms, and perhaps a little in consumer image. But importantly, they can draw on deep pools of management and technical talent and, together with the ability to see across markets and apply industry best practice, they are well placed to resolve local difficulties.

So, the largest banks will expand outside of their home territories, because it is there that they have the best opportunities. The corollary is that outside banks will compete in the UK on the same basis, simply because the large established banks in a country have all the mobility problems, and their public has got as much as it needs of what the bank sells.

9.6   A LOOK OVER THE HORIZON – SOME BRAVER PREDICTIONS

The second part of this book has been all about the influences affecting retail banking and the kind of step changes that we will see over the coming years as a result. But it still only adds up to a business-as-usual scenario with a gradual, rather than step, change.

We do not believe that this round of change will stop there – the pace will accelerate. We expect that the current round will take place over the coming five to ten years. Our final look forward is beyond this in believability, but these are tentative timeframes, and these next predictions could well happen within the same timeframe. Once change takes a grip it tends to happen much faster than people predict.

Change in financial services can be glacial or explosive, so, faites vos jeux – here are some predictions, which may or may not happen. But despite this caveat, the roots of these changes already exist within the retail banking industry.

9.6.1   Customers – their trust, confidence and respect

Banks must be trusted, and confidence in them is a sine qua non – you would think. Trust and confidence cannot be bought – they are earned. The level of trust held by people in their banks has diminished in recent years as banks have become more commercial in the eyes of their customers, and in fact. The drive to create revenue in the last few years, based on the self-interest of the banks' goals, has really messed with the foundations of trust in banks. This trust and confidence was created over a hundred years of integrity, reliability, honesty and predictability. Banks had a responsibility that was honoured, that's what it was.

Responsible banks will make enormous efforts to recreate the trust so that their customers in turn will entrust them with their life events. Fortunately, the investment management and insurance industries failed to establish comparable trust when they had the chance, so bank trust is still the stronger of the three.

Establishing, growing and retaining trust, confidence and respect will require bank staff to change massively. Having been deprofessionalised over a number of years, banking will be reprofessionalised, with promotion for customer-facing staff increasingly dependent on graduating through demanding professional training, enabling staff to advise their customers on complex personal issues. Bank universities and distance learning will be the norms. Salaries will rise in line with achievement. The numbers of staff will decline greatly as a result of the system/process/product/solution improvements, but those reductions will come from cashiers, and middle and back office staff. Transacting will become less and less necessary or desirable for customers, and simplicity will obviate the need for support.

Clerical jobs will disappear, as basic operations become redundant, fully automated and/or outsourced.

9.6.2   Regulation

Banking goes through regulatory cycles – deregulation in the 1980s and reregulation during the 1990s and currently. We believe that the regulatory tide will turn again, with a major shift back to industry self-regulation, particularly as the industry perceives that there is a clear competitive advantage in compliance, and in trust and fairness to customers. The industry will give its industry bodies real teeth to name and shame, and banks will be able to consult expert panels rapidly to ensure that new products meet industry standards for fairness to customers and pre-empt mis-selling risk. The reactive nature of regulation, allowing the horse to bolt first and then trying to get it back, is the problem. It seems logical that before a truly new product or service is put to the consumer market it should be examined to ensure that it conforms to some regulatory level. That could be an industry or government standard and would give confidence to both the banks and their customers.

9.6.3   Customers

Choice is generally good for consumers. Hurdles, laws, penalties, changed laws, taxation consequences, fine print and misunderstood risks are not. All these are increasing.

The state is becoming less interventionist (they say) and more interventionist (in fact). As the government (supposedly) allows individuals greater choice in the management of key elements in their lives, customers will want and need advice and financial solutions from trusted providers in respect of key life events. They will require trustworthy solutions from experienced providers whose advice can be relied upon. Sophisticated financial engineering will enable the creation of a new wave of life event products incorporating financing, investment, actuarial risk and a new generation of derivatives.

The plunge in consumer savings of recent years, the rapid rise in taxes of all sorts, and the government predation over all funds will drive customers to seek help. Already it is estimated that one million people have debts that they cannot service, and a further five million are struggling. How will that play out?

There will be a consumer flight towards trusted banks. Far from disintermediation into the securities and insurance industries, the opposite will be true. For instance, trusted banks could easily invent insurance products that actually provide consumers with what they want to achieve in terms of insurance and protection needs. You could argue that the investment management and insurance sectors have had their go at retail banking and both came up quite short.

9.6.4   Staff

There will be a dramatic upgrading of staff effectiveness which will be achieved through education and the accompanying confidence that they really are in the mainstream of retail banking. As clerical and transactional jobs disappear, bank staff will become better respected, and better paid. Most new entrants will typically be graduates.

This is not going to be easy for banks to achieve. In effect, banks will need to provide recruits and existing staff with a tertiary education in personal finance. Many staff will be able to rise to this, others not, but banks have a good track record of taking employees, graduates or not, and training them to do what their existing business models need.

In effect, staff are going to become financial advisors. It is not possible to be a mini financial adviser. They have to either know the subject, or not be in it. We are therefore looking at intensive education, coupled with external professional and structured career development to become qualified.

There are at least two ways to achieve this. One is for banks to undertake the education of staff themselves and award diplomas. Another is to fund colleges and universities to run degree/diploma courses in personal finance. There are no such courses in UK education today. Such courses would focus on accounting, banking, insurance, securities, financial markets, personal finance, solution creation, systems, taxation, law, ethics, sales, operations, finance theory, management and what have you. Such a diploma/degree will give the holder far more opportunity in the world than many alternative qualifications, and would be portable across the industry.

9.6.5 IT engineering

The latter part of the 20th century was the age of data processing engineering, where manual or mechanised processes were automated. The next 'last' frontier of data processing is now straight through processing (STP) and full automation will be conquered in the next few years. The operational re-engineering of banking will then be complete for a few decades, pretty much along the lines that banks are already working on, as explained earlier. And then, at last, banks can seriously move into information technology. There are immense opportunities here. We say that even today, most of what is called IT is, in fact, data processing. There is little today that is remarkable. Browsing the Internet, enquiring on accounts, initiating transactions, sending emails and so on are all twenty or more years old. There are remarkable things to come from the smart usage of IT. It will be coming from the usage of IT, not the IT itself though.

9.6.6 Financial engineering

In parallel, the spotlight will also move to financial engineering, which is still in its infancy, despite the recent growth of new financial instruments, capital markets and investment banking. As it relates to retail banking, there will be massive growth in capital markets and their ability to bring together all manner of risks to create new instruments to support life events. These products will be appreciated by an increasingly sophisticated retail banking customer base.

For savings to grow in a low inflation and interest rate environment, institutional investors will be searching out new investment instruments. These will, in turn, support the development of new retail banking products. At its extreme, we see new classes of money being created with purchasing power characteristics specific to consumers' life event needs, such as house purchase/capital accumulation/pension creation for the earning part of their lifetime, and pension income/long-term health and care provision/inheritance planning for later life.

The R&D function should be adopted in retail banking, chop chop. Financial engineering is far more important than the design of the credit card and the logo of the bank, and product developers are going to have to be experts in both the art and science of retail banking.

As far as technology goes, we think that this is a played out thing on an entirely lower plane than all the other stuff. Just at the moment, IT technology in particular has a critical importance; but it must now be used to escape from the immense gravitational pull of legacy systems. This is now on the road to resolution, and will be done and dusted in five to ten years. After that, we all hope it will be plainer sailing and that IT will be more contributive to supporting the business proper. As for all the other robots, autobots, infobots, AI, heuristic and other stuff – there's no magic. They can be used where they perform properly and make sense. Why oh why do we all go doolally when it gets to technology? What surprises have we had in reading about 'the branch of the future'? It's much more interesting to read about 'the house of the future', at least that promises to do all the cooking, washing up and make the beds.

The R&D function will drive technology and IT. The questions for them remain 'what does the bank want to be able to do?' and 'what do consumers think and need?'

And what of the IT industry? Well, their boxes and basic systems will be a commodity. The smallest banks will need a comprehensive and universal off-the-shelf core system. But the large banks will know, and get, what they want – probably less so from traditional core system vendors, but rather from specialists in areas such as front-end delivery, credit, treasury, risk, business process management, and so on. They will take on more themselves. As much as we believe in competitive advantage, scale economies, security, cost management, and all the rest of the positives of using third parties, the onus is on these IT vendors to prove it. They have been slow and complacent, and will reap the consequences. IT systems, and their ability to support the banks' missions, are absolute fundamentals of a bank, and the larger the bank, the more that is so. Caveat emptor.

With the new architectures in place, what the banks need are components, not the whole enchilada. IT companies had better get good at knowing about banking. Knowing about IT is less important by the month. Of particular importance is project management, and this is vendor neutral. So, how they architect their applications solutions, how they can effect rapid returns on their costs, how they can avoid risks, how they can give the bank flexibility 'to do anything' without the bank being dependent on them are important. Banks will want IT partners who can do things, not vendors that sell things.

IT usage will become a competitive issue. It will be apparent to customers.

9.6.7   Risk

Technology gives banks both better information on risk and the ability to manage risk better. So, the more traditional risks, such as credit and treasury risks, will diminish in their potential impacts.

Conversely, we see technology creating two major new(ish) risks, which will make banks vulnerable in new ways, until they are tamed.

The first is the creation of new financial instruments, bringing new risks and, no doubt, some unexpected individual or collective capital market meltdowns as new instruments and markets settle in. The ride will be hairy at times and the regulators will be kept busy ensuring that there are adequate controls over newly emerging systemic risks, which are feared above all else. Also, the creation of new products and product combos will bring its own risks, both financial and reputational if they fail to perform as designed and expose the banks and their customers to unexpected loss. This will generate a new class of risk – product risk.

Secondly, IT systems security will become a major issue. Today's threat is largely from hacker vandals trying to break in from outside, and mostly kept at bay by firewalls, virus protection, tamper proofing and the like. The major threat going forward will be from insiders backed by organised crime. As systems are increasingly consolidated into mega processing engines, so the threat rises to core operating systems that are broadly unprotected from insiders. The danger will come from individuals able to corrupt operating systems through cracking, reverse engineering, Trojan horses or whatever. New scams will emerge and thereby perpetrate major frauds on the bank and its customers. Teenage hackers eventually have mortgages to pay and insider fraud orchestrated by organised crime will be a potent threat.

Strange then, that an opportunity to control this risk would be outsourced with development done outside of the bank. Still, that appears to be how some lessons have to be learned. This is not about skimming ATMs. Extraordinary cash flows will be caught and reputations lost overnight after major hits.

9.6.8   Outsourcing

Over the horizon, we see a massive break-up of core banking and the rise of mega shared service providers undertaking the basic operational processing better and cheaper than individual banks are able to achieve. There will be lights-out, low manpower and high-volume data processing factories with a small number of providers servicing the industry in the following areas:

- cards;
- payments/settlement/clearing;
- custody and back office securities processing for banking, insurance and fund managers;
- mortgages;
- core back office account maintenance;
- shared branches;
- shared ATMs;
- financial Internet service provision.

This move is already underway domestically, and we see the large venture capital and IT houses becoming catalysts in the creation of a new processing sector within financial services, carving out and consolidating major chunks of the back offices of banks and also of fund managers and insurance companies. As the engineering and systems become commoditised, we see this moving from a domestic to an international business operating cross-border.

Banks will then become brand, customer, product and marketing, risk, capital and supplier management businesses.

With improvements in IT, there will be fewer IT staff, and a far greater proportion of their time will be spent on go-forward products. This development will not be outsourced. We see this resource as truly providing competitive advantage as creative solutions to customer life events and lifestyle needs are introduced.

9.6.9   Payments

Just how can a book like this not predict the arrival of the 'cashless' society? There seems to us no doubt that the direction of the 'less cash' society has now been set, and that the long march towards it is finally picking up momentum. The moves in ATM ownership and deployment, the introduction of the chip/PIN cards, and the growth in Internet purchases will encourage increased card transactions. As the numbers in Table 3.2 earlier in the book show, just a 10 % move from cash to debit cards will amount to some 2.5 billion new debit card payments, which itself will be a 75 % growth in debit card transaction volumes, as compared to the 12.4 % growth of 2003. We are now into the less cash society, and public confidence will take hold and drive the change.

Although they'll fight hard, the banks' grip on payments will come to an end. Payments are too large a business not to attract competition. The revenues from payments are substantial, and with 20 billion automated payments per year forecast in the UK within five years, the business will be worth several billion pounds of revenue annually.

The change could take one or more of a number of forms, but clearly the banks have a major mobility problem as wireless communications and mobiles get their acts straight. The large retailers themselves account for many of the payments. It's easy to see an alternative payment mechanism coming from that direction. In fact, either of these and others look highly possible.

9.6.10   Industry consolidation

Banks will continue to merge with banks, but the time is close when the opportunities will run out in any single country.

Bancassurance, the combination of banking with insurance, has largely been a failure. We think that this is because none of the attempts have involved the creation of a proper, new, and appropriate business model. Retail banking and insurance have been brought together in an uneasy cohabitation, but the two core business models have remained untouched. If you want eggs and bacon, you may as well put them on the same plate. Just because bancassurance has failed in the execution, does not invalidate the concept and we believe that as customer needs converge, so banks, life companies and investment managers will need to come together in a new business model, which, although fascinating to explore, is unfortunately beyond the scope of this book. But look at it this way. A twenty-something-year-old male with a new family will want to know that, were anything horrible to happen to him, his wife and child would be financially secure. That's all he wants at that life event/decision. He doesn't specifically want a £100 000 life insurance policy. A little R&D could go a long way to meeting that requirement. Between their bank and insurance skills you can imagine a fit-for-purpose product quite easily.

Also, the insurance and investment management industries have fallen well short of the banks in two key areas: trust, where public perception is much lower, and legacy engineering systems and processing costs, which are substantially less efficient (honest guv) than the banks. For these reasons, and the inevitable merging of the bank 'cash' products with fund managers and insurance companies securities and actuarial based products, the banks will be acquisitive and force the pace on bancassurance. As with investment banking in the late 1980s and early 1990s, we foresee a bancassurance industry 'big bang'.

So, over the horizon we see a wave of cross-industry consolidation, which will keep the current generation of investment bankers in Ferraris well into their retirement.

9.6.11   Investors and banks – the end game

The risk of all books presumptive enough to make predictions about the future is that after taking readers through a couple of hundred pages of analysis, argument and prediction, the final reaction is a rather flat 'so what?' We hope that this, our final, final prediction addresses the 'so what?'

Our view is that investors will continue to invest in banking and financial services, which will continue to grow ahead of the rate of growth of the underlying economy. As suggested above, banks will now be bancassurers – banking/insurance/investment management combos – and will have outsourced the major part of their operational infrastructure to specialist providers. And, increasingly with securitisation, investors, particularly the pension funds and institutional funds such as unit trusts, will have the opportunity to invest in individual classes of banking assets – card and motor receivables, mortgages, corporate loans and so on, without needing to invest in a bank itself. They will have the choice either to invest in efficient well-run banks, which will do the portfolio management for them, or alternatively to create portfolios of banking assets themselves, probably leveraged, thereby relegating banks to the role of intermediaries, not principles.

Equally, many banks will decide that instead of a business model where banks take deposits and make loans, they become financial high street retailers. They will take in customer funds and investments and package them for investment in a wide range of structured money market and investment funds, some with an insurance/protection dimension on a fiduciary basis, i.e. off balance sheet. In many cases, these funds will be unit trust, insurance and pension funds, structured and managed by the banks/bancassurers themselves on behalf of their personal, corporate and institutional customers. Conversely, although they will still make loans to customers, they will no longer hold these on balance sheet, but rather bundle them up and securitise (i.e. sell) them to institutional investors. A direct consequence of this will be a massive excess of (expensive to service) capital as banks downsize their balance sheets. That capital goes away, back to the investors to place elsewhere.

This leaves a final thought, that whilst bank brands will continue in business, serving customers and providing payment, deposit, loan and investment products, they will undergo a massive operational transformation from banking to become just-in-time retailers on the one hand, and money and investment managers on the other, on a grand scale. In so doing, they will have moved themselves conclusively from the data processing to the information age, and from retail banking to bank retailing.

10
Conclusions

This book comes down to three forces and the interactions (Figure 10.1). What will the bank leadership decide in achieving their balance between consumers, investors and themselves? How will they attract and retain customers, and how will investors view the bank? What will attract customers, and what will help the bank retain those customers that they want to retain?

The bank itself has a balancing act between its investor owners and its customers. The bank's leadership team is going to have to make decisions emanating from their views of the retail banking market, and the roles that they want their bank to play. Of course, this is a normal activity for them, but it does appear that 'more of the same' is less likely to be successful than in the past, and that new opportunities are abundant. There are perhaps 'safe' options for established banks – like going with the flow.

Through the last ten years and more, there has been the major drag of legacy systems to any changes, and these have blunted the forward progress of banks. It hasn't only been the legacy systems that gave the drag, it was also the legacy thinking that they engendered. With those constraints being removed over the next five years, banks will enjoy more freedom to compete. They are going to need it. The tempo of competition will increase from established UK competitors, and from European and US banks, from real retailers led by the supermarkets, and from new banks, probably with filthy rich parents.

Just how proactive, reactive or passive a bank will choose to be will alter the personality of the bank.

Retail and small business banking is up for grabs, and will be driven by the banks' skills at marketing banking products and services, and the consumers' perception of value. This perception includes rates, transparency of charges, and flexibility in terms of conditions and penalties. For consumers, there has to be a real feeling that the bank is on their side. This includes a view by the consumer that the bank is a trusted and valued adviser, a cocreator of their financial solution(s). Marketing, which we see as responsible for defining and selling the products and services, will have its work cut out, and be upgraded in importance.

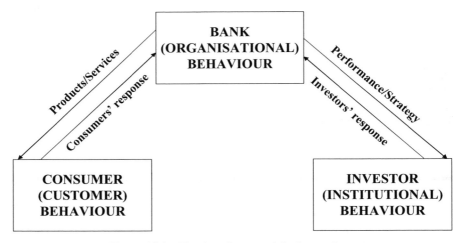

Figure 10.1   The three forces and the interactions

At the moment, competition is a little like the Round the World Yacht Race, where each team has an identical boat. In banking today, products are largely commodity in nature, the staff are pretty similar from one bank to another, the technology is similar whichever vendor it is from, the systems all follow the same ideas, and the skills have become normalised across the banking industry. So it is largely down to the skipper of the boat to read the charts, study the weather, choose the right course and perhaps be a little lucky. Within a retail banking market, as in the yacht race, it comes down to judgement and skill, and perhaps a little luck. Skippers can learn much of this. There is a lot of science and engineering to it.

The opportunity is now to build a new boat, develop your own systems and staff skills, offer new products and services, and the rest. It's not unreasonable to think that the banking fleet will sail all over the globe. Neither is it as certain that the best skippers will continue to win, because there are all these other factors in play over which they have no control. There's art thrown in now. Art is human, creative skill, concerned with the production of imaginative designs and workmanship. That's a lot of room for a new yacht design. However, good teams still win more, whatever the conditions.

Large banks have more difficulties in responding to the challenge than do their smaller brethren. If their margins and market effectiveness were cut they would suffer badly – a 10 % reduction in their retail and small business deposit and loan balances would seriously hurt them. In fact, it would lead to a major realignment of investor capital.

The value of brand and large size is diminishing. The importance of regulators and goodness is growing.

There are plenty of new customer propositions to be developed. Just what planet will the new propositions come from if not from Planet Earth? How can we encourage creativity and channel it properly?

Imagine you have to live with reduced margins – as much as halved in big banks, seriously shaved in mortgage banks. What will you have to do? We have to start thinking and acting on it now, because it is going to happen. Sure, some of them will stumble. If transparency of pricing is introduced, then the lending or borrowing of funds will be priced separately from the fees. The customer appreciation of fees will come down directly to the added value of the bank staff.

The customers are quite rightly on their own side, and whilst the demutualisation of the building society movement is a pity, you have to say it was a rational decision, as all customer decisions en masse are. Decisions on personal finance have huge consequences for consumers – individually and collectively. It's one thing to show that Bank A saves £ 189 over 36 months for a loan versus Bank B. But with pensions, savings, insurance, mortgages and taxation, the sums to be saved could easily be in the tens of thousands of pounds over an individual's adult lifetime. Now, that is worth a consumer's consideration. The payment of fees will become a rational expense.

The likelihood is that mid-sized banks, new banks and building societies could be a major force. They need to respond first, insofar as they have fewer buffers to fall back upon. They also have greater manoeuvrability than the biggies, and proportionally their success is more important in relative terms than it is for the large banks. IT allows a small organisation to punch well above its weight, as does its staff.

New banks can be obliterated quite easily. It will only be because of the strength and commitment of their parents that new banks will be able to stay the course. It is not wise for a new entrant to only have 'just enough' capital; they will need substantially more than that, or a terrific customer proposition deployed rapidly.

Don't expect any help from the government, whatever they say. It is the big banks that finance the government, and the government needs them on their side. All these high-profile debates on credit cards and concerns about the exclusion from banking services for a modest percentage of the population may be well intentioned by the movers, but totally irrelevant to the powers that be. We do not have joined up government when it comes to banking.

Ever creative, financial markets will engineer new ways of managing capital and consumer funds, and this will lead to massive restructuring possibilities.

UK banking really is inviting in foreign banks if it acts passively or reactively. This country will be a happy hunting ground for the right customer value propositions, and UK customers need not worry about the national origin of a major bank. Money is a global commodity.

The big trigger to all this will be gaining freedom from legacy systems and legacy thinking. That opens up the oceans. We think that gaining that freedom is the race that matters, to be followed by a wider marketing remit and the upgrading of staff capabilities. There will be huge staffing consequences, and most of them good.

There are going to be some mighty impacts across other businesses, such as the media, IT and consulting industries – and a lot of it may not be pleasant. On the other hand, the opportunities that are coming along as the result of these changes are immense. Those that are prepared to think open mindedly, and immensely, will do immensely well! But that's another story.

Meantime, we consumers will all benefit from better banking from many aspects. And it is our belief and hope that banks will too.

Finally, we do hope that this book interested our target readership – that was its objective. We have tried to frame the subject of retail banking so as to give perspective to what you know or suspect already, and hopefully it has helped to read it is different words. We thank you for having chosen to read the book. All feedback is welcome. Please send it to croxfordh@aol.com with the word 'book' in the subject line so that your e-mail doesn't get despammed.

Many thanks.

Appendix A: List of Acronyms

ABC	Activity-based costing
ADP	Automatic data processing
AI	Artificial intelligence
AIB	Allied Irish Bank
APACS	Association for Payment Clearing Services
ATM	Automated teller machine
BA	British Airways
BACS	Banks' automated clearing system
BAU	Business as usual
BCCI	Bank of Credit and Commerce International
BIS	Bank for International Settlements
BoI	Bank of Ireland
BoS	Bank of Scotland
BP	British Petroleum
BPR	Business process re-engineering
BSCH	Banco Santander Central Hispano
BT	British Telecom
CEO	Chief Executive Officer
CHAPS	Clearing house automated payment system
CIF	Customer information file
CIS	Co-operative Insurance Society
CMA	Cash management account
CRM	Customer relationship management
DASD	Direct access storage device
DBMS	Database management software
E&Y	Ernst & Young
EDP	Electronic data processing
EDS	Electronic Data Systems Corporation
EFT	Electronic funds transfer

ERM	Electronic relationship management
EU	European Union
FCE	Ford Credit Europe
FMCG	Fast moving consumer goods
FSA	Financial Services Authority
FTE	Full-time equivalent
FTSE	Financial Times/London Stock Exchange (UK stock index)
GDP	Gross domestic product
GE	General Electric
GM	General Motors
HBOS	Halifax/Bank of Scotland
HP	Hewlett Packard
HR	Human resources
HSBC	Hong Kong and Shanghai Banking Corporation
IBM	International Business Machines Corporation
IF	Intelligent Finance
IFA	Independent financial adviser
IPO	Initial public offering
ISA	Individual savings account
IT	Information technology
IVR	Interactive voice response
KLM	Koninklijke Luchtvaart Maatschappij (Royal Dutch Airlines)
KPI	Key performance indicator
LTSB	Lloyds/Trustee Savings Bank
M&A	Mergers and acquisitions
MBNA	Maryland Bank North America
MBO	Management buy-out
MIS	Management information system
NAG	National Australia Group
NHS	National Health Service
NYCE	New York Cash Exchange
P/E	Price/earnings ratio
PEP	Personal equity plan
PIMS	Profit Impact of Market Strategy
PIN	Personal identification number
POS	Point of sale
R&D	Research and development
RAROC	Risk adjusted return on capital
RBS	Royal Bank of Scotland
RBSG	Royal Bank of Scotland Group
ROA	Return on assets
ROE	Return on equity
ROEC	Return on economic capital

ROI	Return on investment
SAP	Systeme, Anwendungen, Produkte in der Datenverarbeitung (Systems, Applications and Products in Data Processing)
SME	Small and medium-sized enterprise
STP	Straight through processing
SWIFT	Society for Worldwide Interbank Financial Telecommunication
SWOT	Strengths, weaknesses, opportunities, threats
T&Cs	Terms and conditions
TSB	Trustee Savings Bank
VARONE	Value added return on net equity
Y2K	The year 2000

Appendix B: Glossary

Bancassurance	The combination of banking and insurance.
Bridging loan	A loan made to cover the period between two transactions – usually between buying a new house and sale of the previous property.
Capital requirement	The amount of capital that a bank is legally required to maintain in order to protect customers' deposits in the event of the bank's failure. This figure is set by the banking regulatory authorities and is set internationally, not on a country-by-country basis.
Clearing bank	Any bank that makes use of the banks' central payments clearing systems.
Commercial bank	A bank that makes and accepts payments and deposits from the general public and companies and also lends them money.
Corporate banking	Banking services for large companies.
Credit union	A financial organisation, usually founded by co-workers or fellow union members. The organisation takes deposits from members, pays dividends on the deposits and makes loans to members.
Demutualisation	The process of converting from a building society or insurance company into a bank.
De novo bank	A new bank.
Derivative	A financial instrument whose price is dependent upon the underlying product – this can be interest rates, commodities, etc. They involve the trading of rights or obligations, but do not involve the transfer of property. Derivatives are commonly used to hedge risk.
Dividend	A payment made to a company's shareholders from the net profit of the company.

Expected loss	An amount built into the price of a loan by banks to cover the expected cost of people not repaying loans.
Friendly society	An association whereby people pay regular sums of money in return for pensions, sickness benefits, etc.
Goodwill	The difference between the amount a bank paid for an acquisition and the book value of that acquisition.
Interest rate spread	The difference between the interest rate paid to savers and that charged to borrowers.
Interest rate swap	Another term for an interest rate derivative.
Investment banking	Businesses that specialise in the formation of capital. This involves the purchase and sale of bonds, shares, derivatives, companies etc.
Lien	The legal right to take possession of a property or funds if a debt is not repaid.
Micro-banking market	Our preferred term for the non-prime market.
Net interest income	Bank income derived from the difference in interest rates paid to depositors and charged to lenders.
Non-interest income	Bank income derived from fees and commissions paid by customers and others.
Non-prime market	A growing sector of the banking market involving smaller sums of money. For example, customers who need a few hundred pounds to resolve problems.
Private banking	Services provided by banks to their wealthiest customers. This involves investment advice, securities safekeeping and lending.
Retail banking	Commercial banks dealing with individual customers and small businesses.
Secured loan	A loan in which some collateral (often property) is pledged in the event that the customer defaults. A mortgage is the most common example, but there are also secured personal loans.
Securitisation	A scheme by which investors buy certain bank assets and revenue streams, thus freeing up capital for the bank to make further loans, mortgages, etc.
Silos	End-to-end, self-contained systems that handle every aspect of an account, from delivery to processing.
Stress testing	Complex computer-based analytical techniques measuring overall risk and testing how this might change in different scenarios.
Swap	Another term for an interest rate or foreign exchange derivative.
Tier I capital	The core capital of a bank, including equity capital and reserves.

Tier II capital	Secondary bank capital, typically bonds with various characteristics.
Transfer pricing	The price at which the various units of a bank can 'trade' the assets and liabilities generated from one business unit to another or at which they charge the other unit for services provided.
Unexpected loss	A series of losses incurred which is greater than the norm for loans of this type.
Unsecured loan	A loan made with no collateral. This is much more risky for the bank, as they have much less reliable comeback if the customer defaults.
Zero-based budgeting	An approach by which each group of staff functions is questioned with a view to designing them out of a new model.

References

APACS (2004) *The Way We Pay – A Market Review of the Plastic Card Industry in 2003*.

Clear Capital Limited (2004) *UK Non-Prime Lending*, research note, January 26th.

Frost, S.M. (2004) *The Bank Analyst's Handbook*, John Wiley & Sons, Ltd, Chichester.

Howcroft, J.B. and Lavis, J. (1986) *Retail Banking: The New Revolution in Structure and Strategy*, Basil Blackwell, Oxford.

Matten, C. (2000) *Managing Bank Capital*, Second Edition, John Wiley & Sons, Ltd, Chichester.

The Banker (2004) *Top 1000 World Banks*, FT Business, July.

Index

Index compiled by Terry Halliday